AN INTRODUCTION TO THE STUDY OF

SOUTHWESTERN ARCHAEOLOGY

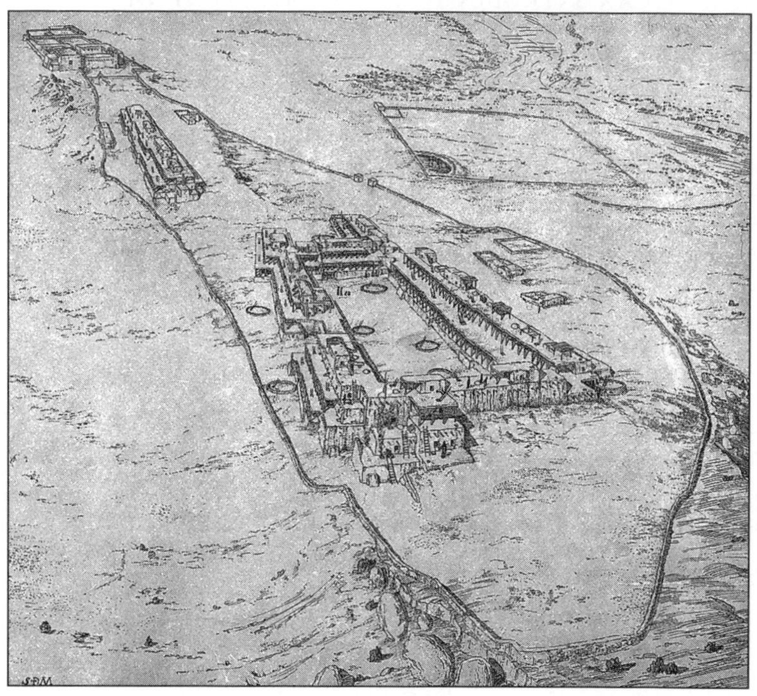

PLATE 1. Pecos from the north: North and South Pueblos, with mission and convent beyond. Restoration by S. P. Moorehead as of about 1700 (courtesy of R. S. Peabody Foundation).

AN INTRODUCTION TO THE STUDY OF

# SOUTHWESTERN ARCHAEOLOGY

ALFRED VINCENT KIDDER

With a new essay by
DOUGLAS W. SCHWARTZ

Yale University Press/New Haven & London

Set in Baskerville type by The Composing Room of Michigan, Inc.
Printed in the United States of America.

Library of Congress Cataloging-in-Publication Data

Kidder, Alfred Vincent, 1885–1963.
An introduction to the study of Southwestern archaeology / Alfred Vincent Kidder; with a new essay by Douglas W. Schwartz; [foreword by James W. Bradley].
p. cm.
Includes bibliographical references.
ISBN 0-300-08297-5 (pbk.: alk. paper)
1. Indians of North America—Southwest, New—Antiquities.
2. Southwest, New—Antiquities. 3. Pueblo Indians—Antiquities.
4. Pecos (N.M.) I. Title.
E78.S7 K5 2000
979'.01—dc21 99-046927

A catalogue record for this book is available from the British Library.

The paper in this book meets the guidelines for permanence and durability of the Committee on Production Guidelines for Book Longevity of the Council on Library Resources.

10 9 8 7 6 5 4 3 2 1

# Contents

List of Illustrations vii

Foreword by James W. Bradley xi

Kidder and the Synthesis of Southwestern Archaeology by Douglas W. Schwartz 1

Preface 56

History of Pecos 61

Field work at Pecos: previous investigations, field work of Phillips Academy, summary of results 88

The modern pueblos 140

The prehistoric pueblos 158

The San Juan: Pueblo ruins—Chaco Canyon, Mesa Verde, Kayenta; pre-Pueblo ruins; post–Basket Maker ruins; Basket Maker sites; Northern Peripheral district 165

The Rio Grande; Eastern Peripheral district 254

The Little Colorado 266

The Upper Gila 280

The Mimbres 289

The Lower Gila 298

The Chihuahua basin 316
Conclusions 323
Bibliography 353
Schwartz References 379

# Illustrations

PLATES


1. Pecos from the north: Restoration by S. P. Moorehead as of about 1700 *frontispiece*
2. General view of Pecos from the north 65
3. *a.* View across Arroyo de Pecos. *b.* The ruin mounds from the church 72
4. Pecos in 1846. *a.* Church and monastery. *b.* Plaza 84
5. Model of Pecos 90
6. The Pecos church. *a.* From the pueblo. *b.* Interior 92
7. Sketch plan of the Pecos ruins 99
8. The eastern trenches in the great Pecos rubbish heap. *a.* The opening cut. *b.* Trench at twelve feet deep. *c.* Trench at nineteen feet deep 106
9. A stratigraphic section in the deep rubbish. *a.* Cut 3, Test X. *b.* Cut 5, Test X 110
10. Typical burials. *a.* Extended burial of late period. *b.* Partly flexed burial of Glaze 4 period. *c.* Closely flexed burial, Glaze 3 period 114
11. Skeletons in the deep rubbish 120
12. North terrace excavation. *a.* From the top of the ruin mound. *b.* From the north 124
13. Architectural details. *a.* Typical Pecos masonry. *b.* Conditions in the Great Quadrangle 130
14. The west cross-cut trench, 1920 135
15. Modern Pueblo villages. *a.* Taos. *b.* Tesuque 146
16. Modern pueblos. *a.* Harvest dance at San Ildefonso. *b.* Kiva at San Ildefonso 148
17. Pueblo costumes. *a.* Woman of San Ildefonso in everyday dress. *b.* Corn dancers at Santo Domingo 152

18. Modern Pueblo pottery 156
19. Pueblo Bonito *a.* Restoration. *b.* Ground plan 168
20. Masonry of San Juan ruins. *a.* Chaco Canyon. *b.* Mesa Verde. *c.* Kayenta 174
21. The great kiva of the Chaco Canyon culture. *a.* Plan of the great kiva at Aztec. *b.* The great kiva at Chettro Kettle 180
22. Chaco Canyon black-on-white ware 183
23. Designs of Chaco Canyon black-on-white ware 187
24. Cliff Palace, Mesa Verde, Colorado 193
25. Black-on-white bowls of the Mesa Verde culture 200
26. Designs of Mesa Verde black-on-white ware 204
27. *a.* Proto-Mesa Verde pottery. *b.* Towers in Ruin Canyon, Utah 208
28. Section of a kiva and dwelling house 212
29. Kayenta cliff houses. *a.* Betatakin. *b.* Kietsiel 216
30. Kayenta black-on-white pottery 221
31. Designs of Kayenta black-on-white ware 223
32. Designs of Kayenta polychrome ware 225
33. Deformed and undeformed skulls 231
34. Pre-Pueblo pottery 233
35. Designs of pre-Pueblo black-on-white pottery 235
36. Sandals. *a.* Pueblo. *b.* Pre-Pueblo. *c.* Basket Maker 237
37. A Basket Maker storage and burial cave 247
38. Basket Maker specimens 250
39. Pecos pottery, chronological series 258
40. Designs of Pecos pottery, chronological series 259
41. Rio Grande habitations. *a.* A large circular pueblo, Tyuonyi. *b.* Artificial caves used as dwellings near Tyuonyi 262
42. Little Colorado pottery 269
43. Typical terraced pueblo, Oraibi 274
44. Black-on-white and corrugated wares of Upper Gila type 286
45. Designs of Mimbres black-on-white ware 293

46. The Casa Grande ruin 295
47. Model of a typical compound (Casa Grande) 303
48. Lower Gila pottery 307
49. Designs of Lower Gila polychrome ware 311
50. Pottery of the Chihuahua basin 320

FIGURES

1. Alfred Vincent Kidder at Pecos in 1920 2
2. (*top*) Pecos Valley. (*bottom*) Excavations on North Terrace, Pecos, about 1920 20
3. Typical projectile points of the Paleo-Indian and Desert traditions 33
4. Pithouse and artifacts of the Hohokam tradition 38
5. Pithouse and pottery of the Mogollon tradition 41
6. Hogan and pottery of the Athabaskan tradition 43
7. Supposed and actual extent of rubbish 96
8. Cross-section, superposition of walls, burials, etc. 103
9. Approximate limits of the Southwestern culture area 141
10. Present-day distribution of the Pueblo tribes 143
11. The culture areas of the Southwest 163
12. The San Juan area 167
13. Chaco Canyon vessel shapes 176
14. Ground plan of Cliff Palace 191
15. Mesa Verde vessel shapes 198
16. Exterior decorations of Mesa Verde bowls 203
17. Ground plan of unit-type dwelling 210
18. Ground plan of Kietsiel 218
19. Kayenta vessel shapes 220
20. Proto-Kayenta pottery designs 227
21. Distribution of remains in Northern Peripheral district 245
22. The Rio Grande area 256
23. The Little Colorado area 267
24. The Upper Gila and Mimbres areas 281
25. The Lower Gila area 299

26. Lower Gila vessel shapes 304
27. Lower Gila red-on-gray designs 310
28. Distribution of Basket Maker sites 327
29. Distribution of post–Basket Maker sites 328
30. Distribution of pre-Pueblo sites 331
31. Distribution of Pueblo population at various periods 339

# Foreword

On February 9, 1915, a young scholar named Alfred Vincent Kidder approached the trustees of Phillips Academy in Andover, Massachusetts, with a proposal. His plan was to excavate the ruins of the Pecos Pueblo under the auspices of the Academy's Department of Archaeology (now the Robert S. Peabody Museum of Archaeology), established in 1901 through the bequest of alumnus Robert Singleton Peabody. The trustees had encouraged this proposal in accordance with Peabody's wishes that the department he funded should promote new sciences "such as archaeology" through research as well as education.

What is remarkable as one rereads Kidder's handwritten proposal is the clarity of his vision. Kidder knew exactly why excavating at Pecos would be important. "Culture histories," he noted, had already been worked out in other parts of the world. What was needed in the Southwest was a site where the relationships among the other known sites could be established. If we could "reconstruct the development of Southwestern culture," Kidder argued, "we should have made a contribution of the greatest importance, not only to Southwestern history but also to the study of human institutions in a much broader sense; sociology, technology and art, all would derive direct benefit."

Kidder's acuity did not diminish as the Andover/Pecos Expedition continued over the next fourteen years. In 1927, Kidder invited several coworkers from the Southwest, as well as some students, to meet at Pecos. The goal was to pool their knowledge, discuss problems within the region, and plan out how to work together. From this modest start, the

Pecos Conference has become *the* premier educational conference in twentieth-century American archaeology, introducing and training at least three generations of new scholars.

Although much has changed in the culture of this country and the profession of archaeology, the standards of excellence and inclusion established by Kidder and his colleagues early in this century continue today. With the passage of the Native American Graves Protection and Repatriation Act in 1990, the Pueblo of Jemez finally became a full participant in this piece of its own past. Today, the Pueblo, the Robert S. Peabody Museum, and the Pecos National Historical Park are developing plans for a ten-year education and outreach partnership, one that will allow us to share our mutual resources of information most appropriately with students and scholars of all ages, backgrounds, and levels of expertise.

It is our hope that this new partnership will continue the tradition begun by Kidder eighty years ago. As always, those who come after us will judge our success.

—James W. Bradley

# Kidder and the Synthesis of Southwestern Archaeology

DOUGLAS W. SCHWARTZ

## INTRODUCTION

Alfred Vincent Kidder was an extraordinary figure in American prehistory. In addition to his contributions to field archaeology and scholarly communication, Kidder demonstrated exceptional skill in archaeological synthesis. His superb *Introduction to the Study of Southwestern Archaeology,* published in 1924, is a landmark in the history of Southwestern studies. Written as a preliminary report on Kidder's first ten years of excavation at the northern New Mexico pueblo of Pecos, the book also serves as an introduction to the prehistory of the whole Southwest. In 1927 Kidder made another contribution by initiating an annual gathering called the Pecos Conference at which current archaeological fieldwork could be discussed.

Kidder's synthesis of Southwestern archaeology and the harvest of new ideas that emanated from the conference stimulated research by a legion of archaeologists working throughout the Southwest. As a result, our understanding of the region's prehistory has blossomed in ways that Kidder could never have imagined.

Human prehistory in the American Southwest extends back at least eleven thousand years, with lifeways ranging from mobile hunters and gatherers to sedentary agriculturists. Although the earliest periods of human settlement were roughly similar, it was the Southwest's geographical diversity that influenced the development of what became a cluster of regionally distinct cultural traditions within the Southwest.

Fig. 1. Alfred Vincent Kidder at Pecos in 1920 (courtesy of Museum of Indian Arts and Culture/Laboratory of Anthropology, Museum of New Mexico).

The Southwest is a dappled landscape of deserts, mountains, high plateaus, and sometimes lush river valleys. Each of these regions has a distinctive ecology and remains home to modern Native Americans. The Sonoran desert region, which today generally centers around Phoenix, Arizona, is drained by the Gila and Salt Rivers. This is a land of blistering summers, mild winters, and scant rainfall. Historically it was the home of Pima and O'Odham (formally Papago) people.

In the central parts of Arizona and New Mexico lie impressive mountain ranges and intervening grassy meadows.

Rainfall here is two to three times as great as that of the Sonoran desert, reflected in its great forests of ponderosa pine and pinyon and juniper. Historically, some of this region has been the home of Apache peoples.

In the northern Southwest, the vast Colorado Plateau region has a quite variable climate and ecology, its topography ranging mainly between four thousand and eight thousand feet, with mountain peaks rising to twelve thousand feet. The area includes extremely dissected sandstone plateaus with slender canyons and sweeping, meagerly vegetated valleys with only sporadic flowing water. In the cooler and wetter areas vast stands of pinyon and juniper trees cover the landscape. Most of the region has a long dry spring and early summer, broken by heavy thundershowers, with chilly winters accompanied by considerable amounts of snow. This area was the traditional home of the ancient Pueblo peoples, and, in early historic times, Athabaskan- and Shoshonian-speaking peoples.

To the far west, on both sides of the Lower Colorado River, ranging from the Grand Canyon southward, is the hot, desert extension of the Basin and Range country. The region has been the home of Yuman-speaking people, including the Cocopahs, Mohaves, Maracopa, and, further to the east, the Walapai, Yavapai, and Havasupai.

It was in this Southwest region, with its excellent preservation of prehistoric remains and variety of contemporary native people, many of whom have been resident since early prehistoric times, that Kidder found an unparalleled opportunity to study archaeology. When he began his work there was not yet the precise chronological control or the detailed understanding of past climates that later became available, but in this singular province for research, and with his tenacious persistence, brilliant organizational ability, and gift for synthesis, Kidder became a model scholar that few have equaled.

But Kidder was not the first archaeologist to work in the Southwest, and his groundbreaking work was built firmly on the research of several talented predecessors. Five earlier researchers stand out as forerunners and contributors to Kidder's later ideas (Schwartz 1981, 251–73).

## EARLY HISTORY OF SOUTHWESTERN ARCHAEOLOGY

The foundation for modern scholarship in the archaeology and ethnology of the northern Rio Grande region was laid by Adolph Bandelier. This energetic young scholar previously had been a part-time library scholar working in his father's southern Illinois business. In August 1880 Bandelier traveled to New Mexico, where he was soon reporting to his sponsors, the Archaeological Institute of America, that this was an exceptional place to carry out research since "enough is left to make New Mexico the objective point of serious, practical archaeologists; for, besides the living pueblo Indians, besides the numerous ruins of their past, the very history of the changes they have undergone is partly in existence" (Bandelier 1881, 28–29).

Bandelier visited, observed, and studied several northern Rio Grande pueblos and explored archaeological sites in the nearby Jemez Mountains and along the Pecos River valley to the east, where he visited Pecos Pueblo in 1880. He separated the archaeological sites he was visiting into prehistoric and historic periods (Bandelier 1881, 104). Later he recognized that not all of the prehistoric sites were simultaneously occupied and tried to date them through their associated painted and plain pottery, which he recognized as having a rough chronological significance (Bandelier 1883, 29).

Bandelier postulated a sequence of architectural change from "the many-storied communal houses" to "the one-story buildings of stone" and concluded that "small-house dwellers . . . became extinct before the conquest" (Bandelier 1883, 30–31). Implicit in Bandelier's reconstruction was the assumption of continuity between the peoples of the past in this region and the historic and present Native Americans.

This seemingly obvious point was nevertheless worth making because at the time some writers were attributing prehistoric American ruins to the Welsh, Egyptians, Phoenicians, and the lost tribes of Israel. The concept of continuity with the past and the idea that the indigenous people had been able to create these great ancient villages were groundbreaking at the time. Bandelier's extensive published descriptions of prehistoric materials and historical records provide an early, substantial base on which Southwestern and especially northern Rio Grande archaeology could grow.

Four years after Bandelier left the Southwest, Edgar Lee Hewett, a young classics teacher from Colorado, began exploring the archaeological sites on the high mesas east of the Jemez Mountains, an area he later named the Pajarito Plateau. For eight years he recorded sites in this area and began publishing comprehensive reports on architecture, with good site maps and comments on the form, location, building sequence, and comparisons with sites outside the Jemez Mountain region. Hewett made no mention, however, of the artifacts associated with these sites. His early contribution was his publication of the first comprehensive descriptions of archaeological sites in the northern Rio Grande (Hewett 1902, 1903, 1904, 1905, 1906).

Hewett was also interested in the chronological ordering of the prehistoric sites he was discovering. Beginning with his work in the Jemez Mountains Hewett applied his approach to the whole prehistoric Pueblo world, as it was then known. He concluded that "there is an evolutionary and chronological sequence to be seen in the construction and occupancy of the domiciliary structures of Pajarito Park" (1904b, 657). His sequence was divided into three epochs, with an emphasis on type of habitation. First, the *Pretraditionary Epoch*: "An obscure, archaic epoch of semisedentary occupation" based upon scant evidence from rock shelters and natural caves that sheltered a population "in the most primitive stages of culture on the American continent" (Hewett 1904a, 438). Next, the long *Epoch of Diffusion* was one in which "small communities were distributed over the semi-desert areas; devoted to agriculture; under matronymic social organization; dwelling in fairly substantial houses" with "strictly utilitarian" pottery (Hewett 1904a, 438). Finally, the *Epoch of Concentration,* the most recent period, began with "the concentration of clans for defensive purposes into the great communal houses, made expedient by the arrival of the nomadic, predatory tribes." Hewett (1904a, 437–38) felt this was the time when "the present Pueblo languages were formed and the great ritualistic ceremonies were elaborated."

Hewett was also interested in cultural variety and differentiated the Southwest into a number of separate cultural areas. The culmination of all his work was presented in his doctoral dissertation, completed at the University of Geneva in 1908, which preceded Kidder's regional ordering of Southwestern archaeology in 1924 by nearly two decades. Hewett felt strongly that climate was a key to understanding the hundreds of depopulated archaeological ruins scattered throughout the Southwest, and their abandonment he saw as "principally a question of subsistence" (Hewett 1904b, 659), resulting from "climatic modifications by reason of which the hardships of living at these sites became unendurable" (Hewett 1906, 13), a modification characterized by "a slow, progressive drying up of this region" (Hewett 1909a, 22).

Hewett's work was flawed, however, by his lack of understanding of smooth cultural succession. Others, like Bandelier, were seeing continuity between the prehistoric and historic Pueblo cultures, while Hewett felt strongly that the Pueblo tribes were related to the occupants of the prehistoric sites only in a "qualified" way (Hewett 1906, 12). He saw nonconformities in symbolism and physical type and in what he saw as clues in Tewa Pueblo mythology. Combining all of these, he could not accept the conclusion of continuity: "That there was relationship is not questioned, but the degree of relationship is yet to be determined" (Hewett 1909b, 340).

Following his perceptive early descriptive work and his

synthesis, Hewett moved on to diverse interests, mainly in administration. He became the first director of the School of American Research, and he began leaving to others the task of pursuing the implications of his work on the culture areas of the prehistoric Southwest.

Just as Hewett was abandoning his concentration on northern Rio Grande field archaeology, Nels C. Nelson, who received his training at the universities of Chicago and California–Berkeley, began six field seasons of work there that greatly influenced the future of archaeology in the area and helped create a revolution in American archaeology (Willey and Sabloff 1974, 94). Nelson was a young archaeologist at the American Museum of Natural History in New York when he was sent to the Southwest in the summer of 1912 as part of the museum's extensive field research program. He immediately began the systematic excavation of seven pueblo ruins in the Galisteo basin south of Santa Fe, directing the excavation of approximately 448 rooms, plus ceremonial chambers called kivas, and digging exploratory trenches through trash mounds (Nelson 1914, 7). His meticulous notes were far more complete than those of Hewett and were consistent with Nelson's goal to see this project as "an opportunity to prosecute a piece of research work in the most scientific manner" (Nelson 1914, 9).

From his excavated material Nelson was able to identify a series of discrete pottery types, and his primary concern was the chronological sequence in which these occurred. In 1914 he returned to continue his Herculean excavation efforts, feeling "reasonably certain what was the chronological order of the four apparent pottery types," though the "tangible proof" he was searching for in the form of stratigraphic support for their temporal differences "was still wanting" (Nelson 1916, 162).

At the ancient San Cristóbal Pueblo, Nelson dug ten-foot-deep trash deposits in arbitrary layers and then classified and recorded the pottery fragments by levels. Using this stratigraphic method, he could see how the character of the sherd collection changed as the depth of the trash mound increased. He found a succession of pottery types from black-on-white ware, through glaze-on-gray, white, yellow, or red, to a later glaze polychrome (Nelson 1916, 162–64). That winter his supervisor at the museum excitedly described Nelson's work in the *American Museum Journal:* "It can now be told at what relative date each of these (ruins) was built" (Wissler 1917, 100).

Nelson's seminal work made clear the importance of the stratigraphic method and the use of pottery types as chronological markers. His results prepared the way for a northern Rio Grande regional chronology that could date surface collections from other archaeological sites. In fact, this breakthrough provided all of Southwestern archaeology with a new field method and a basis for constructing a series of hypotheses on cultural succession. Furthermore, Nelson's own interpretative conclusion that there had been a continuity of Pueblo population in the region from prehistoric to historic times agreed with Bandelier's conclusion and rejected that of Hewett.

While Nelson's work was being hailed by some as eminent, another reaction came from those who paid his salary, his sponsors at the American Museum of Natural History. For them Nelson's approach may have been too scientific. Some feel (Richard Woodbury, personal communication) that Nelson left the Southwest after 1917, unable to capitalize on his breakthrough, because his sponsors at the museum were less impressed by Nelson's work than by the spectacular display of "quality artifacts," that is, whole pots, being collected by Earl Morris at Aztec Ruin and other Southwestern sites. The museum officials, therefore, shifted their support from Nelson to Morris. The study of Southwestern prehistory and probably the whole discipline of archaeology lost an important scholar through this decision, and it was left to others who followed him to build upon Nelson's critical insights.

Two other important scholars who added to the intellectual tool kit that was built in the Southwest—and who were later to be critical of Kidder's work at Pecos Pueblo—were Alfred Kroeber and Leslie Spier. While Nelson was working in the Galisteo Basin, Kroeber was conducting research at Zuni Pueblo to the west. After comparing the contemporary pottery used at Zuni to progressively older Zuni area settlements, Kroeber observed that pottery types changed through time. By using the "direct historical approach," moving backward from the pottery used at contemporary Zuni to the pottery of lesser-known local settlements, it was possible to put these settlements in a chronological sequence (Kroeber 1916).

Building on Nelson's insight from archaeological stratigraphy and on the successive, patterned changes in pottery types through time discovered by Kroeber, the work of Leslie Spier added another important perception by applying the method of seriation. Spier, like Kroeber working for the American Museum of Natural History in New York and also in the Zuni area, made stratigraphy excavations at some of the sites where Kroeber had collected his pottery types.

Spier, however, took the successive appearance and disappearance of pottery types through time beyond the observations of Kroeber, noting that the frequency of pottery types also changed through time. This perception led him to examine the pottery at small settlements with short occupations, and by determining the percentage of various types of pottery in each he placed them in chronological order (Spier 1917). Like the earlier work of Bandelier, Hewett, and Nelson, the new insights about chronology were to be important in the development of Kidder's research at Pecos Pueblo.

## KIDDER'S EARLY CAREER

Alfred Kidder was the next major figure to emerge in Southwestern archaeology, and his contributions further revolutionized the field (Woodbury 1973). His personal and educational background gave him real advantages that allowed him to capitalize on preceding research. Kidder was born in 1885, the son of a mining engineer. He received an excellent education in Cambridge, Massachusetts, in Switzerland, and then at Harvard. Beginning as a premedical student, he soon began studying archaeology.

In the summer of 1907, while only a junior at Harvard, Kidder, a good-natured, strong, and healthy young man, was invited by Edgar Hewett, along with two other Harvard undergraduates, Sylvanus Morley and Jesse Nusbaum, to participate in a series of archaeological projects in the Southwest. Kidder reported that Hewett took him and his schoolmates, three completely inexperienced young men, to the edge of a mesa in the region around Mesa Verde in southern Colorado, "gestured at the vast landscape below, and said, 'I want you boys to make an archaeological survey of this country. I'll be back in three weeks'" (Woodbury 1981, 16). With virtually no instructions or direction, this trio of novices made an exhaustive survey of the remote, fascinating ruins of the region. That summer Kidder characterized Hewett as "one of the most learned men for his age I have ever met." Hewett gave these young students an unprecedented opportunity (Woodbury 1973, 12).

After this survey, Kidder and the others assisted Hewett in mapping several sites at Mesa Verde, and finally they participated in excavations at Puye on the Pajarito Plateau. The following summer, Kidder was back in the Southwest, this time to work in southeastern Utah under another early dean of Southwestern archaeology, Byron Cummings. During these two summers Kidder received an excellent introduction to Southwestern archaeology and, more important, came under the spell of the Southwest.

In 1909, Kidder entered graduate school at Harvard to study anthropology and was influenced by two scholars who furthered his intellectual development. George Chase showed Kidder the potential of ceramic analysis as practiced on classical Greek vessels, and the Egyptologist George Reisner introduced him to a much more sophisticated understanding of research design and advanced field techniques than he had been exposed to under Hewett or Cummings (Wauchope 1965, 151; Woodbury 1973, 20–21).

Kidder was also fortunate to visit many archaeological projects in Europe, America, and the Middle East and began to see firsthand several new field techniques, like the more refined use of stratigraphy. The influence of Chase and Reisner was to become integral to Kidder's doctoral dissertation, which emphasized pottery, and later to his work at Pecos Pueblo with the importance he placed on stratigraphy as a key technique of excavation.

In 1910 Kidder joined Kenneth M. Chapman of Santa Fe, a principal authority on Pueblo pottery. Later, in reflecting on that visit, Kidder wrote, "We made a large collection of potsherds at Pecos. We were very much struck by the variety of types represented at the site; there being specimens of all varieties then known in the Rio Grande, from the ancient black-on-white to the obvious modern. . . . I felt that here if anywhere could be found the stratified remains which were so badly needed to straighten out the chronological problems of the district. Accordingly, when the chance came in 1915 to undertake an extensive piece of excavation, I at once recommended Pecos" (quoted in Woodbury 1981, 17).

Kidder's dissertation, completed in 1914, shows the effect of his considerable field experience and the extent of his intellectual growth. The topic he chose was not a modest one: "Southwestern Ceramics: Their Value in Constructing the History of the Ancient Cliff Dwelling and Pueblo Tribes: From the Point of View of Type Distinctions." Recognizing that "no adequate descriptions of the pottery" had been published, Kidder wanted to remedy "this condition: by providing a short description of the known wares" based on a careful analysis of ceramic collections from a wide area of the Southwest (Kidder 1914, 411–12). He devoted more than fifty pages to the pottery of the Pajarito Plateau alone, which contrasted sharply with Hewett's single page on the pottery from that area, which had appeared only a few years earlier (Hewett 1906, 52).

Kidder discussed the relation between pottery and culture and speculated on the chronology of the wares from distribution and design clues. He pointed out that his temporal conclusions were tentative because he found no stratified finds that could give him absolute proof. Kidder had visited Nelson's excavations and in a footnote near the end of the dissertation, clearly inserted after the main work had been completed, Kidder reported that Nelson had just published on his San Cristóbal Pueblo excavations and "it can hardly be doubted that this most important discovery will throw light upon the sequence of the types described in this paper" (Kidder 1914, 461).

Within a relatively short period of time, several archaeologists were recognizing the importance of pottery as a tool that could contribute to placing prehistoric occupations in time and assessing cultural relationships. Nelson's approach stressed extensive excavation at many sites and the use of stratigraphy, with little emphasis on pottery description. Kroeber and Spier focused on the direct historic approach and seriation. Kidder used pottery construction, design, and distribution to hypothesize temporal relationships, while recognizing that stratigraphic data were needed to validate his ideas. All of these approaches were to mesh perfectly for Kidder at Pecos and enable him to take an important new step in the development of archaeology far beyond the northern Rio Grande.

After receiving his doctorate, Kidder worked with Samuel Guernsey of Harvard's Peabody Museum exploring the archaeological materials in rock shelters in northeastern Arizona. Their benchmark reports, scrupulously recording an amazing range of perishable materials, foreshadow the talents that made Kidder one of the Southwest's premier field archaeologists and scholarly writers.

In 1915 the trustees of Phillips Academy in Andover, Massachusetts, and the Robert S. Peabody Foundation for Archaeology decided to support a major archaeological project in the Southwest. Two of the academy's trustees, Roland B. Dixon of Harvard and Hiram Bingham of Yale, were impressed with Kidder's performance as a student and with his work with Samuel Guernsey. They recommended that this affable twenty-nine-year-old be the leader of the important research initiative that would foster a novel kind of archaeology focused more on ideas than on excavation. The trustees had no way of knowing that by choosing Kidder they would help to transform Southwestern archaeology.

Accepting the invitation to lead this major new effort and drawing on his earlier enthusiasm, Kidder chose Pecos Pueblo as the centerpiece for his research. Situated seven thousand feet above sea level at the foot of the snow-capped Sangre de Cristo Mountains, the pueblo had been established just above the Pecos River, in a dramatic location of rosy-colored cliffs surrounded by grasses and shrubs and bordered by thick stands of dark green pinyon and juniper trees. Furthermore, it lay at the eastern edge of the Pueblo domain and on the edge of the Great Plains, where trade with the Plains tribes was an important part of its economy. He felt Pecos possessed all the elements necessary, including a rich historical record from the Spanish, for making an auspicious contribution to understanding Southwestern prehistory.

## HISTORIC PECOS PUEBLO

In the spring of 1540 Francisco Vásquez de Coronado led the initial Spanish incursion of *conquistadores* into the Southwest. Searching for the Seven Cities of Cibola, he hoped to find a treasure trove of gold equal to those found in Mexico and Peru. He traveled north and was the first European to reach Pecos Pueblo about thirty miles southeast of what was later to become Santa Fe, New Mexico. It was one of the biggest and most majestic Indian villages in the region, with a population of more than two thousand. Like the people of the other pueblos the Spanish visited, the people of Pecos farmed corn, beans, and squash. They also traded with the Plains Indians to the east, exchanging cotton, turkeys, and farm products for meat and hides.

Coronado was struck by the number of people living there, by its rock-walled fortification, and by its military strength. He observed a community composed of blocks of rooms four to five stories high built around a central plaza containing several semisubterranean ceremonial chambers; these later came to be called kivas. The encounter was peaceful because Coronado reasoned that Pecos was well protected by some five hundred warriors. His composed demeanor undoubtedly was due to his experience with Southwest Indians at Hawikuh, near Zuni, the first pueblo he encountered. The people protected themselves from the strange foreigners by retreating to the roof of the pueblo and attacking the Spanish from above.

After a four-decade gap, Pecos was visited by Antonio de Espejo in a more aggressive encounter between the two cultures. Espejo compelled the inhabitants to provide his soldiers with food and abducted two of the pueblo's males.

The third Spanish visit to Pecos Pueblo brought further deterioration of relations with the local people. On the morning of December 31, 1590, a party of thirty-seven men headed by Gaspar Castaño de Sosa arrived and was greeted with deep suspicion. In his advance on the pueblo, de Sosa spent five hours marching around the pueblo displaying some pageantry and trying to give gifts to pacify the community. When his efforts failed, he began a raid and gained a commanding position on the roof of the pueblo. The next night, however, while the Spaniards slept, all of the village occupants secretly slipped away. Four days later de Sosa, defeated in his efforts to gain control, left Pecos in search of other communities.

The writings of de Sosa were published in 1965 by the School of American Research under the title *A Colony on the Move.* This excellent translation was edited and annotated by Albert H. Schroeder and Dan S. Matson. A portion of this chronicle is quoted here, as it provides such a rich introduction to the life of the Pecos community that Kidder was to spend so many years uncovering:

> The houses in this pueblo are (arranged) in the manner of houseblocks. They have doors to the outside all around, and the houses are (set) back to back. The houses are of four and five stories. In the galleries there are no doors to the streets. They go up little ladders that can be pulled up by hand through the hatchways. Every house has 3 or 4 apartments (on each story) so that from top to bottom each house has 15 or 16 rooms. The rooms are worthy of note, being well whitewashed.
>
> In the arrangements for its grinding, each house has three and four grindstones (usually referred to as *metates* . . . ), which are placed and fitted into little bins, and the *manos* (handstones) for grinding, and (they [the bins] are) well whitewashed. They grind with this peculiarity that they pass along from one to the other the flour which they grind, and they do not make *ixtamal,* but with this flour they make their bread in many ways and not *atole* and *tamales.*
>
> There were in this pueblo five plazas. There was a very great amount of maize which, as it seemed to all, was a thing to be wondered at. There were persons who thought and said that there (must be) more than 30,000 *fanegas* of maize, because every house had 2 or 3 rooms full. It is the best maize that was seen. There were many beans. The corn was of many colors, and the same (is true of) the beans. Apparently there was corn from the two previous years. They have many green herbs (*quilites* . . . ) and *calabaza* (pumpkins or gourds) in their houses (and) many things for the cultivation of their corn fields.

After de Sosa's visit, the people of Pecos were subjected to a long series of incursions by Europeans that some two hundred years later would lead to the abandonment of the community. They were ravaged by smallpox and other diseases introduced by the Spanish. Pecos, like other pueblos, was also fiercely missionized during the seventeenth century, and the tyrannical Catholic friars were an important impetus to the revolt of the Southwestern pueblos against the Spaniards in 1680, causing all Europeans to withdraw from the region.

The Spanish did not reenter the Southwest until they were led back by Don Diego de Vargas in 1692–93. By this time the Apache, Navajo, and Plains Indians had become much stronger, acquiring guns and horses and periodically raiding Pecos and the other pueblos.

A new period of European contact began with the advent of the Santa Fe Trail in 1821, whose path from Missouri to Santa Fe lay quite near the pueblo. Now "Pecos had a steady stream of visitors—merchants from Missouri at first, then later soldiers, immigrants to California, and stagecoach passengers. On the flats surrounding the pueblo could be found an abundance of wood, water, and grass, the essentials for a comfortable camp. If the caravan got a good rest at Pecos, it could usually make Santa Fe with another hard day's push" (Simmons 1981, 3).

Eventually the ravages of European disease, raids by Plains Indians, the impact of the Santa Fe Trail, and the encroachment of Hispanic settlers put such pressure on the pueblo's lands and peoples that serious domestic conflicts were arising. Irreversible damage had now been done to Pecos society. The pueblo lost nearly 75 percent of its population, and in 1838 the last Pecos Indians vacated their once splendid settlement, moving west across the Rio Grande to join the Pueblo people of Jemez. The untended pueblo of Pecos gradually fell into ruin.

## KIDDER'S RESEARCH AT PECOS

Kidder built his work at Pecos on the valuable historical records and on the earlier archaeological work of Bandelier,

Hewett, Nelson, Kroeber, Spier, and others. But in several ways Kidder's singular work at Pecos moved far beyond that of any of his predecessors: in its long concentration on a single settlement; in the grand scale of his research efforts; in its thoughtful research design and organization of resources; and in the employment of experts on a range of subjects outside of archaeology. Kidder's Pecos work was to be the largest excavation of its time north of Mexico, and still today it stands as an important chapter in American archaeology.

Richard Woodbury, in his excellent biography, spells out Kidder's ambitious research plan for Pecos and his interests in using it to examine much broader issues:

> Kidder was not going to excavate Pecos only for the sake of learning more about Pecos. He planned to use the knowledge he gained, particularly the stratigraphic sequence that would give its pottery types a precise chronological placement, to put all the other Indian ruins of the Rio Grande area into a regional chronology. His plan was for intensive research at Pecos, followed by extensive explorations to locate as many sites in the Rio Grande drainage as possible. Although he never completed the second part, his sequence at Pecos still laid the foundation for all future Rio Grande archaeology and his pottery classifications became familiar and indispensable to generations of students and scholars.
>
> Another of Kidder's aims was to use the Pecos work as a start on an understanding of Plains archaeology which at that time was wholly unknown. Pecos had stood between the Pueblos and the Plains as a military buffer and a trading center and the site could be expected to yield Plains materials in its deposits. Finally, Kidder saw that Pecos could, as he wrote, "epitomize . . . a long period in the culture history of the Southwest . . . an index to consider part of that culture history, and so, it

> seems to me, too much effort cannot be spent on the details of its archaeology. But . . . we must keep constantly in mind the more general problems that it is being used to solve." (Woodbury 1981, 17–18)

Because Pecos had been occupied in such recent times Kidder felt he would be better able to understand what went on during the prehistoric period by comparing his archaeological material to the life that had been recorded there during the historic period. He also hoped to find at Pecos evidence of an "avenue from Middle America into the Southwest" and on "the origin of Pueblo culture."

Kidder selected Pecos as the focus of his research because he felt that its large trash deposit had the potential of revealing the longest record of unbroken settlement of any prehistoric Rio Grande pueblo. From the beginning, Kidder envisioned that he would use the now proven stratigraphic method as a foundation for his whole project, assuming it could offer new insights into the prehistory, not only of Pecos Pueblo, but of the whole Southwest. The importance of stratigraphy for chronological ordering had been demonstrated by Nelson in the Southwest, but Kidder may have already been convinced of the significance of this technique by a course he took at Harvard taught by Reisner. He may also have been influenced by his brother Homer Kidder (Williams 1998, 12).

Kidder did find a deeper accumulation of trash deposits than he had expected, but in the end he was disappointed. They did not produce the indications of notable antiquity he had hoped for.

In consulting the old Spanish accounts of Pecos Pueblo and the descriptions by Bandelier, and from what he saw on the surface, Kidder had a good understanding of the nature of the settlement prior to excavation. He realized that two large buildings made up the bulk of the settlement, a prehistoric compound at the north end of the low mesa on which the settlement was built and, to the south, the seventeenth-century adobe church that the Spanish Franciscan missionaries had directed the Pecos Indians to construct.

The old mission building was in terrible shape because for years the local people had been removing its adobe bricks and roof timbers for their own use. Since Kidder wanted to concentrate his efforts on the prehistoric section of the pueblo, he invited his old friend Jesse Nusbaum, whom he had met in 1907 during his Southwestern adventure with Edgar Hewett, to work on the mission. Hewett was now director of the School of American Research, which then owned the site, and he made it possible for Nusbaum, an excellent builder and craftsman, to work on the stabilization and restoration of the church.

In June 1915 Kidder began his excavations, focusing on the prehistoric pueblo at the north end of the mesa. This four- or five-story masonry structure, which Kidder named the Quadrangle, measured four hundred by two hundred feet. One important issue was the great number of burials that were uncovered during the excavation. While these contained pottery and a wide range of tools and other artifacts which provided insights into the material culture of the inhabitants, there were so many that Kidder felt they should be analyzed by a specialist. By the completion of the project, many years later, some nineteen hundred human remains had been recovered. Kidder asked Earnest Hooton of Harvard to study these intensively, and they revealed a great deal about the length of life, the nutrition, and the health of Pecos's prehistoric inhabitants (Hooton 1930).

Hooton's work on the human remains was significant, for Kidder was realizing that the only way he was going to obtain the essence of the settlement's cultural development was by using insights from a wide range of other social, natural, and environmental disciplines. This multidisciplinary approach to his archaeology became a centerpiece of Kidder's research design.

Kidder continued his work at Pecos through 1929, with a break during 1917–19 when he served in combat in the First

World War. After the first decade of excavation, Kidder wrote, "We have found that the Pecos site is much more extensive and vastly more complicated than had been expected. . . . we must be careful to hold ourselves to a proper balance between the detailed and the general. The details of archaeology are in themselves so interesting that it is fatally easy to become completely absorbed in them." Throughout his work at Pecos, Kidder worked to achieve that balance between the minutiae of the pueblo's remains and the larger questions which drew his interest. In the end his struggle for balance was only partially successful because before he completed his full mission he moved on to other work—but nevertheless he had created with his work at Pecos an admirable model for archaeological research.

## PUBLISHING ON PECOS

Kidder's vision of a well-planned, comprehensive program of research included the conviction that unless his work was exhaustively recorded in print and shared with others, the field excavation would have only been a pleasant adventure. Therefore he conceived and executed a comprehensive publishing program. First, in 1924, he presented his *Introduction to the Study of Southwestern Archaeology,* as number 1 of the Papers of the Southwestern Expedition, Department of Anthropology, Phillips Academy, under the imprint of Yale University Press.

This early summary of the first ten years of his Pecos research, and its placement within the larger framework of Southwestern prehistory, was followed by six other published volumes on Kidder's Pecos research. Together these volumes established an admirable standard for archaeological publication. He asked Carl Guthe to write on Pueblo pottery making (1925). Elsie Clews Parsons conducted research on the pueblo of Jemez (1925), where the last of the Pecos inhabitants migrated in the nineteenth century. Hooton's work on the hundreds of skeletons from the excavation was reported in *The Indians of Pecos Pueblo* (1930). Kidder himself,

Fig. 2. (*Above*) General view of the Pecos Valley taken from an ancient shrine north of the ruins. (*Below*) The excavations on the North Terrace, about 1920. The low walls of the oldest settlement appear in the left foreground. To the right and above are the remains of the great terraced community-house of later times.

along with Charles Amsden, in 1931 reported on the "dull paint" and black-on-white wares in *The Pottery of Pecos,* volume 1. Kidder also analyzed and described the artifacts of Pecos in a book published in 1932. Finally, Kidder and Anna O. Shepard published *The Pottery of Pecos,* volume 2, the Glaze Wares, in 1936.

Kidder's original plan was to publish this series of volumes on various aspects of his Pecos Pueblo research. He intended to write a concluding grand synthesis. This was long delayed, however, and never fully executed owing to Kidder's radical career change in 1929, when he accepted a position with the Carnegie Institution of Washington to administer its research in the Maya area. When Kidder finally retired from this position in 1958, he was no longer the vigorous young man who had begun the Pecos project. He was now in the twilight of his years and had much less energy than he had in his early days. The formative period of northern Rio Grande archaeology had passed, and a great deal of work had been carried out by others during the intervening thirty years. Kidder (1958) did publish a short overview of Pecos in his monograph *Miscellaneous Studies, Pecos, New Mexico: Archaeological Notes.* But with the passage of time, the intervening of Kidder's other responsibilities, and the rapid advancement of Southwestern archaeology, his major synthesis of the Pecos project never materialized.

Kidder's great ability to carry out an extended program of excavation and to foster an extensive agenda of publication was aided by his skill as a synthesizer, most elegantly displayed in his masterful *Introduction to Southwestern Archaeology.* This was the first comprehensive synthesis of the prehistory of Arizona, New Mexico, and the surrounding regions, and it became a model for New World archaeology. As Irving Rouse wrote in his earlier introduction to this volume, it "set the pattern for much subsequent work in other areas" (1962, 1). Kidder brought together what was known at the time about prehistoric life in the American Southwest, but, beyond this portrait of the past, he discussed how life changed over time and differed over the Southwest's vast geographic range. Kidder also discussed where more work was needed. Finally, he laid out what he thought would be a productive program for future research in the continuing study of Southwestern archaeology.

Writing in a thoroughly readable style, Kidder created that unusual combination of a scholarly book that made key advances in understanding and also was completely accessible to a broad public audience. "It is a rarity," wrote Gordon Willey (1967, 299), "in that it introduces systematics to a field previously unsystematized, and, at the same time, it is vitally alive and unpedantic. . . . He wrote a book that was romantic but not ridiculous, scrupulously close to the facts but not a boring recital of them."

Kidder's *Introduction* is roughly divided into three parts: the first 80 pages, nearly one-third of the book, relate to his initial decade of work at Pecos Pueblo, serving almost as a preface to his later, more detailed monographs on Pecos. This section covers the history of the pueblo and the results of his preliminary excavations. The next 180 pages review the then-current knowledge about specific areas of Southwestern prehistory. While 140 pages are devoted to the Pueblo area, only the remaining 40 pages cover the remainder of the Southwest, focusing on the Upper and Lower Gila regions, the Mimbres Valley, and the Chihuahua Basin. Finally, there is a 30-page synthetic overview of Southwestern prehistory.

Kidder's use of the term *Southwestern* in the title of this volume clearly contrasts with its decidedly Puebloan emphasis. In only 40 of just under 300 pages does he deal directly with non-Pueblo archaeology. Of course, this was not just a bias of Kidder's, but it represents the lack of systematic archaeology—or of nearly any work at all—at the time outside the northern Southwest. It also reflects the romantic appeal that the great prehistoric and historic masonry pueblos at Mesa Verde, Chaco Canyon, and on the Pajarito Plateau had for the early archaeologists, especially during this period when ideas were still less important than the spectacular artifacts that could fill museum shelves.

The nine subdivisions of the Southwest which Kidder identified were considered through the use of a uniform chronological ordering: (1) Basket Maker; (2) Post-Basket Maker; (3) Pre-Pueblo; and (4) Pueblo. These reflect the Pueblo focus of Kidder's thinking and in general conform to the periods of the Pecos Classification which emerged from the Pecos Conference in 1927.

Three explanatory themes were central to Kidder's synthesis: the cultural relation between the northern Rio Grande and the rest of the Southwest; the origins of the northern Rio Grande population and culture; and the sequence of the region's cultural development. Even before the introduction of tree-ring dating, later called dendrochronology, Kidder perceived that the cultural climaxes of the San Juan Basin, Mesa Verde, and Chaco Canyon areas predated the appearance of the large population concentrations along the Rio Grande (Kidder 1924, 87). He felt the Rio Grande area contributed little to the cultures of the west. "The Rio Grande," he wrote, "received but apparently gave nothing in return" (Kidder and Shepard 1936, 596).

Kidder initially conceived of the northern Rio Grande population and culture, especially Pecos Pueblo, as having developed locally (M. A. and A. V. Kidder 1917, 354). Later he allowed for a migration from the northern San Juan area, but not specifically from the Mesa Verde or the Chaco regions (Kidder and Amsden 1931, 152). He labored to point out the importance of the San Juan Basin as a "breeding ground" for Anasazi culture, while arguing against an actual migration from that area as an explanation for Pecos culture (Kidder and Shepard 1936, 596–610).

Kidder saw the prehistoric cultural development in the northern Rio Grande area as beginning with "pre-Pueblo type" occupation of small settlements, which he never described in detail. This was followed by the first Pueblo period, characterized by small houses whose residents used black-on-white and corrugated pottery; but this pottery was not closely identified with any specific types from the San Juan or other regions. Next appeared larger Puebloan structures of at least two stories built around courtyards with kivas, with a few red ware pottery types. Glaze pottery was then introduced, and settlements became still larger with great quadrangles or sometimes circular ground plans, though the absolute number of settlements he saw as declining in number. Finally, "toward the close of the glaze-ware period, after many of its most flourishing sites had already been abandoned, came the discovery of the Southwest by the Spaniards" (Kidder 1924, 86).

This summary, which built upon the earlier work of Bandelier, Hewett, and Nelson, was nevertheless a clear step beyond anything that had come before him. Given the relatively few years since Hewett had offered his sequential reconstruction, Kidder had made significant new contributions in detail, chronological ordering, and sensitivity to cultural dynamics. It is important to recognize that his general conception of northern Rio Grande prehistory was not to be substantially improved upon for thirty years, and then only following the development of dendrochronology and the publication of substantial amounts of new data.

In their excellent history of American archaeology, Gordon Willey and Jeremy Sabloff (1993, 131) put Kidder's *Introduction* into perspective: "In spite of its limitations, Kidder's *Introduction* marked the coming of age of the Southwest as an archaeological area. New work could be fitted into a spatial-temporal structure, and such a structure pointed the way to progress." Kidder's *Introduction* and his many contributions to follow led to his recognition as the dean of American archaeology.

While most reviewers were quite positive toward Kidder's prodigious work, later it was severely criticized in Walter

Taylor's "Study of Archaeology" (1948) (Willey and Sabloff 1993, 161). Taylor wrote that Kidder had failed to provide provenience data for artifacts, that he had not followed through on his long-promised grand synthesis of Pecos Pueblo, and had demonstrated no interest in process. Kidder was deeply hurt by this attack (Schwartz 1979, 167–68), yet earlier in his career Kidder had been a critic of his own peers' writing, expressing his opinion that unless they followed his lead in large-scale excavation "archaeology will lap into superficiality" (Kidder and Shepard 1936, 628).

## THE PECOS CONFERENCE

Kidder's ground-breaking work at Pecos and his Southwestern synthesis were two of his three major contributions to Southwestern archaeology. The third, for which he continues to be honored by his peers, was the initiation of a pioneering gathering of Southwestern scholars at what was called the Pecos Conference. This assembly of knowledge sharing has demonstrated its vigor and effectiveness by continuing for nearly seventy-five years.

In the late summer of 1927 Kidder invited active Southwestern archaeologists as well as others from affiliated fields to his field camp at Pecos. His purpose was spelled out in a letter of invitation he asked his colleague Jesse Nusbaum to write: "On September second, third and fourth, there will be held at the Laboratory of Anthropology in Santa Fe an informal conference upon the problems of Southwestern archaeology. It is planned to devote the first day to a discussion of general questions. On the second and third days, it is hoped that smaller groups will meet for consideration of more highly specialized matters" (Woodbury 1993, 116).

Kidder hoped through this gathering to spark a detailed conversation on the central issues of Southwestern archaeology and to arrive at a way of productively approaching these issues. More important, he wanted to "lay foundations for a unified system of nomenclature" (Kidder 1927, 489), so that all Southwestern archaeologists would begin speaking the same language about the wide range of prehistoric material they were discovering.

It was a real tribute to Kidder's professional reputation that most of the principal figures in early Southwestern archaeology attended that first Pecos Conference. The participants included Charles Amsden, who worked at the Galaz Ruin in the Mimbres Valley, New Mexico; Mr. and Mrs. C. B. Cosgrove, who excavated the Swartz Ruin, also in the Mimbres Valley; Byron Cummings, who worked in Utah, established archaeology at the University of Arizona, and worked at Kinishba Pueblo, Arizona, and with early Cochise culture sites; A. E. Douglass, the developer of tree-ring dating; Emil W. Haury, who dug Ventana Cave and the critical Hohokam site of Snaketown; Walter Hough, who did outstanding work in the Hopi country; Neil Judd, who carried out research at Pueblo Bonito in Chaco Canyon, New Mexico; Kidder's old friend from his student days Sylvanus Morley, who worked at the Cannonball Ruins and in Colorado, prior to his distinguished research in the Maya area; Earl Morris, who excavated the Aztec Ruin in northern New Mexico; Jesse Nusbaum, who, in addition to working with Kidder at Pecos, had done substantial research at Mesa Verde; and Frank H. H. Roberts, Jr., who excavated at the pre-Pueblo settlements in Chaco Canyon, as well as at the Paleo-Indian Folsom site in Colorado.

Today the Pecos Conference continues to be a vital element of Southwestern archaeology. Emil Haury, writing in a foreword to Richard Woodbury's comprehensive history of the conference (1993), summed up its importance:

> Through time the Conference evolved into a rich tradition among Southwestern archaeologists of holding meetings in August at the end of most field sessions. It thus served as a forum where from the podium the latest findings, ideas, and interpretations could be informally presented and debated. But more than that, it

> provided the occasion for people with kindred interests to fraternize and exchange views, who otherwise might not have had the opportunity to do so. This led to a cohesiveness in the research effort that pushed Southwestern archaeology ahead of that in other regions. Indeed, it was the model for the development of other regional conferences. (Haury 1993, xviii)

Perhaps the most important result of the first Pecos Conference was the realization of Kidder's goal to develop "a unified system of nomenclature," which came to be called the Pecos Classification, a set of temporal stages for the span of Southwestern prehistory. The system contained eight chronologically sequential stages but did not initially have specific chronological dates:

*Basketmaker I,* or *Early Basketmaker:* An assumed preagricultural stage, now called Archaic.

*Basketmaker II,* or *Basketmaker:* A time when agriculture was added to hunting and gathering, but when there was no pottery, and the spear-thrower was used because the bow and arrow had not yet arrived in the region.

*Basketmaker III,* or *Post-Basketmaker:* Lodging was in pit or slab houses. Pottery was now manufactured, undecorated when used for cooking.

*Pueblo I,* or *Proto-Pueblo:* Groups of dwellings were made up of aboveground, adjoining rectangular rooms of stone. Cooking pottery showed the unsmoothed coils on the outside or bands at the neck of the vessels.

*Pueblo II,* The surface of cooking pots was now corrugated, that is, covered with unsmoothed coils. Villages with only a few inhabitants were spread widely over the region.

*Pueblo III,* or *Great Pueblo:* Large settlements were occupied, and arts and crafts were present in specialized and elaborate forms.

*Pueblo IV,* or *Proto-Historic:* During this time a great deal of the Pueblo area was depopulated, most dramatically the San Juan region in southern Colorado. There was also a decline in artistic embellishment, and corrugated pottery progressively was replaced by plainware.

*Pueblo V,* or *Historic.* Beginning in A.D. 1600, this was the last stage of the Pecos Classification.

The Pecos Classification was an extremely important step in the organization of Southwestern prehistory. But as is true of any early system created in a field's development, as it was applied, problems emerged. It was soon realized that it could not be used as a strict chronological guide to what had occurred over the entire Southwest, for there had been no strict, uniform progression of stages. Rather, the classification was best used as the general trajectory of prehistoric Southwestern culture. Later, Frank H. H. Roberts proposed a revision that emphasized that the Pecos stages, while roughly following one another in time, were not synchronous throughout the Southwest, "nor were all developmental stages expected to be represented in every area (Roberts 1935b).

While the first weakness of the classification was one of chronology, another problem related to the growing awareness of cultural variety over the prehistoric Southwest. When the Pecos Classification was developed in 1927, essentially all of the prehistory of the Southwest was conceptualized as a modification of eastern Pueblo cultural developments, which included the occupations of the northern Rio Grande area. As archaeological research proceeded in the Lower Sonoran Desert, the Mogollon Mountains, and the western Anasazi area, it became clear that the eastern Pueblo pattern was only one of several and that the Pueblo periods were not as generally applicable as had originally been assumed.

With the coming of the 1930s, a new era of archaeological work began in the northern Rio Grande, a period no longer dominated by individuals. Researchers from several institutions were now simultaneously involved in field archaeology. These might be considered the second generation of outstanding archaeologists of the eastern Pueblo area and included H. P. Mera, Marjorie Lambert, Hubert Alexander, Frank Hibben, Florence Ellis, Bertha Dutton, and Paul Reiter. As a group these younger scholars continued to move the region's archaeology forward, building on the solid intellectual accomplishments of Kidder and the remarkable researchers who preceded him.

By the mid 1930s it was apparent that the Basketmaker-Pueblo sequence was an aspect only of the northern Southwest. So to mark off the distinct cultural nature of this area from that of other parts of the Southwest, Kidder (1936a, 590) proposed the designation *Anasazi* for this northern culture. Kidder drew the name from the Navajo word which he had translated as "old people." Unfortunately, his rendering was wrong, for it more accurately translates in Navajo as "enemy ancestors." Nevertheless, the term *Anasazi* became widely popular. Recently, as the correct translation has become clear and the use of a Navajo word as the designation for ancestors of the historic Pueblo people has been criticized, this word has been considered less acceptable. Therefore, the designation *Ancestral Puebloan* is being used in place of *Anasazi*. This change also clears up a great deal of confusion, especially among the general public, who for decades have thought of the Anasazi as some kind of mysterious predecessors unrelated to the historic Pueblo peoples.

## KIDDER'S LATER CAREER

Sylvanus Morley, one of the students that Kidder had worked with under Hewett during his first summer in the Southwest, had shifted his focus of research interest to Mexico. These two men had maintained their friendship, and in 1925 Kidder visited Morley's archaeological field operation at the site of Chichén Itzá, on the Yucatán Peninsula. Morley's work there was being sponsored by the Carnegie Institution of Washington, and Kidder soon became one of the Carnegie's consultants, then later a research associate. In 1927 he accepted the position of chairman of the Carnegie's Division of Historical Research. This gave him the responsibility for directing their whole archaeological program in

Middle America, an association that lasted for nearly thirty years.

Years later, in his final Pecos report, Kidder looked back on his Southwestern work and expressed, rather movingly, his feelings about that phase of his career:

> In 1924 I thought I knew a good deal about the Southwest in general, and Pecos, in particular. . . . how very wrong I was. But, I flatter myself, I was not nearly as wrong as he who advised me, just 50 years ago, to take up work in another field because, he said "The Southwest is a sucked orange." I only wish I could return to that wonderful country and wet my lips once again in the rich juice of a fruit which a half-century of research has little more than begun to tap. (Kidder 1958, 322)

## SOUTHWESTERN ARCHAEOLOGY AFTER PECOS

Gradually a recognition emerged that the Pueblo cultural tradition, with its many variations, was not the only, or even the major, prehistoric way of life in the Southwest, but that there have been several major cultural traditions. The earliest of these hunting and gathering ways of life were distributed over most of the Southwest and were called Paleo-Indian and Archaic. With the development of agriculture four coexistent cultures emerged: the Prehistoric Pueblo, earlier called Anasazi, on and around the Colorado Plateau; the Mogollon, in the central mountain region; the Hohokam, in the southern deserts; and the Patayan, along and to the east of the lower Colorado River. Then in the later protohistoric period two new hunting and gathering groups entered the Southwest. First, from the west, came Shoshonean speakers, the Ute and Paiute. Then Athabaskan speakers arrived from the north. Later this group split to become the Navajo and Apache.

## PALEO-INDIAN

The first realization that there was human population in the New World in the waning years of the Pleistocene Ice Age came in 1926, when stone spear points were found along with the bones of a large extinct bison at the Folsom site in northeastern New Mexico. This association was initially met with deep disbelief by the archaeological community because it meant that the occupation of the New World was much older than previously believed. That same year, however, another stone spear point was found, in place, associated with bison ribs, and this disbelief began to vanish. Work was stopped at this site and leading archaeologists, including Kidder, were invited to inspect the finds. They concluded that the finds were valid, and this began to convince others that human occupation in the New World and the Southwest was much older than previously thought.

Following this extraordinary discovery, there were additional finds of other types of stone lance points, like the beautifully made Clovis points, and the remains of extinct mammoths began to be found in the adjacent high plains of eastern New Mexico, Colorado, and Arizona. Subsequently remains of these early Native Americans were discovered in nearly every part of North America that had been unglaciated during the late Ice Age.

The period associated with these finds has been named Paleo-Indian, and it gradually was concluded that this population was the beginning of all the subsequent New World inhabitants. It was also believed that Paleo-Indians originated from people of Asian descent who traveled over the spacious Bering Strait land bridge at the time of the late Wisconsin glacial period. The land bridge, by geological estimation, could have been crossed at various periods between about 23,000 and 8,000 B.C. The exact date of this entry or series of entries and just who the people were who made this passage or passages remain unsolved puzzles in American archaeology.

Most Paleo-Indian finds have come from "kill sites," where

the early hunters butchered the now-extinct mammoth, giant sloth, large bison, and other Ice Age species. Paleo-Indians are thought to have been exceedingly mobile, expert hunters who undoubtedly supplemented their diet with the gathering of plant foods. While they roamed widely over the New World, they clearly lived in the Southwest from about 11,000 to sometime around 7,500 years ago. By 5500 B.C., when there was a change to a more modern climate, the large Ice Age mammals probably had nearly all disappeared, killed, at least in part, by Paleo-Indians, though there has also been speculation that new diseases brought from Asia may have played a part in their demise. In any case, as the Ice Age animals declined in numbers a new way of life, one that did not depend upon that source of food, was evolving.

## ARCHAIC

About 5500 B.C., as the Pleistocene was ending, as climate and plant growth began to assume modern characteristics, and with the passing of the large Ice Age animals, there was a transition to a new way of life. This was based more on the hunting of small to medium-sized modern game animals and an increased reliance on the gathering of wild plant foods. This more generalized economic pattern and the life that accompanied it has been termed Archaic. It lasted for about five thousand years until the introduction of agriculture sometime around A.D. 200.

While the archaeological clues to the highly nomadic life of the Paleo-Indians were slim, with the somewhat more settled life of the Archaic, a much more varied range of evidence became available to archaeologists about how life was being lived. For example, in cave sites of the Mogollon highlands along the Arizona–New Mexico border, Archaic remains have provided an excellent indication of the foods consumed during this period, including pigweed, hackberry, goosefoot, walnut, juniper berries, prickly pear, Indian rice-

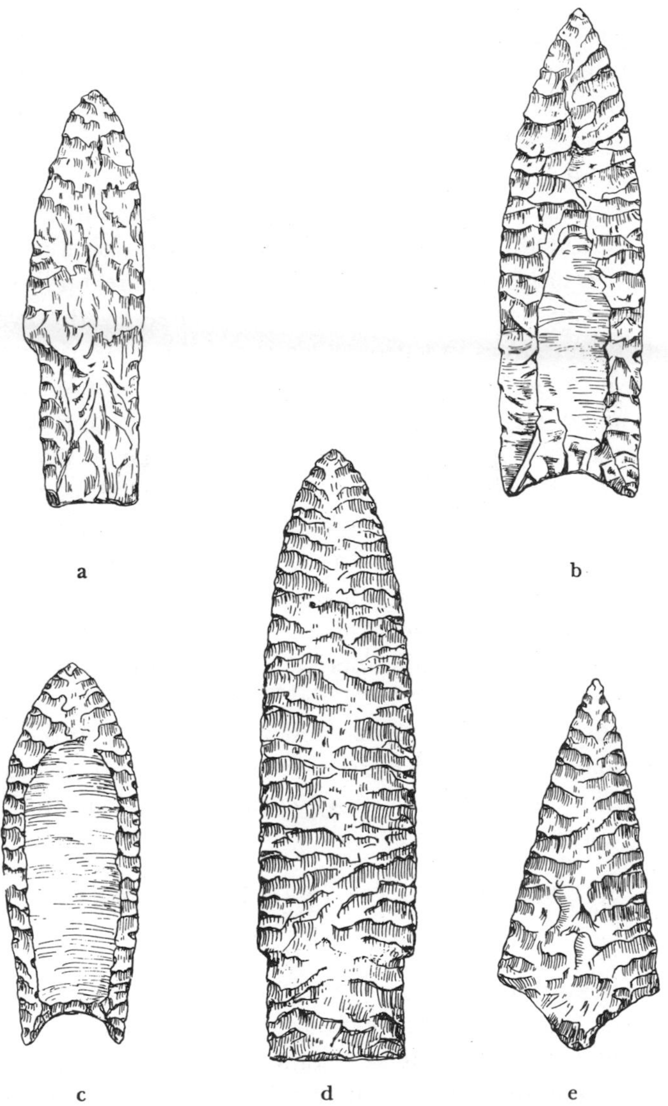


FIG. 3. Typical projectile points of the Paleo-Indian and Desert traditions: *a,* Sandia; *b,* Clovis; *c,* Folsom; *d,* Portales-like; *e,* Gypsum Cave (after Wormington 1957, figs. 68, 70, 72).

grass, yucca, as well as the contemporary animals that were hunted, bison, pronghorn antelope, mountain sheep, Sonoran deer, and mule deer. Also in these caves have been found the digging sticks, baskets, and snares used in connection with food acquisition.

Over time the population of Archaic peoples increased, which meant the territories they were using to obtain food had to become smaller. Movement within these territories was probably seasonal, their rhythm dictated by the availability of resources in various locations, such as seeds in the spring, fruits in the fall, and animal migration routes.

We know that as early as 2000 to 3000 B.C. people in the Southwest were living in small, shallow, circular to oval pithouses, a type of dwelling found widely from Asia to the New World. These subterranean dwellings contained fire hearths for cooking and heating and floorpits that were used for the storage of surplus foods. The stone tools of the Archaic period are more generalized and varied than those of the distinctive Paleo-Indian period. Ground stone tools were now made for grinding plant foods. There were also tools for woodworking, like drills, and smaller stone projectile points that were hafted onto wooden spears. Spears were propelled by a spear-thrower, or *atlatl*; the bow had not yet arrived in the Southwest.

## AGRICULTURE AND REGIONAL DIFFERENTIATION

The next major change in the life of Southwestern peoples came between about 1000 and 1500 B.C., when corn and squash were first cultivated by some of the local people. For the next thousand years the increasing presence of farming, at first a very casual part of the economy, catalyzed a major transition away from the Archaic hunting and gathering way of life to a gradual dependence on agriculture. By about 400 B.C. common beans were also being farmed, and many areas of the Southwest were entering a period of early agriculture, followed by an even more settled way of living with the appearance of pottery and more settlement concentration about A.D. 200.

As the agricultural way of life became the standard over most of the Southwest, the more generalized Archaic cultural pattern gave way to four regional Southwestern cultures:

Ancestral Pueblo—in the northern Southwest, essentially on and around the Colorado Plateau;

Hohokam—in the desert and river basins country of southern Arizona;

Mogollon—in the mountains of southern Arizona and New Mexico;

Patayan—along the southern borders of the Colorado River and into the western reaches of the Colorado Plateau.

## Ancestral Pueblo

The Ancestral Pueblo way of life was concentrated in and around the Colorado Plateau country of northern Arizona, northern New Mexico, southern Utah, and southern Colorado. This was the cultural tradition that gave birth to the historic and modern Pueblo people of the northern Southwest. The Ancestral Pueblo way of life began with the introduction of agriculture and pottery at about A.D. 200. It first appeared in the Four Corners region, then expanded widely over the Colorado Plateau, and eventually withdrew to the historic Pueblo range.

The Ancestral Pueblo people were farmers, mainly of corn, and to a much lesser extent of beans and squash. They also gathered a wide range of wild plants and used the bow and arrow to hunt deer, rabbit, bear, elk, mountain sheep, and many smaller animals. They raised and hunted turkey in part for their feathers, which were probably important in ceremonies. They buried their dead in the ground, sometimes accompanied by pottery, textiles, and ornaments.

The ancient Pueblo people first lived in semisubterranean

pithouses, but about A.D. 700 they began building compact stone or adobe multiroom, and later multistory, apartment settlements. These contained open-air work areas and special ceremonial rooms called kivas, some with painted murals. While many of the original aboveground structures were made of poles and mud, eventually adobe or stone was used in wall construction.

As pueblo dwellings gradually moved above ground, an associated trend was to place a series of two to six rooms in a row, and as the structures became larger they began to resemble what were historically termed pueblos. The rows of connected pueblo rooms have been called unit pueblos and were made in either crescent, L, or U shapes. In the plaza in front of these unit houses a structure like the old pithouse was excavated, but it also gradually changed its nature from a dwelling to a kiva.

Progressively, the Ancestral Pueblo people made increasingly superior pottery. There were a growing number of forms and more differentiation between plain cooking and fancy decorated wares. The pots were fired in a reducing atmosphere, producing a gray or white background on which first black and then other colors were applied. Regional specialization in pottery painting began. To the west, in the Kayenta area, carbon paint was applied to the pots, while in the east, beginning around Chaco Canyon in New Mexico, mineral paint was used, just one of the many differences that grew into a series of definite subcultures throughout the Pueblo area.

By A.D. 1100 large blocks of rooms were being constructed in one concentrated location. These impressive structures gave the name Great Pueblo Period to the time in one classification of Pueblo development. Then, during the fourteenth century, settlements grew to a thousand or more rooms, the precursors to the Pueblo settlements first seen by the Spanish when they entered the region in the sixteenth century.

## Hohokam

Near the middle of the Gila and lower Salt rivers, in the region of the lower Sonoran Desert of Arizona and the adjoining parts of Chihuahua and Sonora, an area that in summer is scorching hot, was the territory of the Hohokam cultural tradition. The word *Hohokam* comes from the Pima language and is translated "all-used-up," but it is customarily paraphrased in English as "ancestors," as first named by Emil Haury, who excavated its major settlement, Snaketown.

Some researchers believe that in the beginning Hohokam culture came directly from Mexico, while others maintain it evolved from the indigenous local hunting and gathering Cochise culture. By 300 B.C. the Hohokam were living in large, semisubterranean square dwellings and later, adjacent rooms were built at ground level. At first the Hohokam farmed by conserving the desert water in earthen dams used to divert water from flowing streams into their fields. Later they learned to control the water of the major rivers in the area, and their small settlements grew to villages of up to a hundred people.

Hohokam settlements were situated along exchange routes that stretched from the coast of California to the Great Plains and from central Mexico to the Rocky Mountains of Colorado. Over these routes were traded animal hides, ocean shells, turquoise, jet, coral, obsidian, parrot feathers, copper bells, and salt.

Gradually, Hohokam water diversions grew into networks of great irrigation canals that reached for hundreds of miles across the landscape. Settlements also grew, covering more than five hundred acres and consisting of a thousand people.

The Hohokam also built ball courts with adobe earthwork walls as high as sixteen feet and two hundred feet long. The game played in these courts was probably similar to that played in central Mexico. Eventually, as they expanded from their Gila and Salt Valley homeland, they constructed

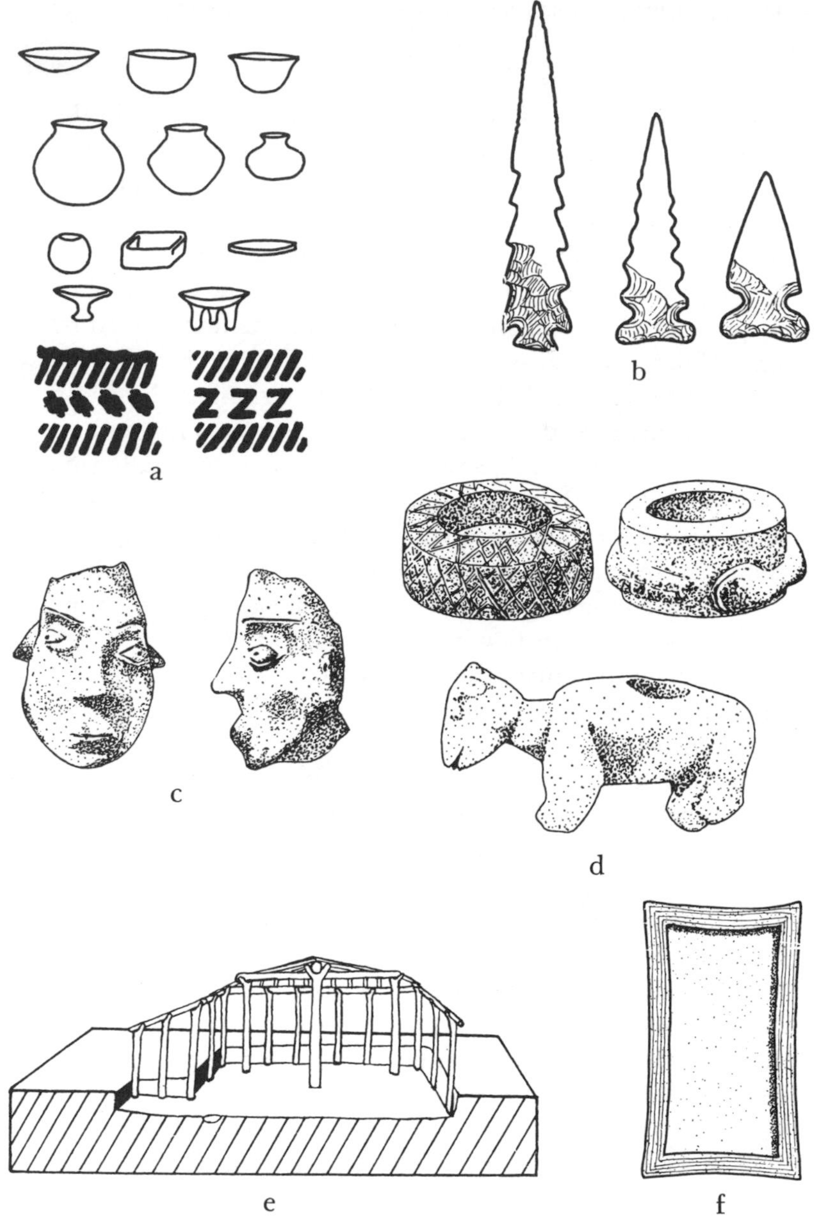


Fig. 4. Pithouse and artifacts of the Hohokam tradition: *a*, pottery; *b*, arrowheads; *c*, clay figurines; *d*, stone bowls; *e*, pithouse; *f*, stone palette (after McGregor 1941, 140, 148, 152, 153, 155, 161).

at least two hundred ball courts reaching from north of present-day Flagstaff to far south of Phoenix.

Prior to A.D. 800 the Hohokam had begun constructing great mounds of earth that may have served as ritual dance platforms. These platforms along with the vast irrigation works and the ball courts represented a huge investment of labor and suggest an extraordinary organization of effort. Beginning about A.D. 1150, however, the whole Hohokam regional system began a major decline. First, the ball court network was abandoned, as were many of the large settlements. The manufacture and use of many crafts were suspended, and some Hohokam even stopped cremating their dead.

Then about A.D. 1300 some individuals, who may have been the upper echelon of Hohokam society, placed their dwellings on the top of the platform mounds, perhaps reflecting a new hierarchical structuring. These lodgings at the tops of the mounds were painted in lively colors with emblems of authority and social position. Now the trade goods from the surrounding regions were employed to embellish only the privileged few. The final stage of these changes began around A.D. 1400, as the Hohokam gradually abandoned their desert settlements as the result of great floods, salt accumulations in the soil from long-term irrigation waters, internal strife, or the dissolution of their long trade routes.

The Hohokam are thought by many to have been the ancestors of the Pima and Tohono O'Odham, once called the Papago, who lived in this same region when the first Europeans visited in the late seventeenth century. They found the Pima making a living, using domiciles, and interring their dead in a fashion similar to that of the Hohokam.

The Pima's own origin stories are quite different from those hypothesized by archaeologists, however. In the words of one investigator, "They deny that the ancient ones, the Hohokam, were their ancestors. Pima oral tradition holds that those who built the mound sites were an evil people they call the *civanos*. The Pima believe that their ancestors arrived from the East, driving the wicked *civanos* out of the Phoenix basin" (Thomas 1994, 118).

## Mogollon

In the high valleys and forests and mountain meadows along the border between Arizona and New Mexico, the Mogollon cultural tradition thrived and struggled between about A.D. 200 and 1400. While some of the Southwest's earliest agriculture, pottery, and dwellings have been found in this area, this rugged upland environment does not seem to have been conducive to the kind of spectacular growth or cultural climax that occurred with the Ancestral Pueblo or Hohokam. Eventually, Mogollon culture was all but submerged by a southward drift of Anasazi traits.

The best-known branch of the Mogollon tradition is the Mimbres culture, who have been recognized around the world as potters. Their elaborate black-on-white geometric designs, while impressive, pale beside their imaginative depictions of humans and animals. The range of species represented and the scope of their dramatic living scenes are truly impressive. Insects, birds, deer, antelope, bighorn sheep, bats, rabbits, and humans are shown in a variety of poses and activities, providing a rare insight into everyday life in the prehistoric Southwest. Mimbres pottery was frequently placed in graves and "killed" by perforating delicate holes through the bottom, which is thought to represent a freeing of the spirits embodied in the pots.

By about A.D. 1000 Mogollon culture begins to look much like that of the Ancestral Pueblo, including white-slipped pottery with black designs and aboveground dwellings of adjacent rectangular roomblocks, grouped around large open plazas. Within these roomblocks rectangular ceremonial kivas also begin to appear.

Most of Mogollon country was unaccountably depopulated about A.D. 1400, the people either leaving or dying off: "A curious development, given the abundance of rich agricultural land and water that seemed everywhere available"

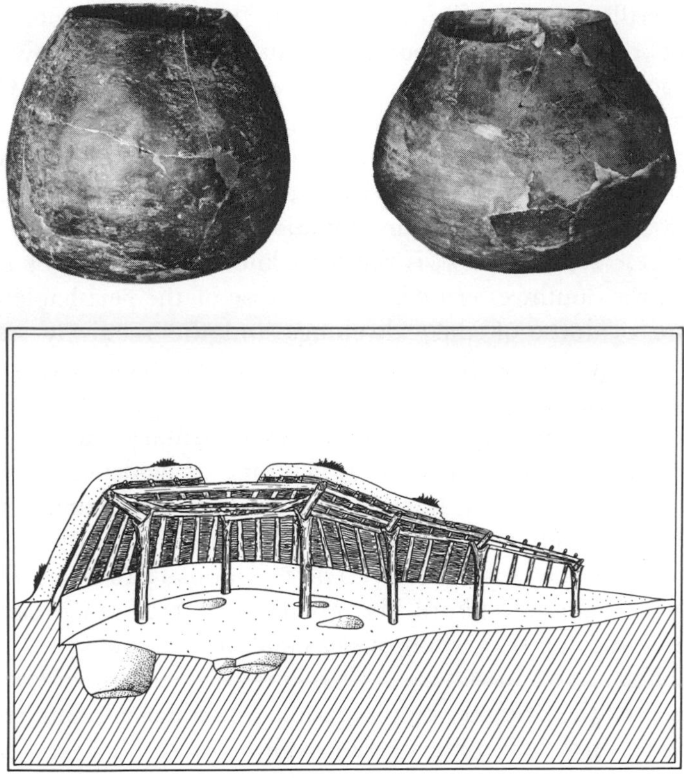

FIG. 5. Pithouse and pottery of the Mogollon tradition (after Martin 1959, 60, 64).

(Thomas 1994, 122). There is no known archaeological relationship between the Mogollon and any historic Indians in the Southwest, nor do any Indians claim to be their descendants.

## PATAYAN

A fourth cultural tradition, the Patayan, extended from the southern side of the western Grand Canyon west over the neighboring uplands and down into the Colorado River Valley (Schroeder 1979). This region was primarily an extension of the basin and range province with a generally desertlike ecology. Shroeder writes, "It contains a considerable diversity of environments with mountains and low flat desert valley with dry lakes in the west, the broad lower Colorado River valley, and the mountains and valleys of the upland area of western Arizona" (1979, 101). Throughout the region there are extremes in seasonal and daily temperatures, and annual precipitation averages less than ten inches. This tradition is the least known of the major prehistoric Southwestern cultures because of the perishable nature of most of their dwellings and the relatively small amount of archaeological research that has been carried out in their territory.

The Patayan people lived a semisedentary way of life, with a low dependence on agriculture, as evidenced by the shallow deposits of trash found at their settlements, their propensity for making jacale or low rock-walled dwellings, the absence of what appear to be ceremonial structures, their sparse material culture, the great number of small campsites, and the suggestion of seasonal occupation.

They lived in diffuse settlements of sunshade ramadas, finished their pottery by the paddle and anvil-thinning technique, fired their pottery in an oxidized atmosphere to a buff to gray color that was rarely decorated, and cremated their dead. It is generally thought that the Patayan tradition is ancestral to the modern Yuman-speaking peoples, who historically lived in this same area, but more research is needed to confirm this hypothesis.

## LATER HUNTING AND GATHERING PEOPLE

### Athabaskan

Two contemporary Southwestern Native American groups speak an Athabaskan language, their main linguistic relatives living in central Canada. The Navajo and the Apache live around the Four Corners area of Arizona, Utah, Colorado, and New Mexico, land that was settled by earlier

FIG. 6. Hogan and pottery of the Athabaskan tradition (after Keur 1941, pls. 4, a; 3, a).

Pueblo people. Although there is no complete agreement on the time when Athabaskans reached the Southwest or the route they traveled, many archaeologists assume they hunted and gathered their way south from central Canada, moving along the eastern front range of the Rocky Mountains, arriving in the Southwest at just about the time of, or just prior to, the arrival of Europeans.

The Diné (the People), as the Athabaskans call themselves, reached their first home in the Southwest, according to Navajo tradition, in northwestern New Mexico, a place they called Dinetah, "among the Navajo" (Trimble 1993, 131). It was here, just north of Pueblo territory, that about 1600 they encountered the Spanish.

By the time the Spanish arrived in the Southwest, the Navajo and Apache had expanded their territory to the rough lands surrounding the Pueblo villages. And when they were not hunting, gathering, or trading with one another, the Dine occasionally raided the Pueblo fields and storage bins. In the early historic period they probably learned to make pottery and farm from their Pueblo neighbors. Some say the word *Navajo* comes from the Tewa/Pueblo word for "planted fields." They also raised goats, sheep, and horses, which they initially acquired from the Spanish. The wool from their sheep was used to improve their weaving, and eventually the Navajo became famous for their expertly made rugs and serapes.

During the first three quarters of the 1700s there was a period of cultural interchange between Navajo and Pueblo people when they lived together in remote canyons of northern New Mexico, trying to protect themselves from the violence of the Spanish Reconquest of New Mexico. Later, during the Long Walk, between 1863 and 1867 the Navajo were removed to the Bosque Redondo in eastern New Mexico. There, at Fort Sumner, they were kept in wretched conditions until they were allowed to travel back to their territory.

## Shoshone/Numic

Sometime around A.D. 1300, just as the Ancestral Pueblo people were leaving southern Utah and southern Colorado, nomadic peoples living a nonagricultural way of life expanded into the Southwest from the west and north. Their role, if any, in the depopulation of the northern Southwest during the thirteenth century has never been clear. These Shoshone/Numic speakers included the Paiute on the west and Ute to the east. Linguistic evidence suggests their ancestors originally came from southeastern California and adjacent southern Nevada. It has been proposed that about A.D. 1000, for unknown reasons, they swelled in numbers and expanded toward the north and east.

By A.D. 1300 these Numic speakers had reached the northern Southwest as well as the southern Plateau country far to the north. In the southern part of their range they lived from just north of Pueblo territory, around the northwestern section of the Grand Canyon, to the east near the northernmost headwaters of the Rio Grande. One tribe, the Comanche, spread as far as the Southern Plains. Historically they traded and sometimes feuded with and raided their Pueblo neighbors to the south, the Navajo, and the Yuman-speaking Havasupai and Walapi who lived to the south of their range across the Colorado River in Arizona.

These people were first referred to collectively as Shoshonean but later reclassified by the linguistic term *Numic*. There were historically as many as fifty separate informal bands, which were never unified politically. Their way of life is well summarized by Stephen Trimble in his excellent book on the peoples of the Southwest (1993, 326–27): "The southern Paiute moved through the land with the seasons and harvests, using every available resource within about ten miles of camp, at a sequence of sites visited each year. . . . The annual cycle of hunting and gathering varied with the ecological zones available to each band."

When Father Escalante crossed their dominion in 1776,

the Ute and probably all of their Numic cousins had no horses and lived in small family clusters, subsisting by gathering wild foods. There was, at this time, no clear separation between the Ute and the southern Paiute. After acquiring horses in the early nineteenth century, however, the Ute of western Colorado and later of northern Utah organized into loose bands of hunters who later preyed on livestock owned by other Native Americans and Europeans.

## RECENT SYNTHESES OF SOUTHWESTERN PREHISTORY

Beginning in the early 1950s some interest in broad regional synthesis reemerged in the Southwest with new attempts to look at the region as a single system, based on a great deal more information than had been available to Kidder and the participants in the early Pecos Conferences. First, Paul Martin and John Rinaldo (1951) used the concept of cotradition, a framework that Wendell Bennett had just pioneered for the Andean area, as a way of excluding the details and focusing on the major trends and characteristics that unified the whole Southwest. This attempt was followed by Hiroshi Daifuku (1952), then by Irving Rouse (1962), and later others also tried to pull all the material together in one understandable system, continuing the earlier efforts of Hewett, Kidder, and Roberts.

In 1983 the School of American Research in Santa Fe sponsored an advanced seminar that "sought to review the general status of archaeological knowledge in 11 key regions of the Southwest . . . to examine a set of broader questions about the region's cultural development, including the themes of cultural change which cross-cut these subregions, and to construct an overall conceptual model of the prehistoric Southwest after the advent of sedentism" (Schwartz 1989, xiii). Out of this effort came a comprehensive attempt to move beyond geographic divisions and characterize the whole pattern of Southwestern prehistory. The synthesis was composed of five regionwide periods, covering the beginning of sedentary occupations to the end of the prehistoric period. This effort can serve as a useful comparison to Kidder's concluding summary over a half century earlier (Cordell and Gummerman 1989):

Initiation—A.D. 200/500 to 750/800
Expansion—A.D. 770/800 to 1000/1050
Differentiation—A.D. 1000/1050 to 1130/1150
Reorganization—A.D. 1130/1150 to 1275/1300
Aggregation—A.D. 1275/1300 to 1540

## Initiation—200/500 to 750/800

Between A.D. 200 and 500 life in the Southwest moved toward a greater dependence on farming and much more permanent settlements. Throughout the region a nondescript brown and gray pottery was made, and pithouses continued to be used as habitations. The reason for the major change in this lifestyle, from the earlier hunting and gathering pattern, is not completely understood or agreed upon, but some feel it relates quite directly to changing physical circumstances, with poor environmental conditions leading to an increased dependence on agriculture and a decrease in residential mobility.

## Expansion—770/800 to 1000/1050

By the beginning of the ninth century there was an even larger increase in the number and density of settlements, and these are found in a wide range of environments. There is some suggestion that during this time of less reliable moisture, at least in the north, settlements were of short duration and there was a planned experimentation that sought out the most agriculturally productive lands.

## Differentiation—1000/1050 to 1130/1150

In the eleventh century, with favorable climatic conditions, the Southwest was transformed into a region with myriad local ceramic styles. Around Chaco Canyon in the north and the Hohokam in the south, large, elaborate regional cultural systems emerged. While the Chaco and Hohokam systems were extensive, it does not appear that they were economically or socially stratified or were moving toward small-scale states. Clearly, in both of these cases and later, further south at Casas Grandes, something different was happening, an experiment in social and political organization on a regional scale, but an experiment that would fail and would never appear in the Southwest again.

## Reorganization—1130/1150 to 1275/1300

During the eleventh century, it appeared that the great Chaco and Hohokam regional systems could evolve into some form of complex social and political developments. With the beginning of the twelfth century, however, the bottom seemed to drop out of this potential. About A.D. 1130 the climate changed, and what appeared to have been quite successful courses of cultural elaboration collapsed. There were at least three different kinds of cultural breakdown at this time: total abandonment in marginal areas like the Grand Canyon (Schwartz 1989, 62); cessation of building and elaboration, as in the Chaco region; and simplification, of the kind that occurred in the Hohokam area. In the latter case, while the old major centers of Southwestern culture, Chaco and Hohokam, were not abandoned, they seem to have greatly declined as sources of new ideas and power.

With lowered precipitation, lower water tables, and an increase in erosion in the Chaco region, no new buildings were constructed, although there was still continued habitation. Marginal areas like the Grand Canyon and Black Mesa, north of the Hopi country, were abandoned completely. Around the Mesa Verde in southern Colorado, however, there was significant new construction and an extension of influence into surrounding areas, until the end of the period, when some not clearly understood disaster seems to have struck.

Something different was happening to the south, however, for while the Hohokam culture showed major changes, there was no abandonment. Rather, there was only a retreat from earlier northern territories and a reduction in the manufacture of elaborate items. Platform mounds, which earlier presumably had been used for ritual purposes, were beginning to be used for habitation, and there may have been an increase in social differentiation.

Near the end of this period of reorganization a great drought created a drastic deterioration of the environment. The drought may only have been a triggering mechanism that, combined with other factors, led the areas of Mesa Verde and Chaco Canyon, along with the San Juan Basin and huge portions of the Western Anasazi territory, to lose all of their settled inhabitants.

## Aggregation—1275/1300 to 1540

By the beginning of the fourteenth century the cultures of the Southwest were being reshaped again. Following the great episodes of depopulation that had just occurred, there now appeared over much of the Southwest radically larger settlements. Arroyo Hondo Pueblo, just south of Santa Fe, illustrates this dramatic change (Schwartz 1993). During the previous century settlements in the Rio Grande Valley, for example, were rarely larger than fifty rooms. Over the first thirty years of the fourteenth century, however, Arroyo Hondo Pueblo and a few similar settlements grew from a few rooms to a thousand, with multiple roomblocks and plazas. Other large settlements were also being constructed and occupied at this time all over the Southwest, including Grasshopper Pueblo, Cibola, Tsegi Canyon, Hopi Mesas, Jeddito Valley, the Little Colorado River Valley, and the southern Hohokam regions.

Although many possible explanations have been proposed for what was occurring during this period, two puzzles still face Southwestern archaeologists. What was the motivation for these large numbers of people coming together? and in what ways were the settlements organized? Some of these settlements may have become purposefully large as a way to provide for their defense against raids from other communities, but some clearly lack evidence of raiding. Also, some sites are made up of large blocks of rooms facing inward around central plazas with restricted access or are surrounded by walls, suggesting a protective posture, much like Pecos. Others are characterized by more open arrangements that appear to have no defensive qualities.

The issue of how these communities functioned is also still an open debate. Some sites are larger than others in the nearby area, and these have been called focal or central pueblos that may have been primary in some way to the political and economic life of the area. Another unsolved puzzle is the degree of social hierarchy, for which the evidence generally is weak or rare. For the most part, the evidence suggests an egalitarian pattern like that of the historic Southwestern pueblos.

Many of the large settlements that began near the start of the fourteenth century lasted for only about a generation. While they may have been reoccupied later, as was the case with Arroyo Hondo Pueblo, most were depopulated prior to the arrival of the Spanish. The success or failure of these settlements may be related to poor ecological adjustment, to environmental change, or to unsolved social problems resulting from large population concentrations. This issue of abandonment cause is a critical research topic for our understanding of late prehistoric cultural dynamics.

## THE NATURE OF KIDDER'S SOUTHWEST CONTRIBUTION

Kidder's work in the Southwest spanned five decades, and by the mid-1930s he had become the most important scholar in the region, carrying on brilliantly where the earlier scholars who had strongly influenced him had left off. Kidder moved Southwestern, and to an important extent New

World, archaeology forward by a quantum leap in research design, publication of artifact descriptions, and local and regional syntheses. He became the preeminent American archaeologist of his generation, building a reputation that has lasted far beyond his lifetime.

Perhaps a more fair appraisal would add that his northern Rio Grande work and especially the Pecos synthesis did not achieve all he had set out to accomplish. For in the tradition of Bandelier and Hewett, later in his life he too had enthusiasms and personal ambitions that took him beyond field archaeology in the Southwest and on to other passions and other areas where he could make a difference. But even so, few scholars approach the level or scope of contribution of Alfred Vincent Kidder.

## POSTSCRIPT

The chronicle of Alfred Kidder's excavations at the ancient pueblo of Pecos has an emotional postscript, an incident that completes the loop of his archaeological work in the Southwest and takes the story from near the beginning of the twentieth century to its end. This final episode involved human remains and other materials Kidder removed from Pecos and their recent return to Native Americans to whom they are sacred.

Pecos Pueblo was a flourishing community and trading center when the Spaniards arrived. Shortly thereafter, however, it began a steady decline, its large population decimated by raiding tribes from the Plains and the smallpox transmitted by European colonizers. By 1821, when the Santa Fe Trail began carrying trade past Pecos between the east and west, the pueblo was already in its death throes. Its population soon fell to a level that could no longer sustain the pueblo's traditional leaders, its religion, or its ancient way of life.

As this decline continued toward even more dangerous levels, Pecos leaders considered consolidation with Jemez Pueblo, to which the Pecos people felt linked by blood, language, spiritual beliefs, and a common origin story. In 1836 a delegation of Pecos Pueblo residents traveled to Jemez, some eighty miles to the west, to discuss the possibility of a merger. Two years later, the last inhabitants, numbering about twenty, left the pueblo. Most of them, including the Pecos governor, joined the Jemez community. A few others moved to nearby Cochiti and Santo Domingo Pueblos, and some settled in the Spanish village that had arisen near the traditional Indian village Pecos.

It would never have occurred to the departing Pecos residents that their ancient burials would be disturbed during the next century by an archaeologist. Yet this part of the story began long after the pueblo was abandoned and its lands taken over by Spanish settlers. Eventually the ancient pueblo and its mission church were purchased by the Gross, Kelly Co., and the title was later given to the School of American Research in Santa Fe, which, in turn, transferred it to the State of New Mexico. In 1965 the site was accepted by the federal government and became Pecos National Monument. But before that occurred, when the site was still in private hands, it became the focus of Kidder's research.

When Kidder began excavating at Pecos Pueblo in 1915, the burials were one focus of his interest. Many bones were found in refuse heaps as well as on the mesa top, wherever there was enough dirt or midden for graves to be dug. Many of the bones had been crushed by the weight of the earth, but many others were well preserved. The remains were of bodies buried from as early as A.D. 800 to about A.D. 1600, when Spanish priests founded the mission and established a Christian graveyard.

Given that workmen at the excavation site were paid $1.50 a day, the importance Kidder placed on the recovery of burials is apparent in this quote: "We were most anxious to discover burials; so a reward of twenty-five cents was offered to the workmen for every skeleton uncovered." So many skeletons were quickly uncovered, however, that Kidder was "forced to discontinue the bonus or go into bankruptcy."

Eventually, the almost inconceivable number of two thousand skeletons were exhumed, mostly Pecos Indians but also some European and other Native American groups.

Phillips Academy in Andover, Massachusetts, under whose auspices Kidder's work was done, originally took possession of these remains. Later they were turned over to the Peabody Museum of Archaeology and Ethnology at Harvard University for study by the anthropologist Earnest Hooton. The collection remained at Harvard for the next seventy years, during which time it was used by several other scholars and researchers.

In the years following Kidder's work, values changed, and calls to redress the (mostly unintentional) wrongs done to the Indians mounted. One result was the Native American Graves Protection and Repatriation Act (NAGPRA), passed by Congress in 1990, which decreed that human remains, burial and sacred objects, and cultural patrimony should be returned to the tribes from which they came.

With this new law in place, the spiritual leaders of Jemez Pueblo began an eight-year campaign of letter writing, telephone calls, and meetings with officials from the Peabody Museum and Andover Academy. The intention was to employ the law to prompt the return of the skeletons and other related materials. Though the talks were mostly friendly, the proceedings were filled with strong emotions. For instance, the anguish experienced by the Jemez representatives upon first entering the section of the Peabody Museum where the remains of two thousand of their forebears were cached was palpable. "When I walked into that room and got together with our ancestors, that was emotionally disturbing. I shed some tears," related Peter Toya, the Jemez War Chief. These feelings, however, were soon followed by a sense of joy. As William Whatley, the tribe's archaeologist, said, it "was a pretty clear indication they were telling us one thing and one thing alone: 'We want to go home.'"

Finally, on May 22, 1999, these transactions were brought to a conclusion when it was agreed that all of the skeletons

Kidder had excavated would be returned to Pecos Pueblo. This transfer is, to date, the single largest repatriation of sacred American Indian material to occur under NAGPRA.

The story's conclusion came in three parts: a final ceremony of transmission and apology, held at Phillips Academy; a 120-mile walk by about two hundred people from Jemez Pueblo to the site of the old Pecos Pueblo, as a symbolic reminder of the walk some of their ancestors had made in the opposite direction 161 years earlier; and the reburial of the skeletons at Pecos. At the transmission ceremony Barbara Landis Chase, head of Phillips Academy, expressed "sadness and regret for unintentional disrespect given by the expedition that exhumed the ancestors' remains from their ancient burial places." She went on, "It is right, just, and fitting to return with greatest reverence and care the remains of the ancestors and burial and sacred objects into the hands of their descendants."

The governor of Jemez Pueblo, Raymond Gachupin, and four of its spiritual leaders received the apology at the ceremony and expressed their feelings on the occasion. Governor Gachupin said, "The ancestors conveyed to us that they wanted to go home." Other Jemez representatives said that the pueblo's traditional members believe that the repatriation will restore a link to the ancestors that has been lost.

The spiritual leaders of Jemez Pueblo decided that the bones and other materials would be reburied at Pecos because it is a sacred ancestral site. But only the human remains and those objects that the spiritual leaders felt were proper were reinterred at Pecos. A large number of other objects were allowed to remain under the curatorial control of Phillips Academy, on condition that they be physically maintained at Pecos National Historic Park. Many are now on display in the museum at the park.

To prepare for the reburial, Jemez officials approved a site selected by National Park Service officials near where the bodies had originally been buried. There were to be no markers to identify their location, which was south of the park headquarters and off limits to the public. The day after the reburial this area began to be monitored by electronic equipment to keep the remains safe. No one will be allowed near the site without the consent of tribal members who have obtained permission from Jemez spiritual leaders to hold offerings and prayers.

Following the instructions of Jemez leaders, the National Park Service staff prepared a trench twelve feet wide, eight feet deep, and about six hundred feet long. This cavity was designed to hold one layer of remains, in a continuous common grave, and be deep enough to protect the remains.

At the interment ceremony, in a voice filled with emotion, an important member of Jemez Pueblo, Ruben Sando, said that the reburial symbolized a new beginning for the Jemez people: "Our ancestors and other tribes who were born here, played here, sang and danced along this beautiful Pecos River valley and mountain, who were taken away for so many years . . . are now home. I guarantee to all of you that they are joyously happy, as we all are."

I didn't know A. V. Kidder, but from all I have read about him, I am convinced that he would have been completely supportive of the Pecos repatriation. Yet there probably would have been a faint ambivalence in the deep recesses of his mind fostered by his concern that with the reburial opportunities for future research would be missed, opportunities that might answer further questions on the subject on which he had so successfully spent such an important part of his professional career: his attempt to understand the prehistory of the peoples of the American Southwest.

# Preface

In 1915 the Trustees of Phillips Academy, at the suggestion of Dr. Roland B. Dixon of Harvard University, and Dr. Hiram Bingham of Yale University, acting as Advisory Committee to the Trustees, for the Department of Archaeology of the Academy, on the foundation of the late Robert Singleton Peabody, determined to undertake excavations in the Pueblo area. It was desired to select a field of operations large enough, and of sufficient scientific importance, to justify work upon it for a number of years. The author was invited to carry out the investigation and to submit proposals as to a site. After the consideration of a number of ruins, Pecos was recommended.

The Pecos ruins lie on the headwaters of the Pecos River in San Miguel County, New Mexico (see map, fig. 10, p. 143); they are the remains of a large Pueblo Indian town, whose people figured prominently in New Mexican history from the time of the first arrival of the Spaniards in 1540, down to the final abandonment of the place in 1838. There was thus a recorded occupation of practically three centuries; and the archaic type of much of the broken pottery that lay scattered about the mounds indicated that Pecos had been inhabited for a great many years before the coming of Europeans. There is, indeed, no known ruin in the Southwest which seems to have been lived in continuously for so long a period. This was a most important consideration, because it gave rise to the hope that remains would there be found so stratified as to make clear the development of the various Pueblo arts, and thus enable us to place in their proper chronological order many other Southwestern ruins whose culture had long been known, but whose time-relations one to another were still problematical. Furthermore, Pecos had been a very large pueblo, and had occupied a commercially strategic position near the edge of the buffalo plains; for this reason it might be expected to have attracted to itself a part at least of any trade which entered the Southwest from other areas, and objects characteristic of those areas were likely to be found in the graves or in the stratified rubbish heaps at Pecos, thus providing evidence as to the chronology of cultures well outside the Pueblo region. From the point of view of specimens also the site was a favorable one, because its large cemeteries had never been despoiled, and the graves promised a rich harvest skeletal material and mortuary offerings. Lastly, the survivors of Pecos had taken refuge at the pueblo of Jemez, where their immediate descendants were still living; and investigations among these people could hardly fail to reveal much of value as to the language, customs, and ceremonies of the old town.

Title to the land upon which the ruins lie had been held for many years by Gross-Kelley and Company of Las Vegas. In 1915 Mr. Harry Kelley of this firm, believing that so important a monument of antiquity should become public property, very generously arranged for the deeding of the ruins to the State Museum of New Mexico. The application of Phillips Academy for permission to excavate was promptly and cordially approved by Dr. E. L. Hewett, Director of the Museum, and on his recommendation was granted by the Board of Regents. No hampering conditions were imposed, but the Regents requested that the old mission church, greatly damaged by the weather and by vandalism, and in immediate danger of entire collapse, be so repaired and protected that no further harm should ensue. They also requested a representative collection of specimens from the ruin. These obligations were gladly assumed, and work was begun in June, 1915.

Excavations were carried on in 1915 and 1916. From 1917 to 1919 operations were suspended, but were resumed in 1920, and have continued to the present time. When the work was started, it was thought that five or six field-seasons would be sufficient to clear the site, and that a final report would be ready for publication about the year 1924. It has now become evident, however, that even without the long interruption of the war, the original schedule could not have been adhered to; for the site has proved to be of vastly greater extent than had been supposed, and the archaeological problems encountered have turned out to be so complex in themselves, and so far-reaching in their application, that it is not yet possible to set even an approximate date for the completion of the field-work. Thus the preparation of a single final report, covering the entire investigation, would be unconscionably delayed, and experience has shown that for one reason or another long-deferred reports often fail to appear at all. Hence it seems wiser to bring out from time to time shorter contributions, dealing with such parts of the work as may be ready for publication. While in some cases they may fail in completeness and finality, they will have, at least, the virtue of freshness.

The present paper, the first of this contemplated series, is designed to give a brief description of Pecos and of its history, to outline the work so far accomplished, and to provide a background, so to speak, for the more specialized monographs which are to follow. The bulk of the work, however, is devoted to a general account of Southwestern archaeology. Because of the vastness of the field and the paucity of our knowledge, this is necessarily far from complete; but it seems worth while to present even so inadequate a summary, because the true value of the excavation of such a site as Pecos cannot properly be appreciated without some knowledge of its bearing on the broader problems of the history of man in the Southwest. The description of the work at Pecos has been placed first in order that those not familiar with this particular field may be better able to visualize the conditions under which archaeological evidence is gathered at a pueblo ruin. The reader who is interested only in the wider aspects of the subject may turn at once to the third section; or, for an even briefer summary, to the conclusions (p. 323), where the results of the investigation are presented in the form of a tentative reconstruction of Southwestern history.

Where everyone concerned has been so helpful it is difficult to single out individuals for thanks, but I cannot let slip this occasion for acknowledging my deep indebtedness to Drs. Dixon and Bingham, who conceived the project of an intensive excavation at a large Southwestern site, and who gave me the opportunity of directing it; nor to Dr. James Hardy Ropes, Chairman of the Committee on Archaeology, whose sympathetic cooperation and support have made my connection with the Department a thoroughly congenial one. Dr. Charles Peabody, Director, and Mr. Warren K. Moorehead, Curator, welcomed me most cordially to the Department, and have placed every facility of the Museum unreservedly at my disposal.

Dr. Carl E. Guthe joined the staff in 1916, and remained with us until 1920, when he was called by the Carnegie Institution of Washington to undertake excavations of great importance in Central America. Whatever success the Pecos expedition may have achieved is in large measure due to Dr. Guthe's scientific acumen, ready resourcefulness, untiring industry, and unquenchable enthusiasm.

Dr. and Mrs. S. K. Lothrop, Dr. E. A. Hooton, and Messrs. G. C. Vaillant and S. K. Moorehead have all worked at Pecos, and each one has contributed assistance of great value. During every field-season, my wife has been with me and has taken practically entire charge of the important and laborious task of cleaning and sorting the hundreds of thousands of potsherds recovered during the digging. My secretary, Miss Ida Sanford, has been indefatigable in the Museum, and during the summer of 1922 accompanied the expedition in the field.

Without the cooperation of the authorities of the State Museum of New Mexico nothing, of course, could have been done; and to the Regents of that Institution, together with its Director, Dr. Hewett, and the members of his staff: Messrs. K. M. Chapman, W. Bradfield, and L. B. Bloom, the hearty thanks of the Department are due. I wish also to express my appreciation of the many services rendered by Messrs. G. D. Hughes, J. F. Miller, J. W. Harrison, Charles Earickson and S. Gray, residents of the Pecos Valley, all of whom have done everything in their power to further the purposes of the expedition.

Alfred Vincent Kidder

# History of Pecos

The Pecos River rises in the Santa Fe range in north-central New Mexico, and flows in a generally southerly direction for nearly 600 miles before it empties into the Rio Grande in Texas. Not more than twenty miles from its source it breaks out of its narrow mountain canyon into a wide, rugged valley, the average elevation of which is about 7,000 feet. To the north the bare summit of Pecos Baldy rises above timberline and is only clear of snow for a few weeks in midsummer; to the east are the lower crests of the Tecolote chain; and to the west the red-cliffed barrier of the Pecos Mesa. Most of these higher lands are covered with fine forests of large yellow pines, and along the river are thick groves of cottonwoods and willows, but the valley itself is a typical bit of the arid Southwest; its soil is red adobe, gashed with deep, dry arroyos; its sandstone ledges are barren; its adobe flats clothed with stunted junipers, pinyons, and cactus (pl. 1, a). About a mile west of the river lies the ruined pueblo. It occupies the flat top of a long, narrow tongue of rock which stands well above the surrounding land and from which one can look out over the whole country. In the broad, sandy bed of an arroyo that swings by the base of the rocks, is a never-failing spring of pure, cold water. Such an ideal combination of easily defensible building site and abundant water supply could not fail to appeal to the ancient village Indian, and the Pecos *mesilla* was settled in very early times. It eventually grew from a small town to a very large one, and at the time of the coming of the Spaniards it contained, without much doubt, more human beings than any other permanent community in what is now the territory of the United States.

Pecos was discovered by the first Spanish expedition that entered the Southwest.[1] The exploration of that country was brought about by rumors of rich cities in the unknown lands to the north of New Spain, circulated by one Cabeza de Vaca, a survivor of an expedition to Florida under Pamfilo de Narvaez. Wrecked on the Gulf coast in 1528, the majority of Narvaez's men lost their lives, but de Vaca, accompanied by a negro called Esteban and two other Spaniards, succeeded after eight years of great hardship in making his way westward from tribe to tribe. He crossed southern Texas, and finally reached the Spanish settlements on the Pacific coast of Mexico. During his wanderings de Vaca had heard stories of large and opulent cities in the north; and these stories so interested Mendoza, then governor of New Spain, that he sent out a Franciscan monk, Fray Marcos de Nizza, to investigate them.

Nizza, with the negro Esteban as interpreter, started north in 1539. On the way he was temporarily delayed; and Esteban, sent ahead to reconnoiter, exceeded his instructions, pushed through to what is now New Mexico, and reached the first of the "cities." Just what occurred there will never be known, but Esteban was doubtless overbearing and arrogant; at all events he was promptly imprisoned and very shortly killed. When Nizza, following a few days' journey behind, arrived in the neighborhood, he was met by some survivors of Esteban's Indian escort in full flight southward, and was told by them of the death of the negro. Not daring to enter the country openly, yet hesitating to return without some definite information, the friar ventured to the edge of the valley in which the

1. Material for the present brief historical sketch has been derived almost entirely from the writings of Bandelier, Bolton, Bancroft, Twitchell, and Winship. References to the original Spanish sources can be found in the copious footnotes of those authors. See Bolton, 1916; Bancroft, 1889; Winship, 1896; Twitchell, 1911, 1914; Bandelier, 1881, 1890a, 1892a. The full titles of works quoted will be found in the bibliography at the end of this volume.

"cities" lay, and obtained a view of one of them from a long distance off. He was much impressed by its apparent size, and by the tales which Esteban's Indians told him; and when he had succeeded at last in making his way back to Mexico, he set the capital on fire with glowing accounts of the "Seven Cities of Cibola." [2]

It must be remembered that at this time the Spanish in Mexico were in just the proper state of mind to be inflamed by stories of golden lands. The glories of the Montezumas were fresh in everyone's memory, and Pizarro had recently dazzled the world with his discovery of the riches of the Incas. Only too willing to believe in the wonders in the north and wishing to profit by them at once, Mendoza immediately equipped a large expedition, placed it under the command of Francisco Vasquez de Coronado, and in the spring of 1540 despatched it upon its journey of discovery and conquest.[3]

After a long and difficult march, hindered by failure of provisions, and the attacks of savage tribes, the army reached the fabled cities. The disappointment of all hands is most graphically expressed by Castañeda, the chronicler of the expedition:

> When they saw the first village, which was Cibola, such were the curses that some hurled at Friar Marcos that I pray God may protect him from them. It is a little unattractive village, looking as if it had been crumpled all up together. There are mansions in New Spain which make a better appearance at a distance.[4]

After overcoming some resistance by the inhabitants, the Spaniards entered the town and took possession of it and the surrounding country in the name of the King.

2. For an account of the wanderings of Cabeza de Vaca see Bandelier, 1890a, chap. 2; Nizza's journey is discussed at length in chap. 4 of the same work.

3. The Coronado expedition is exhaustively treated in Winship, 1896.

4. Winship, 1896, p. 483.

This first pueblo to fall into the power of the white man was Hawikuh, one of the Zuñi villages in western New Mexico (see map, fig. 10, p. 143).[5] Hawikuh was typical of all the other pueblos of that time. They were really huge apartment houses with hundreds of small living rooms grouped closely together, and often terraced to a height of four or five stories. The women built the walls of stone and adobe mud, the men cut and set the roof beams. The women owned the houses, and the unmarried men lived, for the most part, in round, subterranean rooms located in the yards and courts of the town. The people supported themselves by growing corn, beans, and squashes; made fine pottery, raised cotton and wove it into serviceable garments, and kept numbers of domesticated turkeys. The Spanish admired the cleanliness and order of the pueblos, and were struck by the simple democratic form of government, administered by the older men. They were, however, deeply chagrined at the lack of the expected riches of gold and silver, and determined to continue their explorations in the hope of finding better things further on.

They stayed in Cibola for a time to rest themselves and to allow their horses to recuperate. Coronado, in the meantime, instructed the Cibolans to let it be known among all the other Pueblos that he wished them to come to confer with him and render allegiance. There shortly arrived a deputation from Cicuye, as Pecos was called by the earlier conquistadores. Castañeda describes the visit and its results as follows:[6]

> Some Indians came to Cibola from a village which was seventy leagues east of this province, called Cicuye. Among them was a captain who was called Bigotes (Whiskers) by our men, because he wore a long moustache. He was a tall, well-built young fellow,

5. Hodge, 1895.

6. Winship, 1896, narrative of Castañeda. The quotations are literal, but have been pieced together to make a consecutive account.

PLATE 2. General view of Pecos from the north.

with a fine figure. He told the general that they had come in response to the notice which had been given, to offer themselves as friends, and that if we wanted to go through their country they would consider us as their friends. They brought a present of tanned hides and shields and head-pieces, which were very gladly received, and the general gave them some glass dishes and a number of pearls and little bells which they prized highly, because these were things they had never seen. They described some cows which, from a picture that one of them had painted on his skin, seemed to be cows, although from the hides this did not seem possible, because the hair was woolly and snarled so that we could not tell what sort of skins they had.[7] The general ordered Hernando de Alvarado to take twenty companions and go with them, and gave him a commission for eighty days, after which he should return to give an account of what he had found. Captain Alvarado started on his journey and in five days reached a village which was on a rock called Acuco [Acoma, see map, fig. 10, p. 143] having a population of about two hundred men. . . . From here they went to a province called Triguex, three days distant.[8] The people all came out peacefully, seeing that Whiskers was with them. Alvarado sent messengers back from here to advise the general to come and winter in this country. The general was not a little relieved to hear that the country was growing better. Five days from here he came to Cicuye [Pecos, see map, fig. 10, p. 143], a very strong village four stories high, a village of nearly five hundred warriors, who are feared throughout that country. It is square, situated on a rock, with a large court or yard in the middle, containing the estufas. The houses

7. This refers, of course, to the buffalo.
8. Probably near the present site of Bernalillo on the Rio Grande.

are all alike, four stories high. One can go over the top of the whole village without there being a street to hinder. There are corridors going all around it at the first two stories, by which one can go around the whole village. These are like outside balconies, and they are able to protect themselves under these. The houses do not have doors below, but they use ladders, which can be lifted up like a drawbridge, and so go up to the corridors which are on the inside of the village. As the doors of the houses open on the corridor of that story, the corridor serves as a street. The houses that open on the plain are right back of these that open on the court, and in time of war they go through those behind them. The village is inclosed by a low wall of stone. The people of this village boast that no one has been able to conquer them and that they conquer whatever villages they wish. The people and their customs are like those of the other villages. The people came out from the village with signs of joy to welcome Hernando de Alvarado and their captain, and brought them into the town with drums and pipes something like flutes, of which they have a great many. They made many presents of cloth and turquoises, of which there are quantities in that region. The Spaniards enjoyed themselves here for several days and talked with an Indian slave, a native of the country toward Florida.[9] This fellow said that there were large settlements in the farther part of that country. Hernando de Alvarado took him to guide them to the cows; but he told them so many and such great things about the wealth of gold and silver in his country that they did not care about looking for cows, but returned after they had seen some few, to report the rich news to the general. They called the Indian "Turk" because he looked like one. . . . The general

9. This, of course, merely means the country to the east.

> sent Hernando de Alvarado back to Cicuye to demand some gold bracelets which this Turk said they had taken from him at the time they captured him. Alvarado went, and was received as a friend at the village, and when he demanded the bracelets they said they knew nothing at all about them, saying the Turk was deceiving him and was lying. Captain Alvarado, seeing that there were no other means, got the captain Whiskers and the governor to come to his tent, and when they had come he put them in chains. The villagers prepared to fight, and let fly their arrows, denouncing Hernando de Alvarado, and saying that he was a man who had no respect for peace and friendship. Hernando de Alvarado started back to Tiguex, where the general kept them prisoners more than six months. This began the want of confidence in the word of the Spaniards whenever there was talk of peace from this time on, as will be seen by what happened afterward.

Coronado had in the meantime moved his army into winter quarters at Tiguex, near the present site of Bernalillo on the Rio Grande. Here the overbearing conduct of the Spaniards soon resulted in difficulties with the Indians, resulting in the siege of a pueblo and the massacre of its inhabitants. To quote again from Castañeda:

> During the siege of Tiguex, the general decided to go to Cicuye, and take the governor with him, in order to give him his liberty and to promise them that he would give Whiskers his liberty and leave him in the village, as soon as he should start for Quivira. He He was received peacefully when he reached Cicuye, and entered the village with several soldiers. They received their governor with much joy and gratitude. After looking over the village and speaking with the natives he returned to his army, leaving Cicuye at

> peace, in the hope of getting back their captain Whiskers.

In the spring of 1541 Coronado set out with high hopes for the land called Quivira, so glowingly described to him by the Turk.

> The army left Tiguex on the 5th of May, and returned to Cicuye, which, as I have said, is twenty-five leagues from there, taking Whiskers with them. Arrived there, he gave them their captain, who already went about freely with a guard. The village was very glad to see him, and the people were peaceful and offered food. The governor and Whiskers gave the general a young fellow called Xabe, a native of Quivira, who could give them information about the country. This fellow said that there was gold and silver, but not as much of it as the Turk had said. The Turk, however, continued to declare that it was as he had said. He went as a guide, and thus the army started off from here. The army started from Cicuye, leaving the village at peace and, as it seemed, contented, and under obligations to maintain the friendship because their governor and captain had been restored to them.

This journey out into the great buffalo plains was another series of disappointments. Week after week the adventurers traveled across the level wastes, and the further they went the more certain it became that the Turk had been lying to them, undoubtedly prompted thereto by the people of Pecos. He said, indeed, just before he was finally garroted by the exasperated Spaniards

> that the people at Cicuye had asked him to lead them off onto the plains and lose them, so that the horses would die when their provisions gave out, and they

> would be so weak if they ever returned that they could be killed without any trouble, and thus they could take revenge for what had been done to them. This was the reason why he had led them astray, supposing that they did not know how to hunt or to live without corn, while as for the gold, he did not know where there was any of it.

Worn out by their wanderings, and despairing of any success in this direction, the army turned back, and after nearly a month came again to Pecos. Here the advance party was unpleasantly surprised to find the people actively hostile; so they pushed on to Tiguex without stopping. Pecos was, however, reduced to submission by Arellano before the arrival of the main body, and when Coronado reached the place he was well received.

The winter of 1541–42 was spent at Tiguex, and in the spring Coronado decided to return to New Spain. Two devoted Franciscans, however, elected to stay and endeavor to convert the natives to Christianity. Castañeda says:

> Friar Juan de Padilla, a regular brother of the lesser (Franciscan) order, and another, Friar Luis, a lay brother, told the general that they wanted to remain in that country, Friar Juan de Padilla in Quivira, because his teachings seemed to promise fruit there, and Friar Luis at Cicuye. The general sent a company to escort them as far as Cicuye, where Friar Luis stopped, while Friar Juan went on back to Quivira. He was martyred a short time after he arrived there. Friar Luis remained at Cicuye. Nothing more has been heard about him since, but before the army left Tiguex some men who went to take him a number of sheep that were left for him to keep, met him as he was on his way to visit some other villages, which were fifteen or twenty leagues from Cicuye, accompanied

> by some followers. He felt very hopeful that he was liked at the village and that his teachings would bear fruit, although he complained that the old men were falling away from him. I, for my part, believe that they finally killed him.

Thus Pecos was doubtless the scene of one of the first Christian martyrdoms to take place in the United States; and it was certainly the first place in the United States at which livestock was introduced.

After the withdrawal of the Coronado expedition, no Spaniard set foot on New Mexican soil for nearly forty years. In 1581, however, Fray Rodriguez and two other priests, with a small escort of soldiers under Francisco Sanchez Chamuscado, pushed up the Rio Grande to the neighborhood of Bernalillo, and later turned east, where they visited three pueblos and heard of others. One of the three may have been Pecos, but the meager accounts give us no information about it. At the close of the year Chamuscado and his men withdrew to the south, reluctantly leaving the Franciscans to their work of proselytizing among the people of the Rio Grande.

Late in 1582 Antonio de Espejo and Friar Bernadino Beltran led an expedition into the north to determine the fate of the three missionaries. On their arrival at the pueblo of Puara (in the neighborhood of the present town of San Marcial, New Mexico), they learned that Rodriguez and his companions had all been killed by the Indians. Although the real object of the expedition had now been accomplished, Espejo determined to take advantage of the opportunity to make further explorations. With a mere handful of men he set out upon one of the most remarkable journeys on record. He stopped at Acoma, Zuñi, and the Hopi towns, and swinging south passed through what is now central Arizona. He then returned to the Rio Grande via Zuñi and visited the pueblos north of

a

b

PLATE 3a. View northwest across the Arroyo de Pecos. b. The ruin mounds from the top of the church. The remains of the old defense wall may be seen starting in the center foreground and extending along the right edge of the mounds.

Santa Fe. Again turning south he crossed the mountains, and on his way back to Mexico passed through Pecos and followed down the Pecos River.

The next expedition into New Mexico took place in 1590. Its leader was Castaño de Sosa, who took with him a number of Spaniards, both men and women, with the intention of founding a colony. He entered the country via the Rio Grande and the Pecos, traveling up the latter river until he reached the vicinity of the pueblo. A scouting party had preceded him. The events which followed are so interesting, and throw so much light on the condition of Pecos at this time, that I quote the account of them that has been summarized by Miss Hull from de Sosa's report.[10]

> On the 23d of the month (December, 1590), Sosa and his secretary, Andres Perez, who were riding somewhat in advance of the rest of the party, descried in the distance a woeful company, ragged and coatless, approaching on foot with arquebuses reversed. On seeing the lieutenant they made no sign, and even when they reached him, the knowledge of how they had come to such a pass made them most reluctant to speak. From the story which was at last drawn from their unwilling lips Sosa learned that, having followed the trail of which Viruega had brought news, they had at last reached a pueblo. This they had entered notwithstanding the lieutenant's orders to the contrary, because it was very cold, the ground was covered with snow, and they were sadly in need of warmth and shelter, as well as of food. The inhabitants had received them kindly, and had given them grain. But the next morning while they were strolling through the pueblo without their arms which they had left outside in order the better to inspire confidence among the Indians, these latter, having sud-

10. Hull, 1916, pp. 316–23.

denly acquired an utterly unexpected and quite alarming degree of confidence, gave them the war-cry, and let fly a shower of arrows. Taken by surprise, the worthy comrades "stood not upon the order of their going," but fled at once and most precipitately to the spot where they had heaped up their arms and other possessions. Here, too, their dusky hosts had been before them, so that they were able to escape with only five arquebuses, while the Indians carried off the honors of war, together with five arquebuses, eleven swords, the saddles and other trappings for the horses, and the clothes and bedding. Indeed, they felt themselves fortunate to have escaped with their lives, though even life itself, they declared, would have been lost through starvation, had not God in His infinite mercy influenced a squaw whom they met on their way to provide them with food.

In view of their evident distress, the lieutenant did not inflict on them the punishment which their disobedience well merited. Rather, he endeavored to comfort them and to overcome their discouragement by every possible means.

The Indians remained to be dealt with, and he resolved that, leaving the camp at a place which he called La Urraca (The Magpie), he himself with an advance guard of nineteen soldiers and seventeen servants would go to the pueblo to secure the lost possessions and to bring the Indians to submission to his majesty.

On the 26th of December Sosa with this small company left La Urraca, and proceeding up the river arrived on the 30th within a league of the pueblo—evidently Cicuye (Pecos)—where the *maese de campo* and his party had met with disaster.

The next morning the lieutenant gave his final orders before entering the village. He besought his comrades to advance with confidence, believing that they would be kindly received: they had done no harm, so they should fear no evil. But they were to carefully follow the example of the lieutenant, and in no way to depart from his orders. They marched on to the pueblo with lines in order and colors high; but when they reached its environs, they saw all the inhabitants, both men and women, in arms upon the roof, prepared to give battle.

The tactics pursued by Castaño in the face of this crisis are worthy of note. The misfortunes of the *maese de campo* had taught him the value of preparedness. Having pitched his camp within gun-range of the pueblo, he planted his two brass cannon where they would command the strongest position. Thus prepared for all contingencies, he sallied forth with the olive branch in his hand.

He spent five hours in making the rounds of the pueblo, addressing the people with kind words and signs of friendship, and offering them all manner of gifts. But in spite of all these friendly overtures, none would come out from their breastworks and intrenchments. Rather, they gave the war-cry with increased vehemence, and launched stones and arrows at this unlucky advocate of an armed peace. In the end he deemed it expedient to return to his camp and consult with his comrades as to the best *modus operandi*.

They answered with one voice that he should attack these dogs without more ado. But Castaño was still loath to resort to force, not only from the motives of humanity that at all times animated his breast, but for fear of the disapproval of the authorities to whom he was responsible.

Having stationed two of his men on a height to see that the natives should not withdraw, he once more made a circuit of the pueblo, but only to meet with greater contumely than ever. For not only were the cries which heralded his appearance much more derisive, but the stones and arrows fell in a heavier shower; and one squaw went out on a balcony and threw ashes on his head. At . . . his procedure the shouts of her dusky compatriots reached deafening proportions.

Thereupon the lieutenant returned at once to his camp and ordered his men to mount for the attack, and to discharge their arquebuses and the two cannon, to try whether by these means they might affright the Indians. This stratagem was without visible effect, for the defenders of the village only made the more mockery, and hurled the more missiles from behind their breastworks, while Castaño in vain called to them with soothing words.

Now the battle began in earnest. Four men were detailed to ascend with one of the cannon to a quarter of the roof devoid of people, while the lieutenant created a diversion by attacking the Indians in front. Having made the ascent with greatest difficulty because of the desperate resistance offered by the defenders, they proceeded to direct their fire against the neighboring quarters. The Indians responded with showers of stones and arrows, and bravely stuck to their posts, not one showing a sign of fear. The fight waxed hotter. The excitement spread to the Indian followers of Sosa. One let fly an arrow; another followed his example. For the first time the defenders began to show trepidation. Some began to leave their posts which the besiegers quickly occupied, mounting by means of ladders, and at frightful risk, because their arms had to be abandoned before they could pass through the trap-doors that gave access to the roof, swords and shields being afterwards passed up to them by the comrades who remained below. One after another the defenders fell, and the survivors at last fled from the roof, leaving the Spaniards in possession of the breastworks.

The victory won, the lieutenant marched in triumph through the streets and plazas of the pueblo. And the Indians who were congregated in the wooden corridors which connected all the houses no longer showed hostility, but rather, all made the sign of the cross, indicative of friendship, and cried *"Amigos, amigos, amigos!"* They threw down food from the balconies, but they themselves could not be induced to come down into the streets, nor to approach the Spaniards, though Sosa repeatedly signed to them that he would do them no injury, and they need have no fear.

Having found the captain of the pueblo, the lieutenant demanded the restoration of the property taken from the *maese de campo,* but was answered that all had been either destroyed or taken to other villages save some sword blades without guards which he professed himself willing to return. Sosa, however, doubting the veracity of the wily Indian, secretly sent some of his soldiers to search the other quarters of the pueblo, and if possible to seize some Indian from whom more reliable information might be elicited.

Meantime the captain had mounted to the topmost roof and harangued his people in a loud voice. At the conclusion of the speech they showed great joy, and evinced great friendship for the Spaniards, but without descending from the balconies to the plaza. And now the lost property was brought out—a pitiful heap consisting of two swordblades without guards, a large pouch, some pieces of coarse cloth, and a few other little things. Truly, these seemed little worth the battle! But the lieutenant still hoped that his soldiers would succeed in finding the rest; a vain hope, as it proved, for when he shortly returned to his camp it was only to learn of their failure. They had found in the quarter toward which their search was directed a veritable labyrinth of mines and counter-mines extending underground, with so many little openings and trap-doors that a thorough investigation was impossible at that hour when it was already growing dark.

That night a guard was stationed in the pueblo and all remained quiet. The next morning the lieutenant, having thanked his comrades for their faithful service and having given orders that no injury should be done either to the persons or the property of the conquered Indians, proceeded to explore the pueblo, and to examine its contents. It was found to contain five plazas and sixteen kivas, the latter being underground chambers, well-plastered, which Sosa believed to have been made for protection against the cold. The houses, from four to five stories high, were built in the form of *cuarteles* (garrisons), the entrances all on the outside, and the houses standing back to back. They were all connected by wooden corridors or balconies which ran from house to house throughout the village. Intersecting streets were bridged by wooden beams flung from roof to roof. Access to the houses was had by means of small ladders which could afterward be drawn through trap-doors in the roof.

Each house was found to contain a store of grain—the village as a whole possessing an immense supply, estimated at thirty thousand *fanegas,* evidently the product of several years' harvests. The houses also contained a great deal of pottery, both gaily colored and figured, and black, some of it glazed.

As it was winter, the people were warmly clothed—the men in *mantas* of cotton and buffalo skins, while some wore also gaily figured trousers. The women

> wore a *manta* fastened at the shoulder with a wide girdle around the waist, and over this another *manta,* gaily colored, and either embroidered or decorated with furs and feathers.
>
> The pueblo had a large amount of land under cultivation, irrigated by two running streams at the side, while the pool which supplied them with water for drinking lay within a gunshot. A quarter of a league from the pueblo, the Rio Salado flowed.
>
> There can be no doubt that the pueblo thus reached by Sosa on December 31, 1590, was the pueblo of Cicuye or Pecos. His description tallies in the main, not only with that of other explorers, but with modern descriptions of the ruins of Pecos.
>
> That night the Indians, taking advantage of the withdrawal of the guard, fled from the pueblo. For several days Sosa remained in the vicinity, hoping for their return. In the meantime provisions were despatched to the rest of the party at La Urraca. As it at last became evident that the Indians would not return to their pueblo as long as it remained in possession of the Spaniards, the lieutenant determined to move on.

After exploring the Tehua country and penetrating as far north as Taos, de Sosa returned to the Cerillos region near Santa Fe, where he was soon after met by a party sent from Mexico with instructions to arrest him for making unauthorized explorations. The entire expedition was recalled, and the first serious attempt at colonization thus met with failure.

The long-planned settlement of New Mexico was actually brought about in 1598 by Oñate, who established his first town at San Gabriel on the Rio Grande, opposite the pueblo of San Juan. Oñate was a very vigorous executive and was accompanied by a small body of no less energetic priests of the order of Saint Francis. The pueblos were quickly and, with the exception of Acoma, peacefully brought into subjection, and were parceled out for religious administration among the monks. Fray Francisco de San Miguel was given the Pecos district, but beyond the fact that that town was his headquarters and that his parish included a number of other pueblos, nothing is known of his pastorate, Oñate himself visited Pecos on the 24th of July, 1598, and received the submission of its people. Santa Fe was founded about 1605.

Of the events which took place in New Mexico during the first three-quarters of the 17th century very little information has come down to us, as all the church and civil records of the province were destroyed in the revolution of 1680. The "Memorial" of Fray Alonzo de Benavides, however, gives us a glimpse of Pecos at about 1620. He says the town "contains more than two thousand souls. Here there is a monastery and a very splendid temple of distinguished workmanship and beauty, in which a Religious put very great labor and care." [11] This, of course, proves that the great adobe church had already been built, but the exact date of its completion has not yet been established.

The Pueblo revolt took place in 1680. It was caused partly by dissatisfaction with the civil rule of the Spanish, which had been becoming more oppressive year by year, but principally, it would seem, by a deep-rooted hatred of Christianity and a desire to return to the unhampered practice of the ancient native religion. Trouble had evidently been brewing for a long time, and there had been a few minor outbreaks, but it was not until 1680 that real unanimity among the Pueblos was reached under the leadership of one Popé, a medicine man of San Juan. A carefully thought-out plot was hatched; the towns were to rise simultaneously on a given day and every Spaniard in

11. Ayer, 1916, p. 22.

the country was to be exterminated. In spite of the most elaborate precautions to preserve secrecy, the plans of the Indians leaked out at the last moment. But warning came too late to save the Spanish from a most terrible disaster, and on the day of the rising, August 10th, there were killed no less than four hundred men, women, and children. Among this number were twenty-one priests. Those who escaped the first onslaught fled to the capital at Santa Fe, where they were organized for defense by the governor, Otermin.

The priest of Pecos, Fray Fernando de Velasco, a veteran of thirty years' service in New Mexico, was warned by Juan Gé, one of his Indian converts, apparently during the night of August 9–10. He set out at once to notify his superior, who was stationed at Galisteo, a short distance to the west. He crossed the high Pecos mesa, traversed the long pine-covered slopes on the other side, and had almost reached his destination when he was killed within sight of the pueblo of Galisteo. Whether he was pursued and overtaken by his own parishioners, or intercepted by the Indians of Galisteo, is not certain.

At Santa Fe, Governor Otermin and the other survivors were immediately attacked by five hundred warriors from Pecos and the eastern pueblos, shortly reinforced by large numbers of Indians from the north. After being besieged for five days, and having their water supply cut off, the Spaniards determined to abandon the town and attempt a retreat. The Indians fortunately did not oppose them, they made their way to the Rio Grande, and eventually succeeded in reaching the undisturbed settlements north of where the city of El Paso now stands. The victory of the Pueblos was complete; no Spaniard remained in the entire country.

During the next ten years Otermin and his successor, Cruzate, made several ineffectual attempts to reconquer the lost province, but only in 1692, when de Vargas had become governor, were any real results obtained. In that year de Vargas marched northward, and by tactful dealing and a strong display of force succeeded without bloodshed in receiving the submission of all the pueblos. He did not spend the winter, however, and when he returned to resettle the country in 1693, he found his task a very hard one. For the next few years there was almost unceasing war. In spite of the military skill and unflagging energy of de Vargas, revolt followed revolt; quelled in one district, trouble would break out in another, and it was not until 1700 that New Mexico was once more at peace.

While the Spanish were absent from New Mexico, the Pecos, Taos, and Keres had been at war with the Tanos to the west and the Tehua to the north; the hostility of the Pecos, indeed, seems to have been the cause of the abandonment of several of the Tano towns. During the period of the reconquest the Pecos gave no trouble. They fled from their pueblo when de Vargas arrived in 1692, but were not actively hostile; and in 1694 we find their governor, the same Juan Gé who had warned Velasco of the impending revolt, accompanying the army and acting as intermediary between de Vargas and the Indians of Taos.

At the beginning of the eighteenth century Pecos still seems to have held its old position as the largest and strongest of the pueblos, but shortly after 1700 there began a period of decline that ended only with the final abandonment of the town. The chief cause for this was the arrival in the southwestern part of the Great Plains of the Comanche, a warlike, predatory tribe that immediately became the scourge of eastern New Mexico. The Comanche were always, it would seem, particularly hostile to the Pecos, and their raids were a constant source of annoyance and danger. By 1750 the population had shrunk to one thousand. Apparently about this time there occurred a terrible disaster. The Pecos, according to stories still current among the Mexicans in the valley, became infuriated

a

b

PLATE 4. Pecos in 1846. a. Church and monastery. b. Northwest corner of plaza. (Drawn by a member of the American Army of Occupation during the Mexican War. After Emory.)

by the inroads of the Comanche, organized an expedition to carry the war into the enemy's country, and set out with the entire manpower of the pueblo. They would appear to have been ambushed, for they were utterly cut to pieces, only one man escaping. This was the death blow, and when an epidemic of smallpox ravaged the town in 1788, but one hundred and eighty survivors were left. These gradually dwindled away, attacks of mountain fever became more and more severe, until in 1805 the population of the town was reduced to one hundred and four. Gregg in his "Commerce of the Prairies" gives a graphic picture of the dying pueblo:

> This village, anciently so renowned, lies twenty-five miles eastward of Santa Fe, and near the Rio Pecos, to which it gave name. Even so late as ten years ago [i.e. about 1830] when it contained a population of fifty to a hundred souls, the traveler would oftentimes perceive but a solitary Indian, a woman, or a child, standing here and there like so many statues upon the roofs of their houses, with their eyes fixed on the eastern horizon, or leaning against a wall or a fence, listlessly gazing at the passing stranger; while at other times not a soul was to be seen in any direction, and the sepulchral silence of the place was only disturbed by the occasional barking of a dog, or the cackling of hens.[12]

Finally the people of Jemez, a pueblo akin to them in language, invited the remnant of the Pecos to make their home at that place. Accordingly in 1838 the seventeen survivors gave up the struggle, made the eighty-mile journey to the northwest, and abandoned the crumbling ruins of the dwellings that had housed their ancestors for so many centuries.

The town itself, which was doubtless in a ruinous con-

12. Gregg, 1845, vol. 1, p. 272.

dition when it was abandoned, fell quickly into decay, a process aided by the fact that the Mexicans who lived in the vicinity habitually robbed it of beams and timbers for use as firewood. The north building at least kept its form for a few years, as its plaza served for a prison to hold the Texans captured by Armijo in 1841.[13] In 1846 the American army passed through Pecos on its way to the capture of Santa Fe, and in his report Colonel Emory mentions the town and the church (pl. 4, a).[14] One of his pictures (pl. 4, b) shows the kiva in the northwest corner of the plaza; the house walls behind it seem to be still standing to a height of fifteen or twenty feet. Since that time, however, both the church and the pueblo have suffered greatly. The roof beams of the church were removed about 1860, to be used as corral posts, and its adobe walls, unprotected from the rain, have gradually disintegrated. The pueblo went to pieces even faster, the upper walls fell, the timbers below rotted away or were pulled out, and not until a sheltering mound had formed itself over the lower stories was the process of ruin arrested.

13. Kendall, 1844, vol. 1, p. 370.
14. Emory, 1848, p. 30.

# Field Work at Pecos

## PREVIOUS INVESTIGATIONS

In September 1880, Adolf F. Bandelier visited Pecos and obtained material for a report which was published by the Archaeological Institute the following year.[1] Bandelier, with his usual thoroughness and accuracy, described the ruins as they were at that time, and included a most valuable series of measurements of the house-mounds, the church, and the surrounding defense wall. He also prepared tentative elevations of certain parts of the pueblo, upon which he based estimates as to the former size of the buildings and the number of rooms that they contained. While his work was not accompanied by excavation, which would, of course, have solved many of the problems that puzzled him, Bandelier arrived at remarkably accurate conclusions. The traditional and documentary history of Pecos are also summarized; but, perhaps the most valuable part of the report consists of the information which Bandelier was able to obtain from old residents of the valley, particularly from Mariano Ruiz, a man who in his younger days had been an adopted member of the trible. Ruiz remembered clearly the location of the corrals, fields, and gardens of the pueblo; spoke of the governmental organization; and also had some knowledge of the religious rites of the people.

After Bandelier's work, nothing was done at Pecos for nearly twenty years, but in 1904 Dr. E. L. Hewett published a paper dealing with the general problems of the archaeology of the valley, and presenting much useful ethnological information gathered from the two native Pecos Indians then living at Jemez.[2] Hewett discovered

1. Bandelier, 1881.
2. Hewett, 1904.

that the descendants of the Pecos still visited the ruins of the pueblo, and made pilgrimages to a sacred cave somewhere in the vicinity.[3]

In 1910, Mr. K. M. Chapman and the writer made a large collection of potsherds at Pecos. We were very much struck by the variety of types represented at the site; there being specimens of all the varieties then known in the Rio Grande, from the ancient black-on-white to the obviously modern. Accordingly I felt certain that here if anywhere could be found the stratified remains which were so badly needed to straighten out the chronological problems of the district. Accordingly, when the chance came in 1915 to undertake an extensive piece of excavation, I at once recommended Pecos.

The last work done at the site, prior to the beginning of the Phillips Academy expeditions, was a survey by Mr. J. P. Adams, then with the School of American Research at Santa Fe. He and Mr. Chapman spent some time at the ruins and gathered data for a large model, a reconstruction of the pueblo and church, which was made in 1914, exhibited at the San Diego Exposition of 1915, and later returned to the State Museum in Santa Fe. This model is about sixteen feet long, and gives an excellent general idea of what the former appearance of Pecos must have been (pl. 5).

## FIELD WORK OF PHILLIPS ACADEMY

The Pecos ruins occupy the more or less level top of a long, rocky ridge, which stands boldly up above the surrounding land. At the north end this *mesilla* pinches out to a narrow neck of bare sandstone (pl. 12, a); south

3. Mexicans resident in the valley state that the Pecos made such pilgrimages for many years, but that they discontinued the practice about 1910. In 1915, however, there were found, at a shrine near the pueblo, two carved wooden prayersticks. Although these lay in the open, they were so fresh-looking that it seemed as if they could not have been deposited more than a year earlier.

Courtesy Museum of New Mexico

Plate 5. Model of the pueblo of Pecos as it appeared about 1700.

of this there is a rise of ground and a great widening of the top, but still further south it is again constricted and falls away in height until it merges with the uplands that stretch off toward the river.

At the extreme southern end lie the ruins of the church and monastery; the latter has crumbled to a low mound, but the massive six-foot adobe walls of the church have resisted time and vandalism, and still stand, at the transepts, to almost their original height (pl. 6). Directly north of the church is a pile of ruins, four hundred feet long by sixty-five or seventy feet wide (pl. 7). Again to the north, and occupying the highest and broadest part of the *mesilla,* is an enormous quadrangular mound five hundred and fifty feet long by two hundred and fifty wide. These two mounds are the remains of pueblo structures which have fallen so completely into ruin that they appear to be nothing but vast heaps of tumbled stones. Closer examination, however, discloses the tops of walls, and here and there the protruding ends of wooden beams. The mounds are overgrown with grass and cactus. In rainy seasons the wild verbena carpets the ruins with brilliant purple.

The remains of the defense wall mentioned by Casteñeda are still easily traceable (pls. 7; 3, b). It starts and ends at the church, hugging the edge of the *mesilla* and surrounding the entire settlement. Outside the wall the ground falls away more or less steeply, the slopes covered with thousands of potsherds and chips of flint.

## First season (1915)[4]

Work was started on the east side by opening a trench at the foot of the steep slope that runs from the plain up to the defense wall (pl. 8, a). It disclosed six inches to one

4. During the first year Dr. and Mrs. S. K. Lothrop acted as assistants; Mr. J. P. Adams was surveyor, and Mr. J. L. Nussbaum took charge of the repairs on the church.

a

b

PLATE 6. The Pecos church, built about 1617. a. Seen from the ruins of the pueblo. b. Interior after excavation and the reinforcement of the foundations with concrete.

foot of loamy dirt containing potsherds, ashes, and animal bones; below was undisturbed red clay. The deposit deepened as we worked uphill, its surface rising much faster than did the subsoil. When fifty or sixty feet had been covered the depth had increased to four feet, and the nature of the earth began to change. Hitherto it had been featureless mixed stuff, evidently washed down by water from higher up; now ash lenses and firepits appeared, showing that the material was still lying as it had originally been deposited.

Some human bones had been found on the surface, and a few had come from the digging. We were most anxious to discover burials; so a reward of twenty-five cents was offered to the workmen for every skeleton uncovered. The next day one appeared, the following day six; the reward was reduced to ten cents; this brought fifteen more, and in the course of a week or so we were forced to discontinue the bonus or go into bankruptcy. The higher we got uphill the deeper grew the rubbish and the more crowded became the skeletons (pls. 8, b; 11). It was obvious that we were digging in the greatest rubbish heap and cemetery that had ever been found in the Pueblo region; for we were working below the extreme north end of the north building, and the same sort of slope stretched away to the south on the east side alone for nearly a quarter of a mile.

Although we were somewhat overwhelmed by the mere mass of this midden, the conditions it revealed were exactly what we had been hoping for. Such a depth of undisturbed rubbish would be sure to be stratified, the earliest remains at the bottom, later ones above them, and so on up, so that by taking samples from the different levels, we should be able to get evidence as to the exact sequence of the various types of pottery that had been made at Pecos from the time of its foundation down to the beginning of the nineteenth century.

For this reason we gave up all hope of doing any excavation in the building the first year. We confined ourselves to trenching in the rubbish, collecting stratigraphic material, and uncovering and recording skeletons. Our trench was widened to two hundred and fifty feet, and was pushed up toward the defense wall. It was very slow work, for the earth quickly deepened to from ten to twelve feet (pl. 8, b). We soon saw that at our present rate of progress we could not reach the edge of the *mesilla* before snowfall, and concentrated on three narrow salient trenches to explore the deposit ahead and above.

Two of these salients were delayed by skeletons, but the third got on somewhat faster. We had believed that the defense wall was built on the edge of the *mesilla,* and that when we arrived at the wall we should encounter a vertical face of rock. As a matter of fact we reached the defense wall, with a trench twenty feet deep, but no mesa appeared.

After several weeks' digging, rendered very slow by the great depth of the earth and the presence of many skeletons, we found that the whole broad terrace between the ruin mound and the defense wall was made up of nothing but rubbish, and that the rock mesa began directly below the edge of the ruin. We had learned early in the season that the refuse heap was very large, but this latest discovery showed that it was probably at least twice as extensive as had then been estimated (fig. 7). This was the first of the long series of surprises which the Pecos work has furnished. Each one has proved the site to be vastly larger and more complex than had appeared from surface indication.

The earth which has been referred to as rubbish has played so important a part in all the excavations at Pecos, that it merits a brief description. It is a dark, loamy soil, full of charcoal, streaked with thin layers of ashes, and containing an incredible number of potsherds, chips of

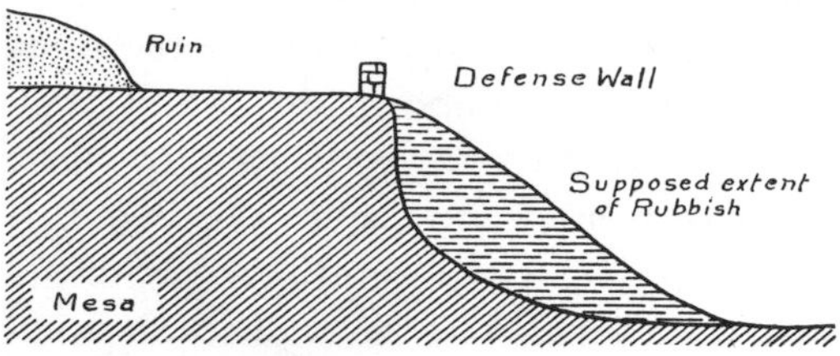
Ruin
Defense Wall
Supposed extent
of Rubbish
Mesa

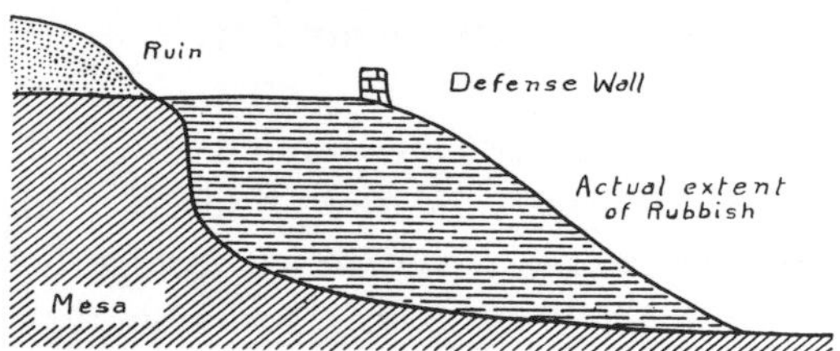
Ruin
Defense Wall
Actual extent
of Rubbish
Mesa

Fig. 7.

flint, animal bones, and broken utensils of all sorts. Its dark appearance is due to the high percentage of decayed vegetable matter, principally corn refuse, which has gone into it; but its largest component, its "body," so to speak, consists of fine windblown sand, and of adobe washed from the walls and roofs of the houses. The beds of rubbish were repositories for ashes, house sweepings, table leavings, broken pottery, and discarded implements; they served, as well, for the burial of the dead. The custom of interment in rubbish heaps is a very general one in the Southwest; it was caused, apparently, by no disrespect for the departed, but rather by the fact that the heaps offered as a rule the only soft earth for gravedigging in a land of bare rocks and hard-packed clays.

The first season, as has been said, was spent in working the rubbish. In comparison to the vast amount of it at the site, the progress, when plotted on the map, was not impressive; but the data and specimens secured were highly satisfactory. The most important results were of course those stratigraphic.

In various parts of the digging columns of earth had been isolated, marked out into horizontal sections, and carefully excavated (pl. 9). The material from each cut was kept separate, and shipped in to the Museum for study. When it was cleaned and examined it was found that the commonest, most easily classifiable, and obviously most significant specimens were the fragments of pottery. Work on these potsherds showed that there had been a steady and uninterrupted growth in the ceramic art of Pecos from the days of its founding down to the period of its abandonment in 1838. It was possible to establish eight major pottery types (see pls. 39, 40),[5] and to determine their exact chronological sequence, thus confirming and in many ways amplifying similar results then

5. The eight types are provisionally named as follows: Black-on-white, Glaze 1, 2, 3, 4, 5, 6, Modern. For description, see Kidder, M. A. and A. V., 1917.

being obtained by Nelson at the ruins of the Galisteo basin a few miles to the west.[6]

We must here consider briefly the application of such stratigraphic data. In the Rio Grande, as in other parts of the Southwest, there are great numbers of prehistoric ruins. Some of these contain one type of pottery, some another, still others show two or more types. It had been inferred that these differences in ceramics represented differences in age, but there was no sure method for arranging the types in their proper chronological order, though such an arrangement was of course necessary as a first step toward a study of the history of the region. With the discovery of the stratified deposits at the Galisteo basin ruins and at Pecos we were at once provided with a key to the whole problem; for they disclosed, as has been explained, an orderly superposition of all these types, the oldest naturally lying at the bottom, later ones above, and the latest at the top. With the sequence of the pottery types thus established, it becomes a perfectly simple matter to arrange all sites containing one or more of them in their true chronological order. The same principle is also used in the local work at Pecos: graves, for example, with offerings of Type 3 pottery must be older than graves containing Type 4; rooms filled with Type 6 rubbish must have been abandoned after rooms filled with refuse of Type 5, etc.

During the trenching of 1915 two hundred skeletons were found.[7] These lay in the rubbish at all levels from just under the grass roots (pl. 10, a) to as deep as twenty and twenty-one feet (pl. 9, b). Their general position in regard to the stratigraphic horizons served to date them relatively to each other; many of them, also, were accom-

6. Nelson, 1916.

7. Exclusive of about one hundred and fifty burials that came to light during Mr. Nussbaum's repair work on the church. A great mass of skeletal material of the historic period still awaits excavation in and near the mission.

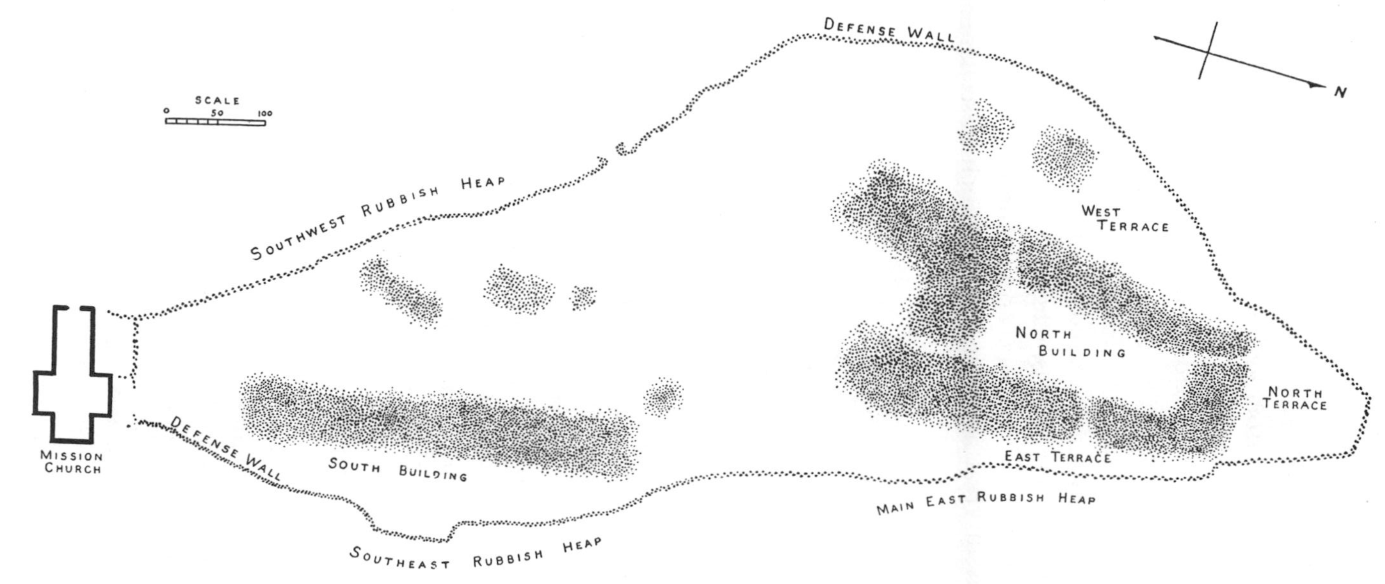


PLATE 7. Sketch plan of the Pecos ruins.

panied by mortuary offerings of pottery, which allowed us to fix their chronological position with even greater accuracy. Although a considerable percentage of the skeletons were in very bad condition, it was possible by careful work to save a large number of them.

The specimens, aside from potsherds and human and animal bones, numbered about three thousand; they included pottery vessels, effigies, pipes; objects of stone such as arrowheads, scrapers, knives and drills; bone and antler tools in great abundance; and much miscellaneous material in the way of ornaments, fetishes, objects of European manufacture, etc.

## Second season (1916)[8]

During the winter of 1915–16 much time was spent in studying the pottery recovered in the stratigraphic tests. It was found that the early types were very poorly represented, and that the later types, which there was no reason to suppose had been made for any greater length of time than the early ones, were present in disproportionately large quantities. It was decided that this was due to the fact that our tests had been made too far downhill and that the thickest deposits of early material must lie at the base of the heavy rubbish close against the mesa. For this reason it was felt that several deep tests must be made. One gang of men, accordingly, was kept testing in the main east diggings all summer, and the rest were used in an attempt to run out the extent of the other rubbish deposits that were thought to surround the pueblo.

Narrow exploratory trenches were cut at intervals of 100 feet or so all along the east slope, and pits were sunk on the terrace east of the north building. These showed

8. In this year Dr. C. E. Guthe acted as assistant, and Mrs. Kidder took charge of the cleaning and sorting of the thousands of potsherds recovered.

that the rubbish heaps extend over these entire areas, but that they are in most places not as deep as they are below the north building.

Trenches were next opened on the west slopes. Here there was found to have been little or no dumpage, a condition undoubtedly due to the strong west winds which prevail in the Pecos Valley, and which would naturally have induced the people to throw their refuse to leeward over the east side.

There now remained to be investigated an area that we called in our field notes the "North Terrace," a smooth, gently sloping surface running from where the defense wall cuts across the narrowing neck of the *mesilla* up to what appeared to be the foundations of the north wall of the main north quadrangle (pls. 7; 12, a). Here there were no signs whatever of house structures except a single low mound, and the place seemed to contain nothing but shallow rubbish and material washed down from the decaying pueblo.

We now received our second annual surprise. The first day's work disclosed house walls; we followed them up, and eventually laid bare, in this innocent-looking place, forty rooms, a kiva, and no less than two hundred burials. Although the actual digging progressed in the opposite direction, it will be simpler to describe the buildings from north to south.

Just within the defense wall, but obviously erected at a very much earlier time, was found a series of chambers, whose walls stood only about eighteen inches high (pls. 1, b; 12, a). These ancient foundations date from the period of the first occupation of the Pecos mesa, a fact that was proved by finding piled *against* them rubbish containing only black-on-white pottery, the type shown by stratigraphy to be the oldest of all. This dwelling, which we may for convenience call the Black-on-white house, extended from the western edge of the mesa across to the eastern; it there turned south and traces of it could be made out here and there under later structures.

Near the northwestern end of the main quadrangle was found a large Black-on-white rubbish heap and cemetery, so that we were led to suspect that the Black-on-white houses turned somewhere near the northeast corner and ran out to the western edge of the mesa, thus forming a three-sided pueblo open to the west and partly surrounding a large courtyard or plaza.

Debris of the Black-on-white period is scanty or even absent at the bottom of most parts of the rubbish deposits along the rest of the Pecos mesa; it is, however, comparatively heavy below the North Terrace, on both east and west sides. I believe, accordingly, that on the North Terrace lay the nucleus of the Pecos pueblo. As to the date of its founding or the length of its occupation we can say little or nothing as yet, but from the fact that at Rowe, and across the Arroyo de Pecos at "Bandelier Bend" and at "Loma Lothrop," there are ruins of what were larger and, in some respects, apparently earlier Black-on-white villages, we can hazard the guess that this mesa settlement was erected toward the close of the Black-on-white period and not long before the beginning of the next, or Glaze 1, stage. At all events the northern wing of the oldest pueblo was abandoned and presumably in ruins during Glaze 1 times, for skeletons accompanied by Glaze 1 pottery were found buried above the floor levels in several of its rooms (fig. 8).

The bulk of the Glaze 1 pueblo seems to have been to the south, where it still lies unexcavated below the mass of the great quadrangle; its approximate position may nevertheless be guessed at from the quantities of Glaze 1 rubbish that cumber the eastern mesa slopes below the quadrangle, and which are also heaped along the southern part of the North Terrace itself. The eastern wing of the old pueblo may have been used, however, to some extent, for there are evidences of repair and rehabilitation of many walls. Whether this was done at the very close of Black-on-white times or during the Glaze 1 stage could not be determined, but in either case the east wing lay abandoned, and probably partly covered up, through the whole long stretch of the next periods: Glaze 2, 3, and 4. This is proved by the presence of burials of these epochs in its rooms and actually above some of its broken-down

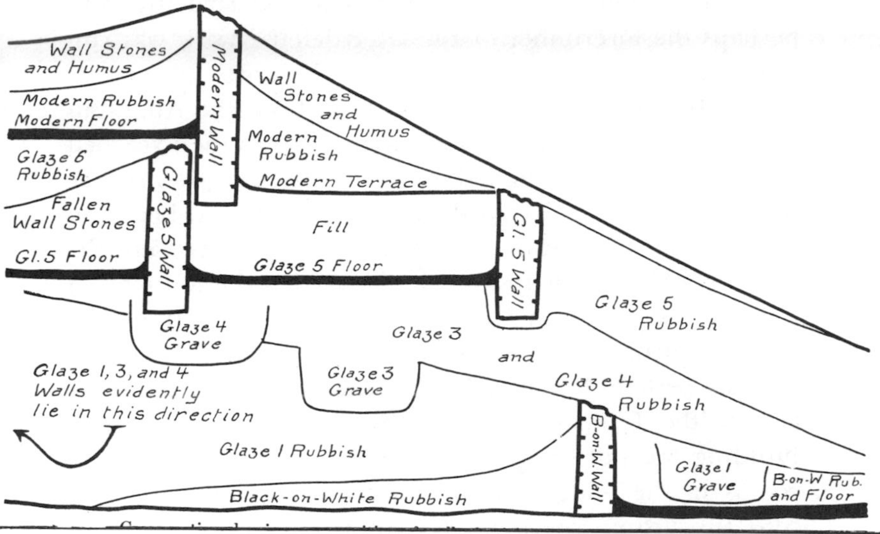


**Fig. 8.** Cross-section showing superposition of walls, burials, etc., on the North Terrace at Pecos.

walls, while the courtyard, usually kept free of rubbish in an inhabited pueblo, is choked with Glaze 3 and 4 debris and burials (fig. 8).

We must infer, then, that during these periods the Pecos pueblo was extending itself to the south, and that the great quadrangle, and perhaps also the long, narrow south house, were gradually assuming their final form. Not until this growth was completed, or at least well under way, did the inhabitants turn again to the North Terrace, the neglected site of what we suppose to have been their earliest homes. Here, in the Glaze 5 period, which began apparently some time before the Conquest and lasted until nearly 1680, were presumably built and surely used the rooms of the south wing near the main north wall. The floors of these lie well above rubbish of earlier times, and they themselves contained on excavation nothing but Glaze 5 pottery. There seems also to have been at this time some repair of the central apartments of the east series, and a long wall, probably a defensive structure and perhaps the forerunner of the later defense wall, was run out across the long-buried rooms of the north series.

The Glaze 5 period appears to have been the Augustan Age, so to speak, of the town, for the houses then reached their maximum size and the layers of Glaze 5 debris are the heaviest of all. Toward its close the pueblo began to draw in on itself again, the south wing rooms were deliberately filled up with stone and served as the foundation for the last addition to the heavy outside wall of the historic quadrangle. In this drawing in and strengthening we may perhaps see the effects of the ever-increasing menace of the Comanche raids. Even then the old north building was not entirely deserted, for the little group of rooms in the middle of the eastern wing was used well into the historic period, as is shown by the finding in them of crockery of Spanish make, bones of domestic animals, and copper implements. The rooms served as a sort of cookhouse annex and contained many manos and metates for corn grinding, while all about them are the remains of ovens sunk through the Glaze 5 rubbish.

In the final dreary years, when the handful of survivors lived huddled together in the few still habitable rooms of the quadrangle, the old north house was evidently given over to decay, for its mound contains none of the latest pottery at all. On its surface, however, we found lying broken a fine large water jar of the very last period, forgotten perhaps, or perhaps deliberately abandoned, by the last of the Pecos when they set out on their final migration to the homes of their kindred at Jemez.

I have gone into detail in describing the conditions that we encountered on the North Terrace, in order that the reader may appreciate the problems by which we were faced at the close of the 1916 season. We had expected to find on the mesa top the remains of a single large pueblo showing, perhaps, signs of repair and rebuilding, but founded on the rock and permitting the easy examination of its walls from top to bottom. Instead of this it had developed that the historic town was erected on the broken and tumbled walls of earlier houses, and that these again had been built over at least two still more ancient ones.

Such conditions were, of course, exceedingly favorable for the recovery of data on the growth of the pueblo, and might also be expected to disclose many important facts as to changes in architecture, house-grouping, etc., at different periods. But they would undoubtedly render the task of excavation infinitely slower and more expensive; and would necessitate the development of entirely new methods of recording. Furthermore, our original plans for repairing the walls of excavated rooms and leaving the pueblo open for inspection by visitors, had definitely to be abandoned. In the first place, to get at and study the older buried structures it would often be necessary to remove parts of walls which lay above them; and, secondly, the old broken-down early houses formed so irregular and unsteady a foundation that the upper walls were in a most precarious condition. Made of crude and badly laid masonry (pl. 13, a), uncoursed, with unbroken joints and with the corners not tied by binding stones, such walls would be hard to save intact even if built on solid, level rock; founded as they were on disintegrated walls of the same type as themselves, they had become, especially since

a

b

c

PLATE 8. The eastern trenches in the great Pecos rubbish heap. a. The opening cut, June 1915. b. Trench at ten feet deep. c. Trench at nineteen feet deep.

the rotting away of their roof beams, so shaky that, the supporting debris once removed, they fell almost of their own weight.

To sum up the work of the season. The eastern rubbish heap was tested and found to run the entire length of the *mesilla;* the western slope under the north building was shown to be practically barren of archaeological deposits; and the North Terrace was almost completely excavated, disclosing a very old ruin and, overlying it and running off under the main north quadrangle, the remains of several other prehistoric structures. Three large stratigraphic tests were carried out in the deepest rubbish obtainable, and several others were taken in places where it was desired to examine certain strata in detail. In the course of the digging four hundred and seventy-five skeletons were encountered, the most important of these belonging to the Black-on-white period.

## Third season (1917)

In this year no excavations were attempted at the main Pecos ruin, but a number of other pieces of work were carried out. I was able, before entering the army, to devote a few weeks to the exploration of the Hopi country in northeastern Arizona, and to locate a site, the ruined pueblo of Awatobi, which resembled Pecos in that its occupancy embraced both the prehistoric and historic periods. Distinct evidences of stratification were noted. Such a site was desirable in order to provide data from a more or less distant region, to use for checking against the Pecos finds.

Dr. Guthe explored the sites along the Pecos River below Pecos, as well as those in the Gallinas drainage to the west. He then investigated many ruins on the upper Rio Grande, and finally ran out the northern limits of Pueblo culture in that direction by following it to its vanishing point in the San Luis Valley of southern Colorado. Returning to Pecos he excavated for six weeks in the ruin at Rowe.

Rowe pueblo lies about four miles south of Pecos. It is a very large ruin which was occupied only during Black-on-white times, a period not extensively represented at Pecos, but a most important one in the history of the Rio Grande. The Black-on-white remains at Pecos are not only relatively scanty, but are also much confused by having been overlaid by, and somewhat mixed with, deposits of later epochs. Hence it was very desirable to collect unmixed data from a pure Black-on-white site. The excavation of Rowe supplied an abundance of such material, clearly illustrating the later phases of the Black-on-white period. The work was far from simple, as there had been several rebuildings accompanied by slight changes in culture. The masonry of Rowe is infinitely superior to that of Pecos.[9]

## Fourth season (1920)[10]

From the autumn of 1917 until July 1919, the Pecos work was at a standstill, and by the time the various loose ends were gathered together, uncatalogued collections arranged, and maps brought up to date, it was too late to take the field. The winter of 1919–20 was spent, accordingly, in studying the specimens already on hand. At this time it was arranged that all skeletal material from Pecos should be turned over to the Peabody Museum of Harvard University, and that Dr. E. A. Hooton, Curator of Physical Anthropology in that institution, should undertake the study of it. The skeletons already recovered numbered nearly seven hundred, future excavations were certain to produce many more, and, as the collection promised to be of great importance, it was desirable to have it in the

9. For a preliminary account of the Rowe excavation, see Guthe, 1917.

10. Dr. Guthe acted as assistant, Dr. Hooton superintended the cemetery work, Mrs. Kidder did the cataloguing and handled the potsherds.

PLATE 9. A stratigraphic test section in the deep rubbish.
a. Working in Cut 3, Test X.

PLATE 9b. Cut 5, Test X, partly removed—the arrows mark the positions of skeletons.

hands of a competent authority. When we took the field in the summer of 1920, Dr. Hooton accompanied us in order to learn the conditions under which the material was found, and also to assist in developing more perfect methods of caring for it.

Advantage was taken of Dr. Hooton's presence in the field to run a number of new trenches in the refuse-heap cemeteries on the east slope. Exploration of the west slope south of the main quadrangle also disclosed a new cemetery of very large proportions. What we have come to call the "annual surprise" was, for 1920, the fact that the upper terrace lying west of the main quadrangle was full of graves, and that part at least of the plaza of the main quadrangle itself was crammed with skeletons, which also ran under the ruins of the later houses.

The greater part of the summer was devoted to excavations in the pueblo itself. Rooms were cleared in both north and south buildings.

The South House work was undertaken with the idea of finding out whether or not that structure dated from prehistoric times. Castañeda, in his description of Pecos, mentions but one pueblo, a large quadrangle which is obviously the North House. That so large a building as the South House should have been overlooked, did not seem likely if it was inhabited at that time. It was thought that it might either have been in ruins in 1541, or perhaps have been built after that date. Excavations proved that both theories were correct, for when the rooms were cleared to bedrock, it was found that there had indeed been an early pueblo on the site, but that it had been abandoned and reduced to a mere heap of ruins long before the coming of the Spaniards. Some time during the late 16th or early 17th centuries, however, a new pueblo was constructed on the same ground. In its rooms were found many objects of European manufacture, such as bits of china, iron and copper implements. In the interior of the mound one ground-floor chamber was uncovered in excellent preservation. Its roof was mostly intact, and from the beams still hung the bark loops that had been used to suspend the goods of the owners; on one smoke-blackened log were a series of handprints, large and small, slapped on in whitewash.

In the North House the excavations were more extensive. The great mound formed by the ruin of this building is quadrangular, and encloses a large level plaza, to which entrance is gained by four gaps in the high-piled ruins. These gaps undoubtedly represent the former presence of passageways giving access to the court.

To explore the mound and the plaza, trenches were started simultaneously at the east entrance and at the west edge of the mesa, so as to cross-cut the entire northern end of the site and meet in the plaza.

The western trench was begun about eighty-five feet from the ruin proper and, like all trenches at Pecos, was run in along bedrock. It was thought that the deposit at this point would be shallow. Rubbish, however, was found at once, quickly deepened to four feet, and contained a number of skeletons of the Glaze 3 period. After passing through this zone of burials, there were encountered the foundation walls of an early building, the presence of which had not been suspected. This was cut through, and the trench continued toward the main mound, only to strike almost immediately a sharp dip in the bedrock. Sinking on the dip we found that we were in a large oval pit filled with rubbishy earth. On complete excavation, which required nearly a week, it proved to be a masonry-lined cistern, fifteen feet deep, ten feet wide, and twenty feet long, built in a natural crevice of the mesa. About its edge was a neatly made coping wall two feet high. The date of the building of the cistern could not then be determined, but it had been abandoned during the Glaze 4 period, and at that time filled full of rubbish. This was

PLATE 10a. Typical extended burial of late period; note shallowness of grave.

Plate 10b. Partly flexed burial typical of Glaze 4 period; mortuary bowl broken and the pieces scattered over the body at the time of interment.

PLATE 10C. Closely flexed burial on face, typical of Glaze 3 period; mortuary bowl unbroken.

a particularly valuable deposit, as it was very rich in potsherds and cast-off implements, and gave us an unusually full and unmixed collection.

When the cistern was cleared it was bridged over and the trench was continued. Another zone of skeletons was at once encountered, part of a large Black-on-white and Glaze 1 cemetery that seems to run all along the western side of the main ruin. Some very fine pottery was taken from these graves.

About fifteen feet west of the high mound we began to meet low walls built on bedrock and not extending to the surface. Resisting the temptation to follow these north and south, we cut through them, and trenched directly into the main ruin. Here we found a most complex state of affairs; a jumble of early walls, some fallen, others partly incorporated into the bases of later structures (pl. 14). The later houses stood about half way to the tops of their second stories, but they were in exceedingly bad condition in consequence of their poor masonry and of the fact that they had been founded on irregularly broken-down earlier walls.

It had been planned to cut the trench straight across to the plaza, but about half way through the mound we uncovered a room with such a finely preserved roof that we were afraid to excavate close about it and thereby weaken its walls. Accordingly we were forced to change direction to the south in order to pass around it. This proved to be a very fortunate circumstance, as it led us into a series of rooms that were most prolific in specimens.

The majority of rooms in a pueblo which, like Pecos, was abandoned slowly, were left empty, as the people naturally took away all their belongings with them. The rooms, however, that we now came into proved to have been the scene of a bad accident at some time in the historic period subsequent to 1680. The entire outer wall of the pueblo had evidently suddenly given way and fallen inward, crushing the rooms to the east of it and burying them with their entire contents under tons of stone (pl. 13, b). No attempt had been made to clear out and refit this section. That the people had some warning of the catastrophe is probable, as there were no skeletons in the debris.

Our finds here were very rich, including a large series of cooking jars, some modern painted ollas and a vessel from Zuñi; all these, of course, were badly broken; but, queerly enough, we found one nest of small ceremonial pots wedged in among the rocks and quite undamaged. With these were many handsome shell ornaments, two sets of bone flutes, two very large tobacco pipes, one of them elaborately carved, thirty-five buffalo horns, part of a wooden dance headdress, and many other specimens.

At this point the western trench encountered the eastern, which had been slowly worked in across the plaza to meet it. The initial progress of the east trench had been rapid, as it was run into the courtyard through an old entryway. Once in the plaza, however, it was as fruitful of labor-making surprises as was the west trench. Instead of a deposit of two to three feet, as had been expected, there was found an average of five feet of very hard-packed fill. Directly in the path of the cut were encountered the long walls of an old pueblo and just beyond were two large underground ceremonial chambers, or kivas. Both kivas had been built during the early occupancy of the Pecos mesa, but one of them was soon abandoned and afterwards served as a burial place, fifteen skeletons being found between its floor and the surface of the plaza. The other was kept in use until after the conquest, undergoing during the many centuries of its history a number of architectural changes. In a sealed recess in the wall of this kiva was found a small granite idol, the only object of its kind that had so far come to light at Pecos and the fourth ever found in New Mexico.

In addition to the two trenches just described, which cross-cut the North Building, a series of rooms about the east entrance was excavated. By very careful observation of the stratified fillings in the lower parts of these rooms, coordinated with an intensive study of the successive increments of masonry that had gone into their construction, Dr. Guthe was able to work out and record by plans and elevations the exact history of the growth of this section of the pueblo from the foundation of the town down to the time of its final abandonment. The methods of observation and recording developed by Dr. Guthe in this piece of work form a distinct addition to archaeological field technique.

The collection of specimens was large and contained many unique objects, and the result of the summer's work on the history of the pueblo and the development of its arts were highly satisfactory. The year's excavations in the North House, however, confirmed our worst fears as to the condition of the building itself. The ruin is in poorer condition than any other pueblo structure that I have seen. The walls of the late rooms stand to heights varying from ten to fifteen feet, but they are of such wretchedly bad masonry, are laid on such insecure foundations, and have been so thoroughly shattered by the falling of their upper stories, that to remove the filling of earth that holds them upright, means to bring about their almost certain collapse. In the few rooms cleared in 1920, we were obliged to pull down a number of tottering walls to avoid imminent danger to our workmen.

## Fifth season (1921)

During the excavations at Pecos, and particularly from the laboratory work on the material recovered, it had become increasingly evident that the surest archaeological results were to be derived from the study of pottery. We were constantly being called upon to classify wares, make

a

b

PLATE 11. Skeletons in the deep rubbish. The crowded condition of burials in certain areas greatly delays excavation, as each grave requires from one to three hours careful work.

comparisons, and form judgments as to the relations between different ceramic groups. We found that in doing this we were severely handicapped by a lack of precise knowledge as to the technology of Pueblo pottery, a lack which could not be supplied by any printed work. Accordingly, when I found in the spring of 1921, that I should be unable to excavate at Pecos that summer, Dr. Guthe went to New Mexico, to make a thorough study of pottery-making as it is practiced among the Pueblo Indians of today.

He chose for his investigation the Tewa pueblo of San Ildefonso, a village on the Rio Grande north of Santa Fe, whose women have for years been recognized as the most skillful and versatile potters of that region. During the weeks that Dr. Guthe spent at San Ildefonso, he recorded every step in the manufacture of pottery, from the digging of the clays to the firing of the completed vessels. His remarkably complete and detailed results will be published in the near future.

A second investigation bearing closely on the problems of Pecos, was also inaugurated in the summer of 1921. This was the study of the ethnology of the pueblo of Jemez.

The Jemez and Pecos were closely allied linguistically and their common dialect was not spoken at any other town. Hence, when Pecos was abandoned, the surviving members of the tribe naturally went to live with the Jemez. There they have gradually increased, until today there is a considerable group of people of more or less pure Pecos descent.

Since the beginning of the Pecos work it had been realized that the investigation could not be considered complete until an attempt had been made to recover from the descendants of the Pecos at Jemez whatever knowledge they still had of their former home and of the life which their ancestors lived there. It was also most desirable to learn something of the ethnology of one of the modern Rio Grande pueblos, for as to the social and religious organization of those towns we really know very little. Such studies could hardly fail to throw light on many of the problems raised by the Pecos excavations. No member of the expedition staff was qualified to undertake this work, and no opportunity to have it done by anyone else presented itself until Dr. Elsie Clews Parsons decided to include Jemez in the intensive ethnological survey which she had been carrying on at the villages further west. She spent the seasons of 1921 and 1922 at that pueblo, where, in spite of great difficulties due to the conservatism and secretiveness of the people, she has collected a mass of most interesting and important data. Dr. Parsons has generously allowed us to publish the results of her work in the Pecos series.

### Sixth season (1922)[11]

The excavation of the main quadrangle was continued north from the narrow cross-cut trench of 1920, particular attention being devoted to architecture, town growth, and the stratigraphy of the beds of early rubbish adjoining the building on the west side. In the course of the latter work an extensive ruin was developed on the West Terrace where enough of it was cleared to show that it dated from Glaze 1 times, and that its main axis ran north and south; but whether it was a simple structure or whether it was quadrangular like the historic pueblo, has not yet been determined.

As a preliminary to the work on the main quadrangle the inner wall of the building was cleared to its foundations all about the north half of the plaza; this served to remove a great deal of loose stone fallen from the ruined

11. During this summer I was assisted in the field by Miss Ida Sanford and Messrs. G. C. Vaillant and S. P. Moorehead. Mrs. Kidder as usual handled the sorting of potsherds.

a

b

PLATE 12. North terrace excavations. a. From the top of the main ruin mound; the remains of the oldest settlement lie just within the later defense wall; from the trenches here visible there were taken over ninety skeletons. b. The main ruin mound seen from the north.

upper walls of the houses and to define the exact limits of the courtyard. Such digging was naturally very unproductive of specimens. The first series of rooms, fronting on the plaza, was then attacked, and here we at once encountered conditions so typical of the whole summer's excavations that it seems worth while to describe part of that work in detail.

Room 39 was the first chamber entered. Under the pile of fallen rock which covered it was found a well preserved roof. The main beams, round poles of yellow pine six to eight inches in diameter, supported a ceiling of split cedar, twigs, and adobe. Tucked in among the roofing were an oak digging stick and two wooden arrows, placed there for safekeeping, and forgotten or abandoned when the owners left. Below the ceiling the upper part of the room was choked with earth, finely stratified, entirely barren of specimens and evidently washed in by rainwater seeping down the walls. Under this, and extending to the adobe floor, was a mass of rubbish two to three feet thick which showed that the room must have been used for a long time as a dumping place; the debris consisted of cornhusks, cobs, and stems, chips of wood, broken and discarded wooden implements and great quantities of animal bones. Remains of sheep and horses as well as fragments of late types of pottery proved the deposit to have been made in post-Spanish times.

In most Rio Grande pueblos when one reaches the floor of a room one's work is over, but at Pecos it is never safe to abandon excavations until bedrock is encountered. In Room 39 a trial pit in one corner showed that there was soft earth below; so digging was continued and was almost immediately rewarded by the finding of a large polished black olla, the mouth covered by a stone slab. This had been hidden under the floor, and contained a pair of turtle-shells perforated for suspension, like those worn by the Santo Domingo corn dancers, and two rattles made of small gourds. Near this was a second jar, also with a lid, but this one, to our great disappointment, was empty.

While we were clearing away the earth about these vessels we encountered human bones, and after careful brushing found that there were two skeletons buried face down in the deposit of dark soil that directly underlay the cached pots. Work from this point downward was very difficult; the light, which came in from a small hole in the roof, was poor, the space uncomfortably cramped, and the bones of the skeletons so badly decayed that the greatest care had to be exercised in cleaning them. The buried individuals proved to be two females, each one with a Glaze 3 bowl inverted over the head. The particular interest of these two skeletons lay in the fact that the head of one of them extended *under* the foundation of the east wall of the room, whereas the earth in which the burial was made had evidently accumulated *against* the much deeper west wall. This showed that the first, or easternmost, series of rooms along the plaza had been added to the building at some time subsequent to the Glaze 3 period, but that the rear rooms had been built at a date enough earlier to allow the growth of a considerable depth of rubbish against them.

How deep the rubbish ran was not ascertained until we had sunk three feet further, taken out three Glaze 1 skeletons, and eventually reached the solid sandstone of the mesa. Even here the work was not quite finished, for in the cracks of the rock were pockets of very early debris, and tucked away in one of them a much rotted skeleton, identified by its accompanying bowl as belonging to the very first period of occupation, the Black-on-white.

By the time all these remains had been cleared, noted, and removed, and their positions recorded on the plan and the cross-section map of the room, we had reached a depth, under the roof beams, of between eight and nine feet. The wall on the west side was decidedly shaky, that on the east had been undermined in taking out the Glaze 3 skeletons, and we were very glad to be able to get out of the deep, narrow, badly lighted hole.

The room just described was typical of the whole east, or plaza-fronting, series, and from each one we took a number of skeletons, ranging in age from Black-on-white down to Glaze 4 times. The most interesting find in these rooms was made in a chamber a few feet south of Number 39. Here, in a cist or bin built partly of masonry and partly of slabs, was a fine sandstone idol surrounded by a collection of pieces of petrified wood, odd-shaped stones, and concretions.

The next rooms to be excavated were those lying to the west, and here the conditions were somewhat simpler, as these chambers for the most part had been founded directly on the rock in early times, and kept in use, and accordingly clear of debris, until the abandonment of the town. Many specimens were found in them, and much was learned from the remains of roofs, fireplaces, and mealing outfits, as to the height of the original structure and the uses of the different rooms. To summarize, it may be said that Casteñeda's description of the town in 1540 was verified in almost every particular, namely, that the building was terraced up from the plaza to a height at the rear of four stories, that there were balconies at the second and third stories, and that the rooms on the ground floor were without doorways, access to the roofs and balconies having been gained by means of ladders.

During the season's work the entire northwest corner of the building was cleared, and several trenches were run in the rubbish heaps to the west. About two hundred and fifty skeletons were uncovered, most of them of early periods. The most notable specimens found were the idol above mentioned, a fine series of tobacco pipes from a ceremonial room at the north end of the pueblo, and a large stone slab from the plaza, upon which is painted in many colors a representation of a masked head, probably a rain god or kachina. The latter is, as far as the writer knows, the only painting of its kind which has ever been found in the Southwest.

Toward the end of the summer a few days were spent at a large but inconspicuous site at "Bandelier Bend" just across the Arroyo de Pecos from the main ruin. Enough was done to get an idea of the nature of the pottery and to determine that the buildings had been low, rambling structures made of adobe. The study of the pottery showed that "Bandelier Bend" was an ancient settlement founded, apparently, quite early in the Pueblo period, and inhabited for a long time. During its occupancy it seems to have grown by accretion from a small community to a very extensive one. It was abandoned at about the time when Pecos was founded, which makes it seem likely that its people merely moved across the arroyo to the more easily defended site on the Pecos mesa. The most interesting feature of our preliminary excavations was the finding of a round subterranean kiva, the oldest example of such a structure so far reported from the Rio Grande.

## SUMMARY OF RESULTS

Let us briefly sum up the results of the field work so far completed. To begin with, we have found that the Pecos site is much more extensive and vastly more complicated than had been expected. The main building mounds, those of the North and South Houses, instead of being the remains of dwellings erected at an early date and kept in use until the abandonment of the pueblo, have been shown to be comparatively late structures which overlie the broken-down walls of several still earlier towns. Where the earth on the mesa-top and along the terraces had been supposed to be a mere skin, it has turned out to be anywhere from five to twenty feet deep, and to cover unsuspected house ruins and cemeteries. The extent of

a

b

PLATE 13. Architectural details. a. Typical Pecos masonry, not coursed and made of untrimmed stones; a sealed doorway appears in the center of the picture. b. Conditions in the rooms of the Great Quadrangle; the badly built lower walls have given way and the upper stones have fallen, crushing the roof timbers.

the rubbish heaps along the east and southwest slopes has hardly yet been gauged. All these facts indicate, of course, a long period of occupancy, a condition which we had suspected from surface signs, but which we had not been able to prove before excavations began. It is now certain, therefore, that the rubbish heaps of Pecos contain the accumulations of several centuries at least; and many of them are so stratified that by careful study of their contents we have been able to trace the development of the arts and industries of the community from beginning to end. Of the various objects found in these stratified heaps, pottery fragments are by far the commonest and most easily classifiable. Hence we have devoted much time, both in the field and in the laboratory, to the study of pottery, and have worked out in considerable detail the changes which have taken place in that art from the unknown date at which Pecos was founded to the early years of the last century.

As originally planned, the work of the Pecos expedition was to be first intensive, then extensive. The intensive phase was to consist of the excavation of the pueblo, and the determination by stratigraphic methods of the sequence of the pottery types found at the site. During the second or extensive phase we were to use our knowledge of the sequence of the pottery types to arrange in their proper chronological order all other ruins which contained those types. This work was to be accomplished by a thorough archaeological reconnaissance of the Rio Grande drainage.

The first phase may, in a sense, be considered complete, since we have determined the sequence of the pottery types; and we should now, if we adhered to the original plan, cease work at Pecos and undertake a general reconnaissance of the Rio Grande. A modification, however, seems advisable. In the first place the Pecos ruin has turned out to be so large that we have as yet succeeded in clearing only about 12 per cent of it. Then, a number of most interesting and important lines of investigation have been suggested by what we have so far done; and none of these can be pursued without continued excavation. But some of these new investigations themselves require the sidelights of reconnaissance. Hence it has been decided to merge the intensive and extensive phases of our work—to continue digging at Pecos and to carry on at the same time as much reconnaissance as possible.

Perhaps the most important of the new lines of investigation just referred to is that of the development of decorative art. Because of the increasing use of pottery, basketry, textiles, etc., as criteria of cultural evolution, the morphology of decoration is receiving more and more attention from anthropologists. But this subject is peculiarly difficult of approach, because to gain a true insight into the development of any decorative complex, one must have not only abundant material but material which is chronologically sequent. Such material for the study of art growth among prehistoric or primitive people has always been exceedingly hard to get. Until now almost all work on the subject has been based on hypothetically arranged series, and conclusions drawn from it are, of course, not to be relied upon. In the Southwest, however, stratigraphic work will eventually provide datable specimens from all districts and of all periods, so that we shall be able to determine with perfect certainty the exact changes which have taken place in the art of that area. The unusually complete pottery series to be had at Pecos will, when carefully studied, make clear the details of the local art growth over a long stretch of time. For this reason alone it seems well worth while to persevere until we have gathered a very large body of data. There enters here, however, the necessity spoken of above for doing concurrent reconnaissance at other sites. The Pecos series, while long, can only be recovered from large, stratified rubbish heaps.

These supply the outline of the development, and also provide abundant material; but, as in all stratified deposits, there has been a certain amount of mixing, so that absolutely pure material from any given period is only to be found under exceptional conditions, as in sealed rooms, quickly filled kivas, cisterns, etc. Hence, to get a perfect series of pure material we must collect pottery from briefly occupied sites of each period, sites which do not contain earlier or later mixtures.

A second investigation which promises much of interest concerns itself with the mechanics of pueblo growth. It was at first supposed that the Pecos ruins were the remains of a single structure, erected *en bloc*, occupied until 1838, and then abandoned. The excavations, however, have shown that we have not only ruin piled on ruin, but that the population kept shifting about from one part of the mesa to another, building and rebuilding. We have uncovered in the course of our limited excavations portions of no less than six distinct towns. While some of these have been nearly obliterated by stone-robbing, all of them can eventually be traced out; and they can all be accurately dated relative to each other by means of the pottery and the burials found in and about them. Furthermore, the later structures, and perhaps some of the earlier ones as well, can undoubtedly be dated absolutely by means of the growth rings of their roof beams.[12] There is also no question but that we shall eventually learn the approximate date for the original founding of Pecos. This will allow us to estimate the number of changes made and the amount of building done during a known number of years, and will give us valuable data on the question of the permanency or impermanency of Pueblo house groups.

The consideration of habitations naturally brings up the matter of population. This, as will be shown in a later chapter, is a question of fundamental importance. We

12. By the Douglass method, see p. 132.

Courtesy National Geographic Society

PLATE 14. The west cross-cut trench, 1920.

must learn as much as possible concerning the size of the prehistoric Pueblo tribes, and also as much as possible regarding their racial affinities. On both problems the excavation of Pecos can shed light. We have already taken out some twelve hundred skeletons, and have as yet barely scratched the cemeteries. While some skeletons are too rotted for laboratory measurement, the age and sex of almost all of them can be determined. As there is no evidence that the Pecos ever cremated their dead, or commonly buried them elsewhere than on the mesa, and as cemeteries were not often greatly disturbed by later use, it would seem that if we excavate the entire site we shall find the bodies of practically all the people who ever lived there. Thus we should be able to estimate roughly the total population of Pecos; and when we learn the date of its foundation, we should be able, by correlating this knowledge with what we find out about the size of the town at different periods, to judge of the number of people who lived there at any given time. Such work will also be greatly aided by the fact that we can usually assign any skeleton to its proper period, either certainly by means of mortuary pottery in its grave, or inferentially by taking into consideration the depth of the interment, the nature of the rubbish surrounding and covering it, and its association with other nearby skeletons.

Even if we cannot gauge the size of the population at every period, the skeletons from Pecos will form a very large addition to the material available for somatologists. Being relatively datable they should provide data as to the unity or heterogeneity of the Pecos people at different times; and, if mixtures have occurred, their period and the effect that they had on the resident population should be discernible. Much of value will also be learned as to length of life, infant mortality, and the effects of certain important diseases.

As in the case of the work on art development, so with

the skeletons, outside excavation must be carried on to supplement the data from Pecos, and to acquire material from periods which are not well represented there. The earlier burials at Pecos are generally in bad condition, because of the great amounts of rubbish which have accumulated above them. By going to contemporaneous sites where, because of brief occupation, the interments are not crushed by so great an overburden, we can recover well-preserved skeletons and so complete our series.

The above lines of investigation can only be carried to completion by clearing the whole Pecos mesa and the rubbish slopes that surround it on all sides, a task that seems beyond the present resources of the Trustees. Furthermore, it is not advisable, it appears to me, that so important a ruin be entirely exhausted at one time or by one excavator. Future work will of course serve to introduce better methods of excavation; and the development of the science of archaeology will inevitably result in the raising of new problems which today are not even suspected. Hence it seems best to leave a considerable portion of Pecos untouched, and so available for the improved technique and the broader knowledge of another generation of archaeologists. We do, however, hope to gather much more material, and at least to make a start toward the solution of the important problems of art development, pueblo growth, and the size of the population at different periods.

In the prosecution of such studies as have just been suggested we must be careful to hold ourselves to a proper balance between the detailed and the general. The details of archaeology are in themselves so interesting that it is fatally easy to become completely absorbed in them, and there is always the excuse that without close and accurate work one cannot arrive at trustworthy conclusions. The result is that too often one arrives at no conclusions at all. It is quite as fatally easy to ignore detail (with the plausible excuse that the close worker cannot see the forest for the trees) and strike out blithely on the primrose path of speculation. If archaeology dealt with phenomena less infinitely variable in themselves and less bewilderingly diverse in their interactions, it might be possible to reduce it to rules and formulas, and to decide just how far to delve into detail, and just how much to generalize. But that is not possible, and apparently never can be. Each problem must be attacked in its own way, and every worker must decide for himself how he shall apportion his efforts.

In the case of Pecos, the way seems fairly clear. The nature of the site and the circumstances of its occupancy have resulted in the laying down of deposits important and interesting in themselves, which also epitomize, as it were, a long period in the culture history of the Southwest. Pecos may be made to serve as an index to a considerable part of that culture history, and so, it seems to me, too much effort cannot be spent upon the details of its archaeology. But for the very reason that it is an index, it cannot be treated as an isolated phenomenon, and we must keep constantly in mind the more general problems that it is being used to solve.

To understand the problems of Southwestern archaeology it is necessary to consider the nature of our knowledge of man in America. Historical information in regard to the American Indian runs back at the farthest for only about four hundred years, and in most parts of the New World the record is very much shorter. Furthermore, where the historical record begins, there, as a rule, the history of the Indian abruptly ceases. There are a few exceptions, such as those provided by the datable monuments of the Maya; and certain instances, as in Peru and Mexico, where native traditionists have set down in European characters the more or less legendary histories of their own particular peoples. At best, then, recorded history for the aborigines of the New World is brief, and in the case of most areas it is entirely lacking. The student has before him data as to the distribution of great numbers of tribes, infinitely diverse in language and customs and ranging in culture from the lowest savagery to a relatively high civilization. This state of affairs must of course be the result of a very long sequence of historical events, and our problem, as Sapir has so admirably phrased it, "may be metaphorically defined as the translation of a two-dimensional photographic picture of reality into the three-dimensional picture which lies back of it. Is it possible," he asks, "to read time perspective into the flat surface of American culture, as we read space perspective into the flat surface of a photograph?" [13] Sapir proceeds to answer his question in the affirmative, basing his deductions largely on the inferential evidence provided by ethnology and linguistics; he emphasizes, however, the great potential importance of archaeological studies. Such studies had not, when Sapir wrote, been prosecuted with any great energy, but during the past decade archaeologists have been devoting more and more attention to the chronological aspects of their work. There has been a very general search for definite information bearing on the time relations of the remains of man in America. Nowhere has this search been more diligently prosecuted than in the Southwest, and the results so far obtained are extremely promising.

To make clear the nature of the chronological problems of the Southwest, and to show how the work at Pecos can be brought to bear upon them, it is necessary to lay before the reader an outline of the data which are already at hand, or in other words to undertake a summary of our present knowledge of Southwestern archaeology.

13. Sapir, 1916, p. 2.

# The Modern Pueblos

The Southwest, archaeologically speaking, comprises those parts of the southwestern United States and northern Mexico which are, or were formerly, inhabited by Indians of Pueblo culture. This culture will be more fully described in the section devoted to the modern Pueblos; for present purposes it suffices to say that its outstanding characteristics are sedentary agricultural life in permanent villages of stone or adobe, the manufacture of excellent pottery, and the use of the hand loom.

When we come to define the limits of the Pueblo area we find our only serious difficulty in the south. This is partly because little exploration has been carried out in northern Mexico; but to an even greater extent because the peoples of that region were also sedentary agriculturists between whose culture and that of the Pueblos there were few very fundamental differences. Were we to use as a criterion the architecture typical of the Pueblos, we should have to establish our boundary at or slightly north of the Gila River in Arizona, and along the international border of New Mexico. Relying upon the evidence of pottery, however, we can extend our limits to include the Gila and southern Arizona, as well as the great inland basin of northern Chihuahua that lies south of New Mexico. Certain well-marked Mexican traits occur in these areas; but the pottery, as will eventually be shown, is definitely Southwestern in type. Accordingly it seems best to accept, provisionally at least, the more extensive southern boundaries.

To the east, north, and west the problem of delimitation is much simpler, for in those directions the surrounding tribes were all in a much lower state of culture than were the Pueblos, and wherever regions adjoining the Southwest show traces of agriculture, permanent stone houses, and pottery, these may safely be ascribed to Pueblo influence. Although much exploration remains to be done, the approximate limits are already apparent. They include, as shown on the accompanying map (fig. 9), most

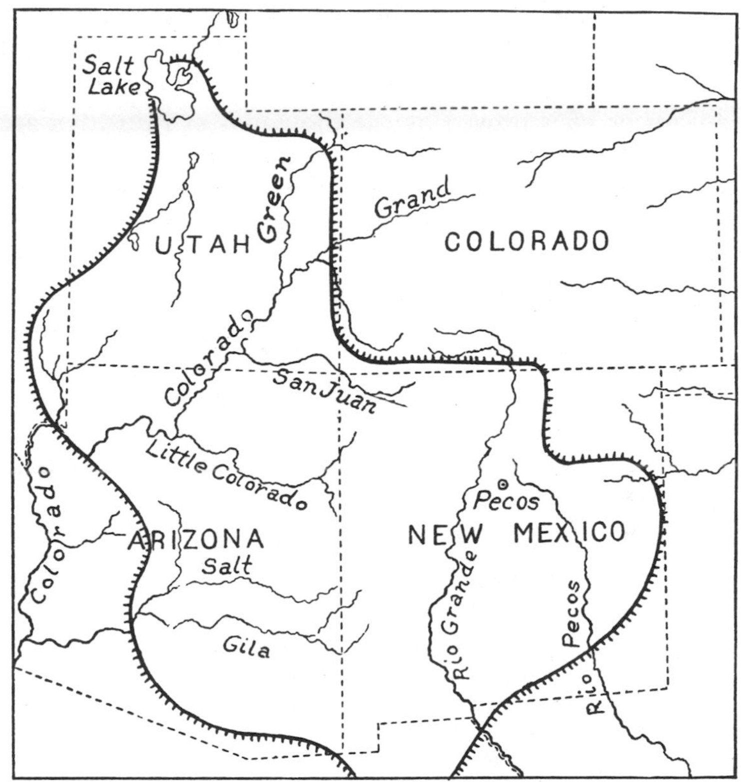


FIG. 9. Approximate extent of the Southwestern culture area.

of Arizona and New Mexico, a small part of Colorado, and a large portion of Utah.

This vast area has very distinct topographic and climatic characteristics; it is essentially a plateau country, high and arid. Much of it is desert. Where conditions are slightly better, the land is clothed with cedars and pinyons. Only the slopes of the eastern mountains and of certain interior ranges are really forested. Grass is everywhere scanty, game is correspondingly scarce; nor are there any wild food-plants of value. Much of the soil, however, is fertile, and where water can be got upon it is surprisingly reproductive. While the country, then, could support only a very limited number of hunting people, it was capable of providing sustenance for a relatively large agricultural population. That this productivity was once fully taken advantage of is proved by the thousands of ruins that are scattered over the length and breadth of the area. In more recent times, however, most of this great territory was abandoned, and when the Spaniards arrived in 1540 they found the Pueblos living in a comparatively restricted region at about the center of their former range.

To trace the history of these people, to discover their origins, to learn how they conquered their harsh environment, how they increased and spread out over the plateau, and how and why they eventually failed to hold their own in the struggle for existence, these are the chief aims of the study of Southwestern archaeology.

A review of the subject matter of Southwestern archaeology must necessarily begin with a consideration of the still inhabited pueblos of New Mexico and Arizona.[1]

1. No attempt has been made to include in the bibliography the enormous literature regarding the modern Pueblos; the following more or less popular works, however, will give the general reader an excellent idea of their life and customs: Bandelier, 1890, 1890b; Donaldson, 1893; Cushing, 1901, 1920; Lummis, 1906, 1910; Hough, 1915; Saunders, 1912; Goddard, 1921. Scientific studies of Pueblo religion, social organization, and material culture are to be found in the writings of Fewkes (*Annual Reports of the Bureau of Ethnology, American Anthropologist, Journal of American Folk-Lore*); J. and M. C. Stevenson (*Annual Reports of the Bureau of Ethnology*); Dorsey and Voth (*Field Columbian Museum Anthropological Series*); E. C. Parsons (*American Anthropologist, Memoirs American Anthropological Association, Journal of American Folk-Lore*); and Kroeber (*Anthropological Papers of the American Museum of Natural History*). See also the articles on the various Pueblo towns and Pueblo linguistic stocks in "Handbook of American Indians" (*Bulletin 30, Bureau of American Ethnology*).

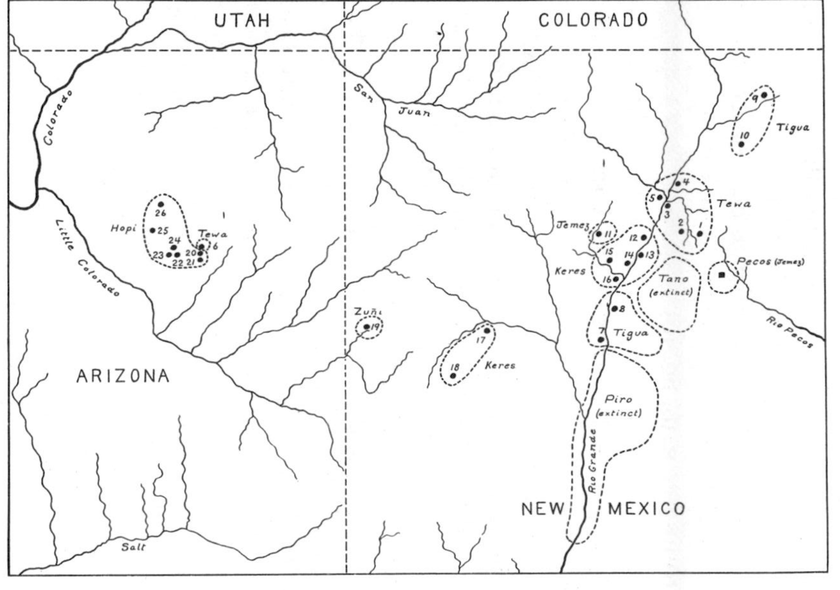


Fig. 10. Map showing the distribution of the Pueblo linguistic stocks and the location of villages inhabited at the present time.

1. Nambe
2. Tesuque
3. San Ildefonso
4. San Juan
5. Santa Clara
6. Hano
7. Isleta
8. Sandia
9. Taos
10. Picuris
11. Jemez
12. Cochiti
13. Santo Domingo
14. San Felipe
15. Sia
16. Santa Ana
17. Laguna
18. Acoma
19. Zuñi
20. Sichomovi
21. Walpi
22. Mishongnovi
23. Shumopovi
24. Shipaulovi
25. Oraibi
26. Hotavilla

These fascinating communities preserve the ancient culture of the Southwest in almost its aboriginal purity; even the most sophisticated of them are little more than veneered by European civilization, and we can still, as Lummis has so aptly phrased it, "catch our archaeology alive."

At the time of the Spanish conquest the Pueblo Indians numbered about 20,000, and lived in some seventy towns. These Indians, although very similar to each other in arts, customs, and religion, were divided into several distinct linguistic groups (see map, fig. 10).

In the northwest lived the Hopi, who spoke a Shoshonean language allied to that of the Utes, Paiutes and Comanches. On the western border of New Mexico were the Zuñi, whose tongue has no known affinities. East of Zuñi came the Keres, divided into two groups, one on the middle waters of the Puerco, the other on the Rio Grande north of the present location of Albuquerque. The Keresan language, like the Zuñian, has no known affinities. All the rest of the Pueblos belong to the Tanoan stock, a group which had five well-marked subdivisions: the Tewa, Tigua, Jemez, Tano, and Piro. Tanoan has recently been suspected to be connected in some way with the Kiowan linguistic stock of the Plains. In general the Tanoan peoples were confined to the Rio Grande and its immediate vicinity. The Tewa subdivision occupied a continuous area north of the Keres. The Tigua were partly to the north of the Tewa at Toas and Picuris, partly to the south of the Keres along the Rio Grande below Albuquerque and west toward the Manzanos Mountains. The Jemez were also divided, one group lying west of the Keres in the Jemez Valley, the other at Pecos far to the east on the upper Pecos River. The Tano occupied the eastern tributaries of the Rio Grande south of the Tewa, and between the Keres and the Pecos branch of the Jemez. The Piro villages began below the country of the southern Tigua and extended down the Rio Grande about half way to El Paso; there were also several towns east of the river in the Salinas Valley.

All these different Pueblo peoples live today in approximately the same places as they did in 1540, with the exception of the Tano and Piro, who have become to all intents and purposes extinct, and the Pecos, who, as we have seen, moved in 1838 to join their kindred at Jemez. There are at the present time only twenty-six villages, and their inhabitants number not over 9,000 souls.

Although reduced in numbers, and to a greater or less extent affected by European contact, the life of the Pueblos of today is surprisingly like that of their ancestors of the sixteenth century, as described by Castañeda and the other early Spanish chroniclers.

The most characteristic feature of Pueblo life is the pueblo itself, that peculiar type of village which has given the culture its name. A pueblo is a closely built agglomeration of rectangular living rooms, a sort of exaggerated beehive, or great apartment house, which shelters an entire community (pl. 15, a). The individual rooms may be grouped in various ways, as in a long row, about a court, or in a solid mass; but close adherence of room to room is always the rule, and for even greater compactness the villages are usually terraced, sometimes to a height of several stories (pl. 43). The people live, cook, and sleep in the outer and upper chambers, and use the inner and lower ones for the storage of their belongings and particularly for their hoards of harvested corn.

The system of architecture is simple. The unit of construction is a rectangular room with walls of heavy masonry set in adobe mud or laid up of pure adobe. Each room is spanned across its short axis by four or five large peeled logs; over these in the opposite direction are placed smaller poles, then twigs or bark for chinking, and finally a layer of adobe. If a second room is to be built above the first, the walls are simply continued upward and the roof

a

b

PLATE 15. Modern Pueblo villages. a. Taos, a terraced village of the old type in northern New Mexico. b. Two-story house in Tesuque pueblo, New Mexico; harvest time, corn heaped at the right, strings of chile drying in the sun, and jerked meat hanging under the balcony.

of the lower serves as the floor of the upper. Lateral rooms are added by merely constructing walls against those already erected. Doorways are small and in old times seldom opened on the ground level, first-story apartments having been entered by trap doors in their roofs. Windows did not exist; little ventilating holes near the fireplaces and smoke vents in the roof kept the air breathable. Although modern frame doors and glazed windows have now appeared at the more progressive towns (pl. 15, b), and the rooms of such pueblos are larger and more comfortable than of old, the people still live largely out-of-doors, in the courtyards, under the balconies, and on the housetops; so much so that even today a person's housetop is still considered a public thoroughfare and no Pueblo ever takes umbrage at its being used as such.

In addition to the rooms of the houses proper, each pueblo of the early historic period possessed several kivas, round or rectangular chambers, usually sunk into the earth so that their roofs were flush with the ground, and entered from above by means of a hatchway and ladder. The kiva is found in practically all the modern towns, and plays a most important role in Pueblo life; it is a social and work room for the men, a council chamber, and (its most important function) the scene of the secret portions of the religious observances; all modern kivas, except those at Taos and the Hopi towns, are above ground (pl. 16, b).

In spite of the solid construction of their towns, and the great labor involved in building them, the Pueblo Indians are (or rather were in the recent past) less firmly anchored to them than might be supposed. As evidence of this we have the fact that none of the modern pueblos, except Acoma and Zuñi, occupy exactly the same sites as they did in 1540. Every other town has moved at least once, and many of them several times. Much of this shifting about was due, of course, to the wars of the re-

a

b

PLATE 16. Modern Pueblos. a. Harvest dance at San Ildefonso, New Mexico. b. The kiva at San Ildefonso.

volt and reconquest between 1680 and 1700; but the Pueblos were always ready to abandon their dwellings on what seem to us the slightest pretexts, and were usually little disposed to return to them again, even under Spanish coercion. Many freshly abandoned villages were seen by the earliest explorers; and in more recent times many shifts have been made for apparently the most trivial reasons. The influence of the priests and the establishment of land grants have served to render the towns of the last two centuries more or less permanent, but it is clear that the Pueblos have little feeling for mere localities and small compunction in abandoning old homes.

This relative impermanency of towns whose construction seems so very permanent is a highly important phenomenon; it helps to explain many otherwise puzzling features of Southwestern archaeology, and will be more fully discussed when we come to consider the subject of the prehistoric ruins.

The Pueblos are primarily agriculturists. They have always hunted to a certain extent, and at present possess more or less livestock, but their main reliance is now, as it was in the past, upon corn. Corn, with beans and squashes, forms the bulk of their sustenance. The Pueblos are expert farmers. They grow crops in places, and under conditions, that at first sight appear to be absolutely hopeless. Irrigation is practiced where possible, but their success depends mostly upon the intelligent choice of ground, deep planting, and the most careful cultivation and weeding. Centuries of selection have resulted in the development of hardy, deep-rooted varieties of corn which will germinate with little moisture and mature quickly after the brief midsummer rains.

After harvest the corn is dried, husked, and stored away on the ear. For use it is ground to meal on a flat stone slab, the metate, and made into various dishes, the most characteristic of which is a thin paper-like bread cooked on a stone griddle.[2]

The governmental, social, and religious organizations of the Pueblos are highly complex and at present are imperfectly understood. The reason for this is that among the Pueblos the secular and the religious are inextricably intertwined, and the people are so exceedingly reticent in regard to their religion that investigators have had the greatest difficulty in finding out the true meaning of what would appear to be the simplest phenomena. To make the most general sort of statement, one can say that each pueblo is a strictly self-contained, closely knit, and autonomous unit, essentially democratic so far as wealth and living conditions are concerned. It is governed by elective officers, whose functions are both religious and civil. Marriage is monogamous, descent is, or was, usually through the mother, and the social unit is the clan, or group of blood relatives in the female line.

The religious system concerns itself principally with the growing of crops; its ceremonies have to do, therefore, with the fertilization of corn and particularly with the production of the ever-needed rain. Minor but still important features are the propagation of game, success in the chase, and the cure of sickness. The ritual is elaborate, involving the use of a great mass of paraphernalia. The public ceremonies are often highly spectacular. During the ceremonies many "prayer sticks" are made and deposited in shrines; much cornmeal is used, both symbolically, and in the form of actual offerings to the gods.

The house building, the agriculture, the religious practices, and the social system of the Pueblos have been relatively little affected by their three hundred years of intercourse with the whites. But their native minor arts, with

2. See *Zuñi Breadstuff* (Cushing, 1920). This is a work remarkable for its completeness of detail, its keen insight into pueblo life, and its literary charm.

the single exception of pottery-making, have disappeared, particularly since the American occupation with its influx of good tools and serviceable textile fabrics. For information as to the old arts we must therefore turn to the narratives of the early Spanish explorers, and to such objects as have been preserved by the people and have found their way into museum collections.

One of the most important industries was weaving. In the sixteenth century cotton was grown at all the pueblos where the local climate was not too rigorous, was spun into yarn, and woven on primitive but efficient hand looms. The cultivation of cotton has now been given up everywhere except in the Hopi country, where a few plants are still raised to provide the native fiber which is considered indispensable for certain ceremonial usages.

Weaving was, and still is, considered man's work, the looms usually being set up in the kivas. Few of the old cotton fabrics survive in everyday use, but ceremonial kilts are still made; the yarn, however, is of American manufacture. After the introduction of sheep, wool largely took the place of cotton; the Hopi were particularly adept in the making of woolen textiles, and even now produce some blankets and a large number of women's dresses, the latter being one of their principal articles of trade.

The clothing of all the Pueblos, except those of the extreme northwest, where contact with the Plains tribes served to make popular the use of fitted skin garments, was essentially alike. Although native clothes are no longer much worn, the ceremonial dress probably reflects older conditions quite accurately (pls. 16, a; 17, b). In dances the men wear a breechcloth and a short kilt fastened about the waist and falling to a little above the knees. The man's short-sleeved cotton shirt, not tailored, but made by simply sewing two square pieces of fabric together and attaching small sleeves, was apparently once in common use; a few such shirts are still in existence as treasured heirlooms,

PLATE 17. Pueblo costumes. a. Woman of San Ildefonso in everyday dress.

PLATE 17b. Corn dancers at Santo Domingo.

and are sometimes worn by the musicians during religious dances. The footgear is a hard-soled moccasin; it is uncertain whether or not the sandal of ancient times survived in the early historic period.

The women are somewhat more conservative in dress than the men. Their principal garment is a sleeveless dress of native (usually Hopi) weave, made in a single piece. When put on, the dress reaches to just below the knees, and is so fastened as to leave the left shoulder and sometimes the left breast exposed (pl. 17, b). During ceremonies the women of some villages go barefoot, but for everyday wear most Pueblo women have moccasins with long attached uppers which are wrapped about the calf of the leg (pl. 17, a). Both sexes complete their costume with a robe thrown over the shoulders; in old times this was of rabbitskin or turkey feathers, now it is either a Navaho blanket or an American shawl.

Basketry is a lost art at most of the pueblos, the requirements of the people being supplied by trade with the Apache, Pima, and Paiute. It is probable that this was to some extent also the case in the early historic period. At the present time heavy coiled basketry is made at the Hopi towns of the Second Mesa, wickerwork trays at Oraibi, and a plaited yucca basket with a wooden ring about the rim is produced at several towns, notably at San Felipe, whose people make a specialty of this particular type.

Pottery, in spite of the growing use of tin oilcans for carrying water, and of cheap American china for serving food, still plays an important part in the domestic economy of the Pueblos. Even today, cooking is largely done in native pots, and earthen ollas serve almost exclusively for the storing and cooling of drinking water. The art of pottery-making, too, has been kept alive by the constant demand for decorated vessels by the traders, who ship them in large quantities to curio dealers. While this commercial demand has naturally resulted in careless work and a certain degeneration in technique and ornamentation, its effects have been less pernicious than might be expected. There are still many expert potters, who turn out fine vessels, even with the knowledge that they are to be sold to white men.

Pottery is now regularly made at some of the Hopi towns, at Zuñi, Acoma, Laguna, Sia, Santo Domingo, Cochiti, San Ildefonso, Tesuque, Santa Clara, and San Juan (pl. 18). Elsewhere it is only manufactured in limited quantities in the form of undecorated cooking jars, or is turned out by women from the pottery-making pueblos who happen to have married away from home. Pottery was formerly, of course, a common product at every village. A detailed report on the subject of pottery-making will be published in an early number of the present series.

To sum up, the Pueblos live in closely knit autonomous groups, a single large building, made up of many small rectangular rooms, often sheltering an entire community. The people are primarily agriculturists, raise corn and grind it on the metate; are excellent and prolific potters; and understand the use of the hand loom.

No description of the Pueblos can be complete without mention of their hereditary enemies, the nomadic tribes of the Southwest. These Indians gained their livelihood principally by hunting, and were not bound down by the possession of permanent towns or cultivated fields. What little agriculture they practiced was of a haphazard sort, and they were always free to shift their range at will. Between the village-dweller and the nomad there has always, and in every part of the world, been bitter enmity; never more bitter, perhaps, than in the Southwest.

Apparently the roaming tribes seldom waged definite wars against the Pueblos, nor did they often carry out organized attacks on their towns. They hung about in the mountains ready at any time to pounce upon outlying

PLATE 18. Modern Pueblo pottery. a. Hopi. b. Cochiti. c. Santo Domingo. d. Acoma. e. Zuñi. f. Santa Clara. g. Tesuque. h. Sia. i. San Ildefonso.

farm settlements, cut off hunting parties, steal women, plunder cornfields, burn crops, and in general make life as miserable as possible for their more sedentary neighbors. Their raids were intermittent, there were often periods of quiet, and even times of actual peace with open trading between the Pueblos and the nomads. But such armistices never lasted long.

Against these tactics the Pueblos were singularly helpless. Good fighters they were, but tied to their villages and fields they could seldom bring their whole force to bear upon enemies so bafflingly elusive. They maintained themselves, however, by constant watchfulness, prompt defensive measures, and the strength of their fortress-like dwellings.

Nomads were present in the Southwest in 1540, for Castañeda records depredations in the Rio Grande country by the Teyas, apparently a Shoshonean Plains tribe, and states that villages had recently been abandoned because of their raids.[3] Since the middle of the seventeenth century the Navaho and Apache have been terrible scourges, the latter having forced the desertion of many Piro and Tigua towns to the west of the Rio Grande. About 1700 the Comanche began to press in from the northeast and east, with disastrous results for Pecos. The Utes and the northern Apache were always troublesome to the Taos and northern Tewa. It is, indeed, only since the American occupation of Arizona and New Mexico that any effective protection has been furnished to the Pueblos, and only in very recent years has the ancient menace of the nomad been entirely removed.

3. Winship, 1896, pp. 323, 324.

# The Prehistoric Pueblos

The Spanish explorers of the Southwest were indefatigable travellers, acute observers and, best of all, accurate recorders of the places they visited and of the things they saw. Their accounts enable us to locate the sites, and in most cases the actual ruins, of practically every pueblo that was inhabited in the sixteenth and seventeenth centuries. That any large or important towns could have escaped their thorough search and careful recording is almost impossible. Hence, any ruin which is not identifiable as a village mentioned in one or another of the documentary sources must, unless it holds internal evidence to the contrary, be considered to have been abandoned prior to the year 1540.

Internal evidence of historic occupancy is usually easy to find, for very soon after the conquest the Spanish introduced horses, sheep, goats, and cattle, whose bones come to light in every refuse heap of historic times; they also traded to the Indians glass beads, iron tools, china, and other objects of European make that turn up in considerable quantities in the rooms of the ruins and in the graves of the dead. While the presence of these things proves white contact, their absence does not certainly prove the contrary; nevertheless any given site containing no object of European provenience may be pretty safely considered prehistoric, particularly if extensive excavations have been carried out in it.

Applying the above two tests to all the known ruins, we find that for every village of the historic period there are literally hundreds which must have been abandoned before 1540. These lie not only in the districts inhabited by the present-day Pueblos and their sixteenth-century ancestors, but are scattered far and wide over the entire Southwest. The ruined dwellings and the specimens found in them show so close a similarity to the houses and artifacts of the modern tribes that there has never been any serious doubt that they are relics of the direct cultural ancestors of the Pueblos. The immense number of the ruins, however, and the vast territory which they occupy make it certain that one of three conditions, or some combination of two or more of them, must have obtained: either the population was formerly very much larger than it was in 1540; or the country was inhabited for a tremendously long time; or the ancient Pueblos occupied their villages for very brief periods. It will be noticed that the time element is the unknown quantity which prevents our choosing between these three possibilities. If we knew the relative date of the founding and abandonment of every ruin in the Southwest, it would be a comparatively simple matter, by estimating the approximate population of each, and plotting the results on a series of maps, to visualize the entire history of the Pueblo peoples. Our task, therefore, is: first, to locate all the ruins and record their size; second, to determine the length of their occupancy, and their age relative to each other; and, third, to establish their age, not only in relative terms, but according to the years of our own calendar. This is a heavy program and one which naturally can never be completely carried out, but it is best to face the situation as it is, and to realize that if our researches are to be worth anything they must be undertaken not only with a clear idea of the end to be attained, but also with a full realization of the difficulties to be encountered.

The location, description, and measurement of ruins can be accomplished by industrious exploration; an arbitrary rule for estimating population according to size of settlements should, if consistently applied, yield more or less valid results; both these things are merely matters of persistent work. The all-important questions of chronology, however, are less obvious in nature and less easy of solution; to settle them we must rank the ruins in the order of their building and determine if possible the length of their occupancy. The following methods of attack have been tried:

*Legendary evidence.* Great dependence has been placed by certain students upon the migration legends of the modern Pueblos, and many prehistoric ruins have been classified as to age and as to cultural affinities by this means alone. Recent ethnological studies, however, seem to show that the Pueblo as an historian is at best unreliable; while archaeological evidence seldom confirms, and often directly refutes, the statements of the native traditionist.

*Preservation.* The state of preservation of ruins is seldom a good criterion of age. The nature of the site, the exposure of walls to the elements and of foundations to surface drainage, conflagrations, the removal of roof beams, all these more or less fortuitous and generally indeterminable factors cause deductions based upon preservation to have very doubtful value.

*Comparison of types.* Crude and primitive-looking remains, when compared with relics of an obviously more advanced type are usually, and doubtless often correctly, assumed to belong to an earlier period. This method of chronological evaluation must, however, be very cautiously applied and should always have the support of corroborative evidence, since in the history of the Southwest many cases of degeneration in culture and of irregularity in culture growth have occurred.[1] Care must also be exercised not to mistake the survival of archaic traits in peripheral regions for evidence of antiquity.

1. For example, the excellent masonry and fine ceramics of the Chaco might easily be considered later than the slipshod building and poor pottery of many actually younger ruins on the upper Rio Grande not far to the east.

*Stratigraphic evidence.* The ideal form of chronological evidence is provided by stratigraphy, i.e., when remains of one type are found lying below those of another. Such evidence is of course conclusive, and has provided us with sure data as to the relative age of several phases of Southwestern culture. If we could find in each district sites containing material running from the very earliest times down to the period of abandonment, our task would be a comparatively simple one; but no such site has ever been discovered. Pecos presents the longest complete series so far known, but Pecos does not carry us back to really remote times. Even short series, covering two or three periods, are rare enough; but they do occur and can be made, by the principle of overlapping, to yield excellent results.

To take full advantage of stratigraphic evidence, whether it be presented in a comparatively long series or by an overlapping of several short ones, the investigator must select for study those phenomena which most accurately reflect changes in culture or, what amounts to the same thing, chronological periods. Pottery has so far provided the most useful material for such studies, as it is abundant at all sites except the very earliest, is readily classifiable, and is a highly sensitive register of cultural change.[2]

Apparently the first application of the principle of stratigraphy to Southwestern problems was made by Richard Wetherill, when in the nineties he defined the Basket Maker culture, and then determined, by discovering its remains below those of cliff houses, that it represented an earlier chronological period rather than a mere local development.[3] Fewkes at Casa Grande[4] and

2. Valuable but much less easily acquired evidence is provided by architecture, physical type, skull deformation, mortuary customs, sandals, etc.; these should all be taken into account and used to check the results obtained from consideration of the pottery.

3. Prudden, 1897, p. 61.

4. Fewkes, 1912, p. 102.

Cummings in the Kayenta district[5] used the evidence of superposition for the relative dating of archaeological material; and in 1914 Guernsey and the writer established the stratigraphic position of the pre-Pueblo.[6] It remained for Nelson, however, to recognize that the most reliable results could be obtained by passing downwards, so to speak, from the known to the unknown. He attacked the problem, accordingly, at the early historic ruins of central New Mexico and worked backwards, basing his conclusions on stratigraphic evidence, and using pottery as the criterion for classification. In this way he was able to arrange in their proper sequence the principal pottery types, and hence the principal chronological periods, of the Rio Grande.[7] Nelson also conducted the first well-thought-out attack on the chronological problems of the Southwest in their broader aspects[8]; and, although his work in this field has unfortunately been interrupted, he has blazed a trail which will be more and more followed as time goes on.

A fifth method for obtaining chronological data has been devised by Prof. A. E. Douglass of the University of Arizona. It depends upon the study of the annual growth rings of coniferous trees. The Douglass system, which holds out the most brilliant prospects for accurate dating, has not yet been extensively employed. For this reason, and also because its application can be more clearly understood when the reader is better acquainted with the nature and distribution of the ruins, discussion of it will be de-

5. Cummings, 1910, p. 10.

6. Kidder-Guernsey, 1919, p. 42.

7. Nelson, 1916. An attempt to do the same thing on the basis of comparative studies of the pottery had been made by the writer (Kidder, 1915); the fact that the sequence of types there suggested was proved by Nelson to be correct is encouraging because it shows that such comparative studies may be of value in regions where no stratigraphic evidence can be discovered. The latter, however, must always be diligently searched for, as it forms the only certain basis for deduction.

8. Nelson, 1919.

ferred until after we have presented such data as we have in regard to the prehistoric remains.

In the following chapters we take up the description of the antiquities of the Southwest by river drainages (fig.

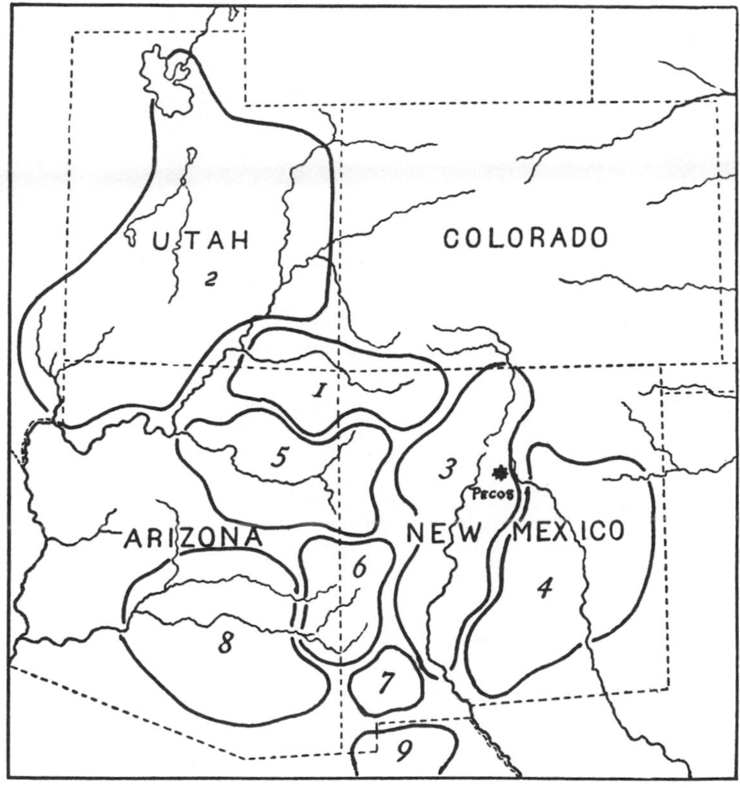


FIG. 11. The culture areas of the Southwest: 1. San Juan; 2. Northern Peripheral; 3. Rio Grande; 4. Eastern Peripheral; 5. Little Colorado; 6. Upper Gila; 7. Mimbres; 8. Lower Gila 9. Chihuahua Basin.

11). This is not only a convenient method for arranging the material but, as will be seen, the river drainages form in most cases definite areas of specialization. At the end of each chapter is given a selected bibliography of the archaeology of the region; the titles included are in most cases modern scientific papers embodying original material; notices of ruins by early travellers, brief references in popular articles, and secondhand descriptions are only listed where better sources are lacking. The most valuable contributions are marked with asterisks.

# The San Juan

The San Juan is considered first because it is in many ways the best known archaeologically of the major territorial divisions of the Southwest. Furthermore, it has yielded a great amount of material in regard to the oldest phases of human development in our area. More important still is the fact that the San Juan appears to have been the breeding ground for many of the basic traits of Southwestern culture and center of dissemination.

The San Juan rises in the mountains of southwestern Colorado, and flows in a generally westerly direction through northern New Mexico and southern Utah to empty at last into the Colorado River. Its watershed, if such a term can be applied to country which normally sheds no water, covers an area of some 30,000 square miles.[1] It is for the most part a high, barren, and arid plateau cut by a multitude of dry, sandy washes and equally dry, gorgelike canyons. The San Juan itself carries water throughout its entire length, but its tributaries, except those upper ones which find their source in the parent mountains, contain no living streams, and only run during the early spring or after the violent downpours of the midsummer rainy season. In spite of this great general aridity, the San Juan country, from its peculiar geological formation, possesses a large number of fine springs of clear, pure water. They usually appear at the heads of gorges or at the bases of cliffs, are seldom large, and their overflow sinks at once into the sand, to seep off thus hidden along the rocky beds of the canyons. But these springs

1. For an excellent description of the topography and climate of the San Juan, see Prudden, 1906. Much useful information, and a very complete bibliography, are also to be found in Gregory, 1916.

redeem a land which would otherwise be hopeless for human occupancy, they furnish abundant drinking water for those who know how and where to find them, and their trickling underflow moistens the earth of the valley bottoms just enough to permit the growing of drought-resisting varieties of corn. Many parts of the mesa tops, also, can in favorable years be cultivated. Hard as these conditions would appear to be for an agricultural people, they did not prevent the ancient Pueblos from occupying the country for a long period of time, or from developing there the greatest achievements of their civilization. No one has attempted to compute the number of ruins in the San Juan drainage, but it must run well into the thousands.

To bring some order into so vast an amount of material, it is necessary to make at least a preliminary classification. For this purpose we have depended primarily upon the evidence of pottery; there are:

1. Sites with well-developed pottery (Pueblo ruins).
2. Sites with less-developed pottery (pre-Pueblo ruins).
3. Sites with crude pottery (post-Basket Maker ruins).
4. Sites with no pottery (Basket Maker sites).

Of the first class there are certain ruins which show evidences of high specialization; these may conveniently be considered under the following heads: Chaco Canyon, Mesa Verde, and Kayenta. Each of the groups is named for the district in which the culture producing the characteristic pottery reached its highest development, but it must be understood that the names are by no means geographically descriptive, for the cultures in question all extended beyond the limits of the type localities and, indeed, in some cases even beyond the confines of the San Juan drainage (fig. 12).

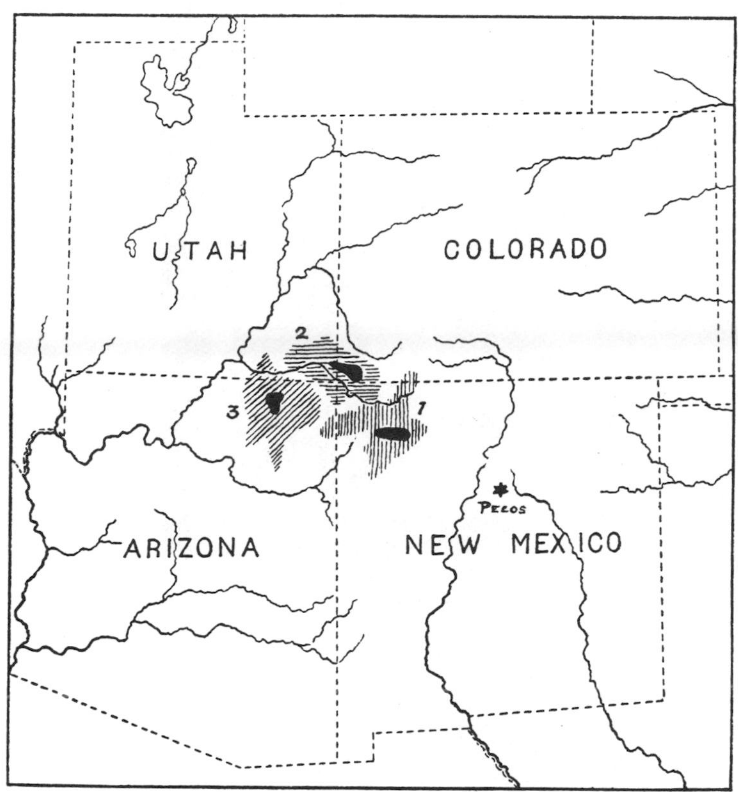


FIG. 12. The San Juan area. The different shadings indicate the three principal subcultures; the districts of highest specialization are shown in black. 1. Chaco Canyon. 2. Mesa Verde. 3. Kayenta.

## PUEBLO RUINS
### (Sites with well-developed pottery)

### CHACO CANYON

The enormous ruins that represent the greatest achievement of this culture lie in and near the Chaco Canyon, a southern tributary of the San Juan in northwestern New Mexico. There are in this locality ten or twelve major sites and a considerable number of smaller ones; some of the latter seem to belong to the Chaco Canyon group, while

a

After Jackson

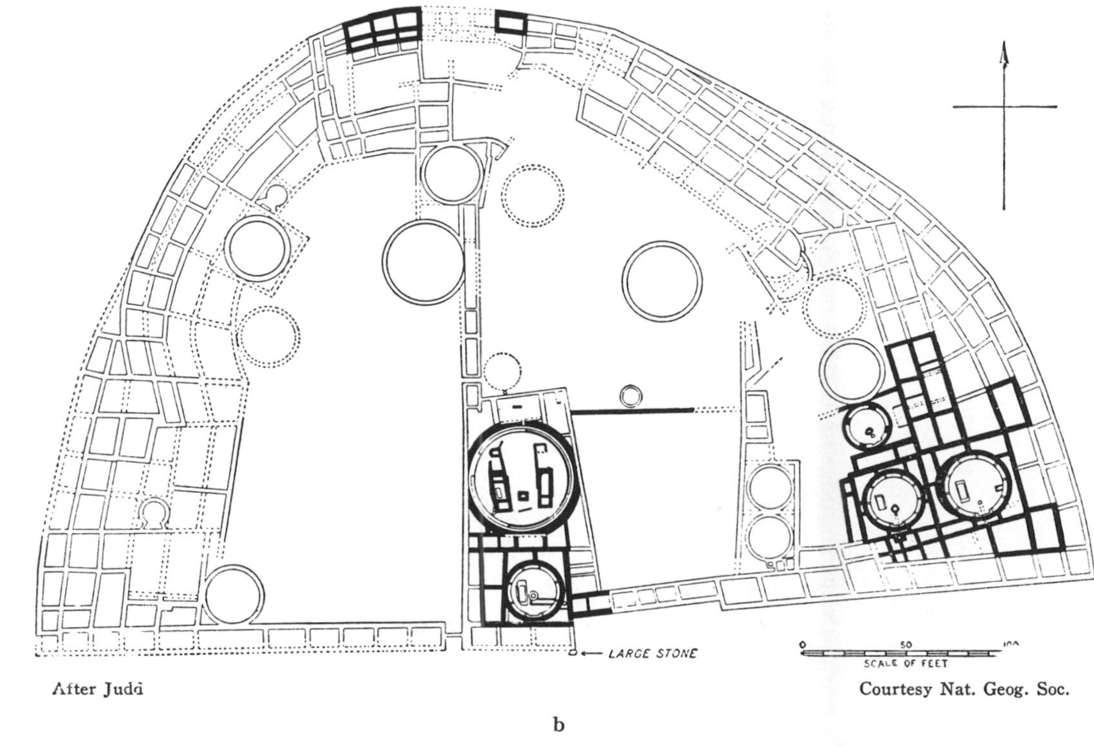


After Judd

Courtesy Nat. Geog. Soc.

b

PLATE 19. Pueblo Bonito. a. Restoration showing interior terracing and high, blank outer wall. b. Ground plan; the circular chambers are kivas, the rectangular structures living rooms.

others are obviously of other types. Of the major ruins the best known are Pueblo Bonito, Chettro Kettle, Pueblo Alto, Peñasca Blanca, and Hungo Pavie. Each of these great buildings contained one hundred or more ground-floor rooms and was terraced from front to back to a height of three, four, or possibly even five stories, thus considerably more than doubling the number of ground-floor chambers. Although they vary considerably in detail, all the Chaco pueblos are alike in general plan. The building normally surrounds three sides of a court, being terraced back from an initial height of one story at the court to three or more stories at the rear, which is always a high blank wall. The third side of the court is enclosed by a tier of one-story rooms, usually bowed outward and connecting the two ends or wings of the main building. Within the court are the kivas, and usually just outside the tier of low rooms lie the rubbish heaps. The frontage is always southerly. The accompanying ground plan and restored elevation (pl. 19) are of Pueblo Bonito, the greatest single structure in the valley; Bonito is in most respects a typical example of Chaco architecture, but differs from the majority of the ruins in being D-shaped rather than rectangular.

Aside from their large size, the Chaco ruins are noteworthy for massive architecture and particularly for excellence of masonry. The walls of the best period are generally made with a hearting of adobe-laid stonework, or rubble, and are finished on the two surfaces with what might be called a veneering of carefully selected tabular stones, evenly arranged in courses that often vary in thickness and thus give the work a very pleasing texture (pl. 20, a). The details of construction, such as the roofs of rooms, the jambs of doorways, and the corners of walls are notable for excellence of finish and accuracy of line. The living rooms are of unusually large size and height.

Our knowledge of the kivas is still incomplete, but they

appear to be of much interest and importance. As we shall often have occasion to refer to the kivas in the various groups of ruins, it may be well to give here a brief description of the principal features of such rooms. The prehistoric kiva was normally a round subterranean chamber, the roof being flush with the ground. Entrance was ordinarily gained by a ladder leading down through a combined hatchway and smoke vent in the roof. In the floor there was always a firepit. Ventilation was supplied by a flue running downwards outside the kiva wall and opening at the floor level. The hot air and smoke from the fireplace passed up and out through the entrance hatchway; fresh, cool air being sucked down the flue and into the room. Such were the essentials of kiva construction; the details of interior arrangement vary greatly from one region to another, but are usually quite uniform for any given culture, thus providing a most useful criterion for classification.

The Chaco Canyon ruins contain kivas of two sorts: great kivas, of which there seems to be but one, or at most two, at each village; and small kivas, of which every village has several. The great kiva is very large, measuring from forty to sixty feet in diameter (pl. 21). The lower part of its wall is encircled by a bench of masonry; near the middle of the floor is a raised fireplace, on either side of which is a rectangular, vaultlike structure of masonry. The central part of the roof was supported by four large pillars. At the north side of each kiva is a sort of antechamber, lying at a higher level, and reached by a ladderlike stairway. In most cases the kiva is surrounded by small rooms, also at a higher level, formed by partitions running out spokelike from the kiva proper to an outer wall surrounding it concentrically.[2]

2. Only three great kivas have so far been excavated, viz. at the Aztec ruin (see Morris, 1921a, for a full description, with discussion of function and relations); at Pueblo Bonito (see Judd, 1922, p. 322, photograph and plan); and at Chettro Kettle (see Hewett, 1922, pp. 121–28).

The small kivas have not as yet been adequately described. Their diameter appears seldom to exceed twenty-five feet. Like the large structures they have a low bench about the base of the wall. On the bench are several (six to ten) small blocks of masonry a foot or so in height, set at equal distances apart, each one enclosing a short heavy beam which runs back into the main wall of the kiva.[3] In the floor there is a central firepit, and under the south side of the wall runs the intake of the ventilator to open through the floor near the firepit. To the west of the firepit is a single rectangular masonry-lined vault (see pl. 19, b, small kivas). The exact system of roofing is problematical, but appears to have been by means of a cribwork of logs, as in Mesa Verde kivas (see p. 196 below, and pl. 28).[4]

One of the many mysteries of the Chaco is the fact that in spite of persistent search the cemeteries of the large ruins have never been found. The burial mounds of the smaller and apparently earlier sites are obvious, and can easily be located; but the rubbish heaps of Bonito, Chettro Kettle, and the other great communities contain no graves whatever. Although a few bodies have been taken from rooms,[5] these do not represent a hundredth part of the number of individuals that must have died during the occupancy of the towns. There is no hint of cremation, and so one can only suppose that the Chacones differed from all other Pueblos of whom we have knowledge in that they buried their dead at a distance from their houses. When the cemeteries are eventually discovered, they should yield a marvellously rich harvest of pottery, ornaments, and utensils.

3. Pepper, 1920, p. 251, and fig. 104.

4. As to the details of Chaco Canyon kiva construction little has so far been published, but these and other now puzzling features will soon be thoroughly understood, when the results of the excavations now being carried on by the National Geographic Society are published.

5. Moorehead, 1906, p. 34; Pepper, 1909.

In the minor arts the ancient people of the Chaco were no less skilled than in architecture. Their work in wood, in stone, and in the weaving of cotton textiles is very superior. They were remarkably expert in the making of turquoise beads and ornaments, and particularly in the production of inlay work on stone, bone, or wood with small bits of turquoise, jet, and shell.[6] The grooved stone axe is rare and, as elsewhere in the San Juan, is always poorly made. Although several types of sandals were produced, the finest and most characteristic were woven of *apocynum* string. These sandals have pointed toes, and each one bears a small jog or offset on the outer edge (pl. 36, a).[7] This is also the case with Mesa Verde, Kayenta, and other San Juan Pueblo period sandals, and provides a ready means of distinguishing them from the footgear of earlier periods.

Chaco Canyon pottery, as found at the large ruins, forms a typical and easily identifiable group.[8] The two principal wares are corrugated and black-on-white; redware appears, but in such small quantities that it may be disregarded in so general a summary as this.

Most Southwestern pottery was made by laying up on each other rings or spirals of clay, each added ring or turn of the spiral carrying the vessel wall a little higher. All trace of this process was usually obliterated before firing by working over the surfaces of the vessels with the fingers or with a smoothing tool. At certain periods, however, the coiled spiral of clay was allowed to remain unobliterated on the exterior of pots, producing a horizontally ridged or corrugated effect. The coils were furthermore often

6. For illustrations of many Chaco Canyon specimens, see Pepper, 1920. Pl. 1, and figs. 50, 71–74 show examples of turquoise and inlay work.

7. The specimen figured illustrates the characteristic shape. It is of yucca, no example of the fine *apocynum* sandal being available for reproduction.

8. Illustrations of Chaco Canyon pottery are to be found in Pepper, 1906, 1909, 1920; Moorehead, 1906; Chapman, 1921; Goddard, 1921, p. 43.

a

b

c

PLATE 20. Masonry of San Juan ruins. a. Chaco Canyon (Pueblo Bonito). b. Mesa Verde (Cliff Palace). c. Kayenta.

pinched and indented as they were applied, giving a still more elaborate texture to the surface. This technique was normally used for the making of cooking pots.[9] Chaco Canyon corrugated ware is well made, the corrugations are unusually sharp and clear-edged, the indentations vary in depth and arrangement to produce a variety of pleasing textures. As to vessel shapes we have as yet few data, but the prevailing form appears to have been a large jar with very wide mouth (fig. 13, a).

Black-on-white ware, which in the Southwest is almost invariably associated with corrugated, occurs in many well-

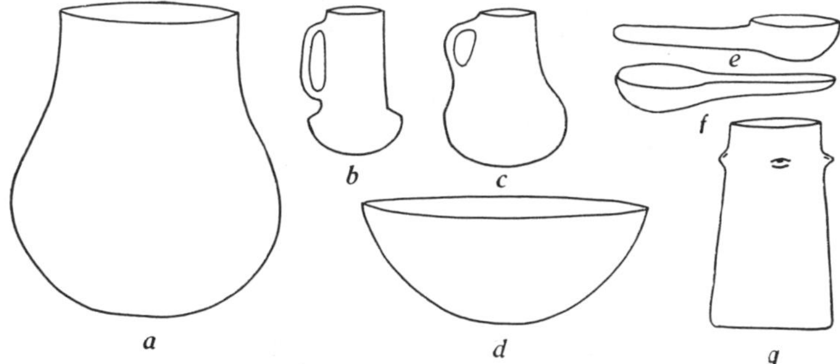


FIG. 13. Chaco Canyon vessel shapes.

defined local varieties. Qualities common to all black-on-white groups are hardness, clear "ring" when struck, surface slips running from light gray to pure white, and prevailingly geometric decoration in sharp black lines.

The most marked characteristics of the Chaco Canyon variety of black-on-white ware are its very white, almost paper-white, slip and the unusually fine lines of its black decoration. The commonest vessels are bowls, pitchers, and ladles; rare but typical forms are human effigy pots and cylindrical vases.

The bowl (fig. 13, d; pl. 22, e-h) approaches the hemi-

9. For an excellent description of the manufacture of corrugated ware, see Holmes, 1886, p. 273.

spherical in shape, with rounded bottom and curving sides. Examples over twelve inches in diameter are uncommon. The rim is "direct," i.e., not bent inward or flared outward; the actual lip is never flat-topped, but is rounded or even brought to a sharpish edge. The exteriors of bowls are undecorated and, indeed, are often left unslipped; or the slip is run down for an inch or two below the rim. The edge of the rim is painted black (this is a useful diagnostic trait for Chaco Canyon pottery); the black of the edge is often interrupted by a tiny space purposely left unpainted, and this space is sometimes emphasized by the turning down of the ends of the encircling line into little dashes or scrolls on the exterior.

Pitchers occur in two varieties, the large bodied and the small bodied. Although intermediate forms appear, the small-bodied type (fig. 13, b; pl. 22, b–d) is the commoner and more characteristic. Examples run from five to eight inches in height. The neck is tall, either cylindrical or in the form of a truncated cone; the body is low (usually about one-third of the total height), with a rather sharply angled shoulder; the handle is a flat strip of clay running from just below the rim to just above the junction between neck and body; the rim is flatter than in bowls and is generally painted black. The large-bodied type (pl. 22, a; fig. 13, c) is a rounder, usually more capacious, vessel with a small handle.

Ladles are either of the "bowl-and-handle" (fig. 13, e) or the "half-gourd" type (fig. 13, f).

Rarer forms, which appear to be confined to the Chaco Canyon culture, are the cylindrical vase (fig. 13, g)[10] and the effigy pot.[11] The large decorated olla or water jar seems to be much less common than in other black-on-white areas; I have never seen a specimen complete enough to give a good idea as to its shape.

10. Pepper, 1920, pls. 2–6.
11. Pepper, 1906.

The decoration of all the black-on-white pottery of the Southwest is preponderatingly geometric and rectilinear. Although the actual number of design elements employed is not great, they are handled in such a great variety of ways, and used in so many different combinations that a thoroughgoing analysis is necessary before one can really understand the system of ornamentation in any single group. Most groups, however, possess certain characteristic features, certain earmarks, so to speak, which enable one after a little practice to recognize them at once. The earmarks of Chaco Canyon decoration are best shown by a few illustrations and explanatory notes.

In plate 23 is presented a selection of typical Chaco Canyon black-on-white designs. The majority of them are band decorations that encircle the interiors of bowls. The bands may be made up of a repetition of identical units (pl. 23, f, g, h, i), or of an alternation of two different units (pl. 23, e). Most bands are framed above and below by a single black line. Very characteristic of Chaco Canyon work is the use of lines dotted along one side (pl. 23, e, h). The interlocking spiral in one form or another (pl. 23, g, h) is also abundant, as is the sharp-pointed "bat wing" figure (pls. 22, a, b; 23, f, j). Large terraced elements are often outlined with a series of two to four or five thin black lines, which follow accurately the angles of the basic figure (pls. 2, g; 23, a, b). Hatching is perhaps the best earmark of Chaco art; the individual lines used are narrow and often slightly wavy, and they are always framed in or enclosed by outer lines much heavier than themselves (pls. 22, a, d, e, h; 23, c, d). All these qualities are much more clearly brought out by the illustrations than by any verbal description. The drawings also show that there are several quite distinct types of decoration: those based on the outlined terrace figure; those making use of interlocking scrolls; hatched ornaments, etc. Whether these were all contemporaneous parts of a single design system or whether they represent successive phases of a changing system cannot be decided at present. Chapman's studies of the sherds from a rubbish-filled kiva at Chettro Kettle, and Nelson's stratigraphic work in the Pueblo Bonito middens, while not extensive enough for definite results, indicate that the ceramic art, even during the occupancy of the great pueblos, was not at a standstill.[12] The intensive excavations now being carried out by the National Geographic Society and the School of American Research will undoubtedly serve to answer this and many other perplexing questions in regard to the Chaco Canyon ruins.

The archaeology of Chaco Canyon presents many baffling problems. To begin with, the district is little better than a desert; many parts of it, indeed, are absolutely barren wastes of sand and rock which do not even support the usual dry-country flora of the Southwest. It is almost devoid of springs, has no permanent streams, is subject to severe sandstorms, is blistering hot in summer and bitterly cold in winter. It is hard to see how life in the Chaco could have been anything but a continual struggle for bare existence. Yet in this harsh and difficult environment Pueblo culture reached its highest development. The towns are large, excellently constructed, and lie in close proximity to each other. If all of them had been inhabited at the same time, they might well have housed more than 10,000 people. But how so large a population could have supplied itself with the mere necessaries of life, and still had time and energy left for the development of so remarkable a civilization, has puzzled every observer who has visited the Chaco country.

The explanation of course suggests itself that the climate of ancient times was moister than that of today. If such an hypothesis could be accepted, all our difficulties would be removed. The truth is, however, that no convincing evidence has yet been presented to warrant a belief in

12. Chapman, 1921; Nelson in Pepper, 1920, p. 383.

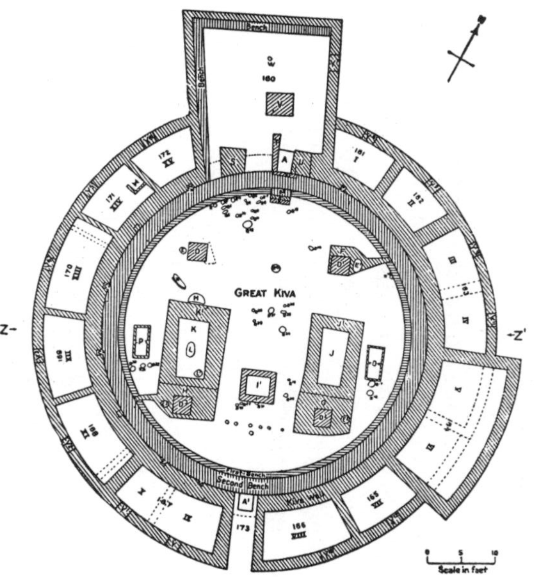


After Morris

After Hewitt | b | Courtesy "Art and Archaeology"

PLATE 21. The great kiva of the Chaco Canyon culture. a. Plan of the great kiva at Aztec. b. The great kiva at Chettro Kettle.

any marked climatic change in the Southwest during the period of its occupancy by man. Those who, like Huntington,[13] have based their conclusions in large part upon the testimony of the ruins, have failed to realize the ability of the Pueblo Indian to support himself quite comfortably in the face of conditions of dryness which would stagger the white farmer. Such investigators have not taken into consideration how little water the Pueblo Indian actually uses, how carefully he conserves his supply, or how little he thinks of climbing up and down steep, precipitous paths to get it. Furthermore, the modern Pueblo often lives many miles from his cornfields; and numbers of ancient ruins are situated at considerable distances from the nearest land which could ever have been cultivated even under the most favorable climatic conditions. One more point which is often not recognized is that the Indian farms only for himself and his family, while every modern cultivator helps to feed an enormous industrial population which produces no foodstuffs whatever; hence the acreage the white farmer must plant is vastly greater, and no comparison between the amount of cultivable land necessary for his support with that necessary for a Pueblo Indian can have any bearing on the subject.

I think there is no ruin in the entire Southwest that one hundred years ago could not have been successfully reinhabited by Hopi Indians in numbers equal to its ancient population. I say one hundred years ago, because during the past century sheep and cattle have been extensively introduced, and have in many places so denuded the country of grass, and so stripped the soil of the binding protection of the grass roots, that the formation of deep, water-cut gullies has everywhere resulted. The destructive action of such gullies is enormous; not only do they rapidly eat away the adobe earth of the valley bottoms, but they carry off the flood water, and also lower the plane

13. Huntington, 1912, 1914.

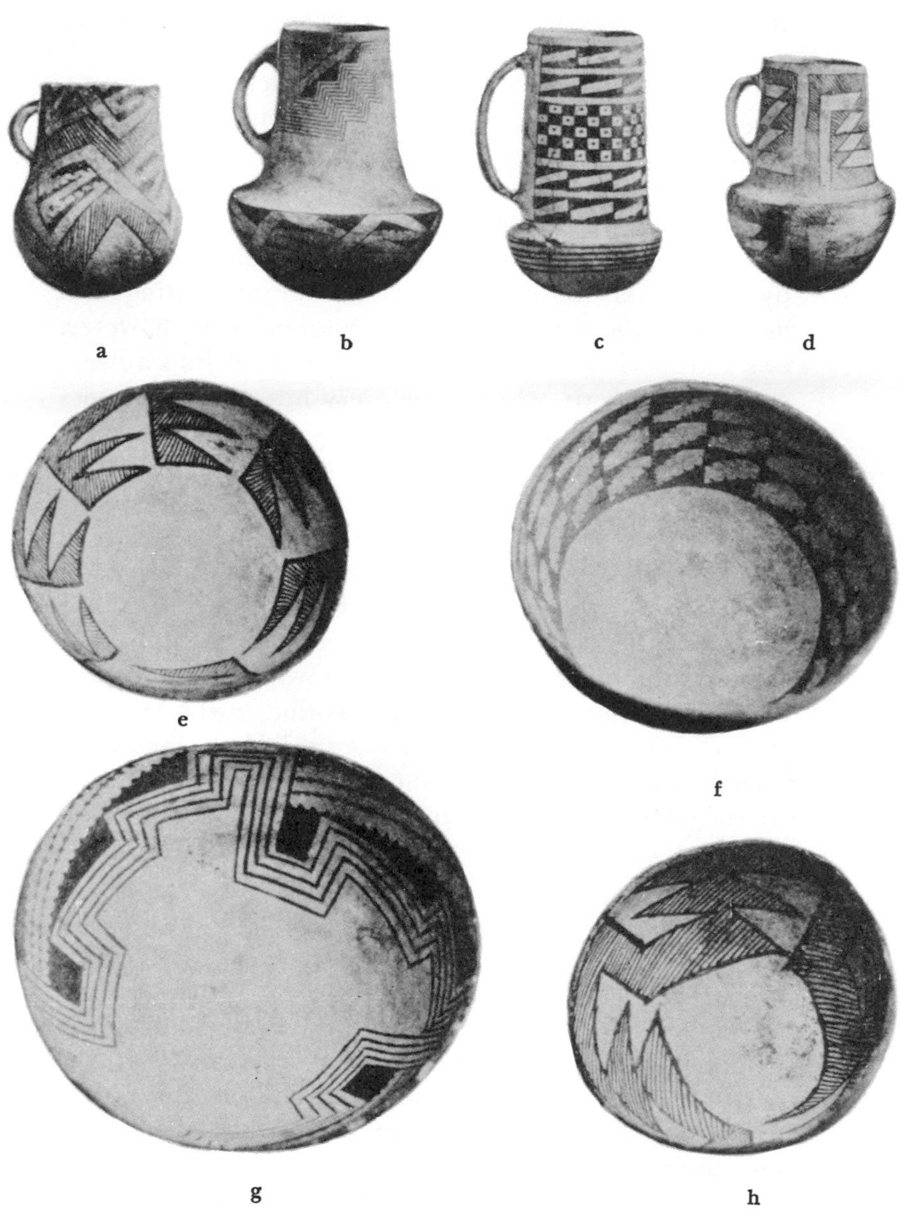


PLATE 22. Chaco Canyon black-on-white ware.

of underground seepage to such an extent that the remaining land on either side of them becomes permanently parched.

This very thing has happened in Chaco Canyon. In former times the spring rains and summer showers spread out evenly over the flat floor of the valley, depositing year by year layers of enriching silt, and penetrating and moistening the earth from top to bottom. Now, however, every drop of water is immediately diverted into a deep, steep-sided arroyo, which after every heavy rain becomes a raging torrent, undermining, cutting down, and carrying away more and more of the cultivable soil of the valley.

Thus, the Chaco has recently become less favorable for agriculture than it was in former times, but even so it could never have furnished what one might call an ideal environment. My feeling is that the population of the valley was never over 5,000 or 6,000 souls and that not more than four or five of the large towns were inhabited at any one time. This impression is due to the fact that each of the great ruins was obviously laid out and completed in a relatively short time and according to a preconceived plan. Some of them have been more or less extensively altered, and Bonito shows signs of much remodelling, but few appear to have grown slowly by the accretions of generation after generation of inhabitants. The small extent of the rubbish heaps, as well as the paucity of burials, tends to confirm the belief that not more than one or two of these ruins was continuously occupied for more than, say, one hundred years.

Definite answers to many of these questions will doubtless be provided by the new methods of research now being applied by Judd and his associates. I should not present speculations on matters so soon to be cleared up, were it not for the fact that the remains of Chaco Valley are so important for the study of other manifestations of Southwestern culture that a proper appreciation of the problems of the Chaco is necessary for a true understanding of the archaeology of the rest of the area.

The groups of great ruins that stand as the type of this culture are strung along the Chaco wash for a distance of some thirty miles. The easternmost of them, Pueblo Pintado, situated on the divide between the San Juan and Rio Grande drainages, marks the eastern limit, so far as is known, of the culture. To the south are no large ruins of Chaco type, but the characteristic pottery appears in collections made in the vicinity of Gallup, N. M.[14] The Kintiel ruin on Leroux Wash in northeastern Arizona has been regarded as allied to the Chaco group;[15] but although it shows distinct Chaco influence in architecture, the pottery found there by Fewkes and that observed by me on the surface are by no means typical of the Chaco culture. Not far from Kintiel, however, in the so-called Red Rock country on Black Creek, sixteen miles south of Fort Defiance, Arizona, are sites which produce absolutely typical Chaco pottery;[16] as to the ruins we know nothing, but they are apparently not large. North from the Red Rocks is the Canyon de Chelley, a district notable for its abundance of cliff houses. These dwellings have not been examined by archaeologists for many years, so that our knowledge of their pottery is confined to collections made by "pothunters." In such collections are a few pieces of Chaco-like pottery, though that type is not the prevailing one.

When we turn to the north we find clearer evidence for extensions of the culture. In many of the lots of pottery, excavated and sold to museums by the commercial diggers

14. Specimens in the Peabody Museum of Harvard University. Chaco influence is also to be seen in certain early kivas in the Zuñi country (Hodge, 1923).

15. Fewkes, 1904, p. 127.

16. Collection in Brooklyn Institute of Arts and Sciences. This district should not be confounded with the Red Rock country of the Verde River, described in Fewkes, 1896.

of the nineties, are pieces from Montezuma Valley, McElmo Canyon and the mesas of southeastern Utah; among these are almost always to be found examples which more or less resemble Chaco vessels. These pots are seldom of the most pronounced Chaco types; they give one the impression of being either the product of a peripheral development affected by Chaco influence, or of an earlier and less specialized stage of the Chaco culture. Morris has recently demonstrated that the great kiva with radiating rooms about it is an integral part of the Chaco Canyon system of architecture, and has called attention to the apparent extension of this kiva form across the Mesa Verde and west into the Montezuma Valley.[17] Although we do not know the exact provenience of the Chaco-like vessels in the pothunters' collections from this district, it is probable that both they and the great kivas may indicate a northwestern spread or a northwestern origin of the Chaco culture.

In the northeast there is definite evidence of Chaco influence, shown by the architecture and ceramics of a ruin discovered by Jeancon in the Pagosa Springs region of Archuleta County, Colorado.[18] The actual building is not large, yet its masonry is distinctly Chacoan, and its kivas are of the same low-benched type as the small kivas of the Chaco; although not built in a radiating manner, there is a hint of great-kiva arrangement in the small rooms surrounding one of them.[19]

The clearest and most interesting occurrence of Chaco culture outside the limits of the actual Chaco Canyon district is furnished by the great Aztec ruin. This site lies about sixty-five miles north of Pueblo Bonito on the lower waters of the Animas River, a northern tributary of the San Juan. The Aztec ruin is architecturally a perfect ex-

17. Morris, 1921a, p. 138.
18. Jeancon, 1922, pp. 14 ff.
19. Roberts, 1922, pl. 3.

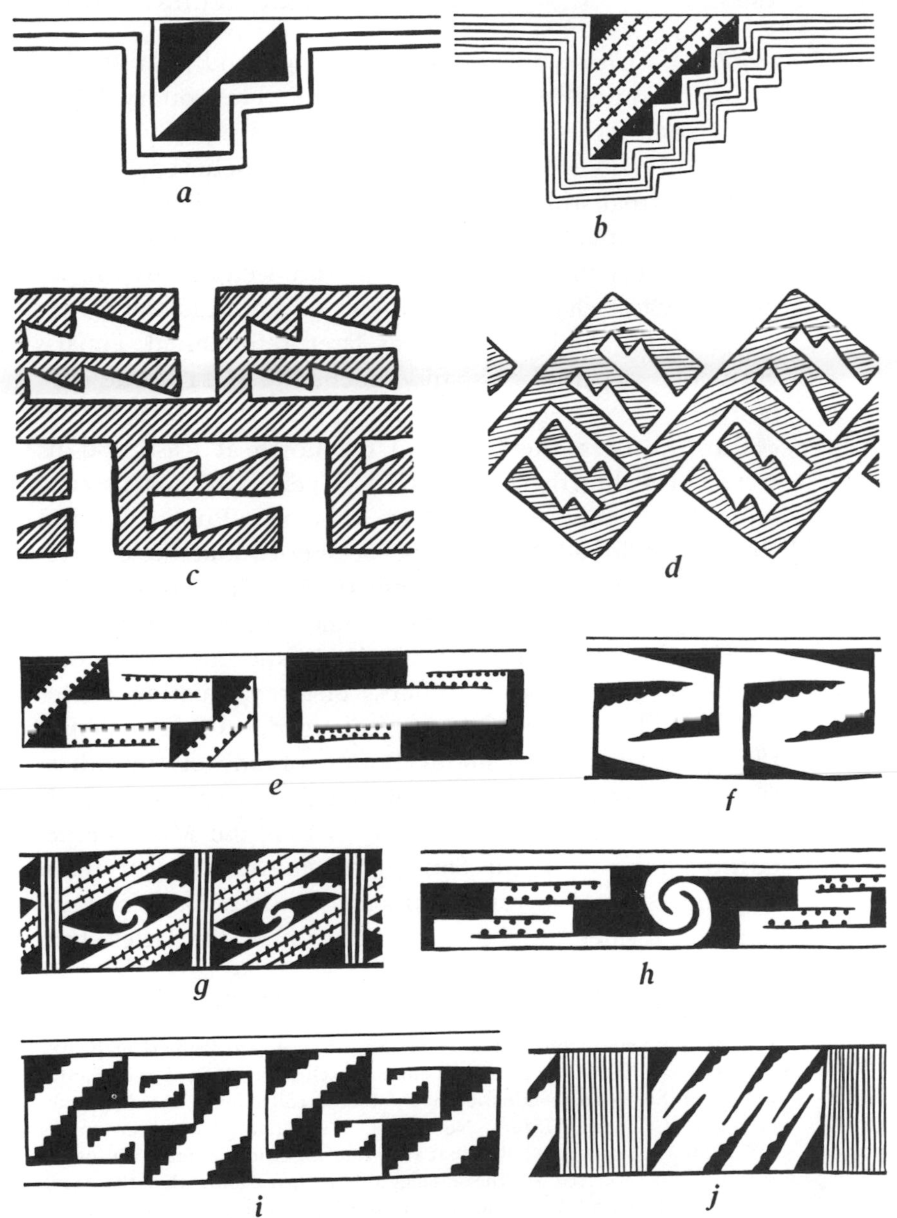


**Plate 23.** Designs of Chaco Canyon black-on-white ware.

ample of a Chaco pueblo, not only in ground plan but in the most minute details of construction. The pottery, however, from the surface of the mounds is equally typical of the Mesa Verde culture. I formerly believed, as did Morris,[20] that this indicated a hybrid settlement, but Morris's thorough excavations have resulted in the important discovery that Aztec was built and occupied by Chaco people, whose characteristic pottery he found in the lower strata of the rubbish; and was later reinhabited, apparently after a period of abandonment, by Mesa Verde colonists.[21] Thus we can be certain that the Mesa Verde culture outlived the Chaco in the north at least, and it seems probable that it survived it generally, for in certain of the rooms excavated by Pepper at Pueblo Bonito there were found Mesa Verde potsherds, and these were in sufficient abundance to indicate that those rooms had actually been occupied for some time by Mesa Verde people at a time subsequent to the abandonment of the pueblo by its original builders. The reoccupation could not have been extensive or prolonged, as Mesa Verde sherds are not found about Bonito or any of the other Chaco ruins to the extent to which they occur at Aztec.[22]

While the above evidence shows that the Mesa Verde culture held on in the San Juan somewhat longer than did the Chaco Canyon civilization, it is equally certain that the former was not an outgrowth of the latter, but

20. Kidder-Guernsey, 1919, p. 201; Morris, 1919a, p. 106.

21. Morris, 1921a, p. 136.

22. The rooms in question are nos. 59, 88, 109 (see Pepper, map, fig. 155); the fact that they contained almost exclusively Mesa Verde sherds was noted during an examination of the Bonito collection in the American Museum of Natural History, New York. I did not go over the entire collection, so that it is possible that the same conditions obtained in other rooms. I have inferred, on the analogy of the Aztec finds, that the Mesa Verde sherds are of late date; but it is of course conceivable that the reverse may have been the case; Judd's excavations will undoubtedly clear up this important question of relative chronology.

that the two more or less overlapped in time. This is proved by the finding by Nelson of Mesa Verde sherds in the middle strata of the Bonito rubbish heap.[23]

We have so far concerned ourselves principally with the larger ruins which architecturally or ceramically seem to belong to the Chaco Canyon culture. In the Chaco Canyon itself, however, and out from it in all directions to a distance not yet established by exploration, are other ruins, smaller in size, less elaborate architecturally, and containing less highly specialized pottery. A few of the larger of these may well be of the true Chaco culture; but the majority are small, are very badly ruined, and as regards pottery are obviously different from the great dwellings. Their wares are corrugated and black-on-white. The corrugated is often very elaborately decorated with wavings and indentations of the coil; it is, in fact, in many ways the finest corrugated pottery of the entire Southwest. The black-on-white is hard to characterize, partly because so few well located whole pieces are available, partly because it seems to be of a generalized type vaguely resembling Chaco ware, but without any readily grasped peculiarities. As to the structure of these small ruins in and near the Chaco region, nothing is known, as none of them have yet been excavated. Morris,[24] however, has demonstrated the presence of an early black-on-white Pueblo period in the San Juan, a period antedating that of the large ruins; and from his description of its characteristics (small houses, excellent coiled ware, etc.) it would seem that these little sites must belong to it, and must therefore represent a stage in culture antecedent to that of the great Chaco pueblos, which would thus appear to have been the latest inhabited dwellings in the district. The studies of San Juan archaeology now being carried on by Morris can con-

23. Pepper, 1920, p. 384.
24. Morris, 1921.

fidently be expected to settle the age and affinities of these inconspicuous but most important sites.

## Mesa Verde

The type locality for this culture is the Mesa Verde, a large plateau in the drainage of the Mancos River in southwestern Colorado. This country is a much better one than the Chaco Canyon. It is higher, nearer the mountains, and so receives considerably more rainfall in summer and more snow in winter. The top of the mesa supports a heavy growth of cedar and pinyon, in certain favorable spots there are good stands of spruce; springs are relatively abundant. The mesa is cut by a series of deep canyons, in the upper walls of which are many very large caves. Although a number of ruins are found on the level uplands of the plateau, the largest and most characteristic settlements are the great cliff houses that are built in the shelter of the caves. Cliff Palace and Sprucetree House are excellent examples, which may well serve as types.

The ground plan of a cliff house is naturally dependent upon the shape of the cave which contains it. Most caves, not only in the Mesa Verde, but also throughout the sandstone formations of the Southwest in general, lie at the top of rocky talus. The floor slopes upward more or less steeply, and at the rear often flattens out to a semicircular platform hugging the back wall of the cave. The roof arches high overhead.

When such caves were used as village sites the first houses were naturally built along the flatter portions of the rear platform, then the irregular places were levelled up and utilized, and finally terraces were constructed upon the sloping front floor to provide still further space for foundations. Because of the cramped conditions room was often piled on room, sometimes clear to the roof of the caves, the buildings reaching a height of several stories. So strongly does the structure of such caves influence the

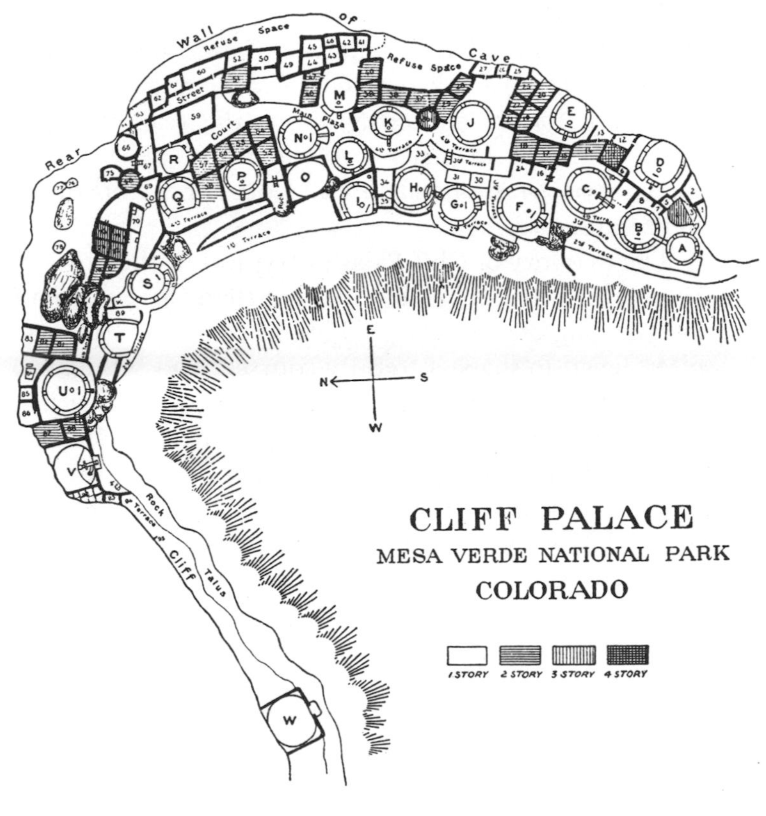


Fig. 14.

shapes of the buildings that it has been thought that the peculiar crowded room grouping and terraced arrangement typical of pueblo architecture must have originated in the cliff houses.[25]

The accompanying ground plan (fig. 14) is that of Cliff

25. Cushing, 1886, p. 479. The arguments advanced are very convincing. This is, however, a question which involves the entire history of pueblo architecture. It cannot be discussed in the present paper, but it may be pointed out that there surely was no such thing as a true cliff-dwelling period, when all houses were built in caves. The cave, as a house site, has always been the exception rather than the rule; and while cave occupation may have had some influence on the form of pueblo dwellings, their basic peculiarities will, I feel sure, eventually be traced to other sources.

Palace, one of the largest known cliff dwellings. It contains about ninety-five ground-floor rooms and twenty-three kivas, the former clustering about the rear of the cave, the latter lying in general to the front (pl. 24). This is the normal arrangement in cliff houses both on the Mesa Verde and elsewhere.

The masonry of Cliff Palace is typical of the other Mesa Verde ruins. It is much less massive than Chaco stonework, but is composed of larger individual stones (pl. 20, b), often hewn to shape, carefully coursed, and brought to an even surface on the face of the wall by a pecking process that results in a characteristic dimpled texture. Rooms are more irregular in shape and smaller in size than those of the Chaco ruins; they appear to have been added on as needed. Mesa Verde villages seem always to have started in a modest way and grown by accretion; I do not know of a single large secular building of this culture that gives evidence of having been erected at one time and according to a preconceived plan.

The Mesa Verde kivas are fairly uniform in size, and in the details of interior arrangement. They average about thirteen feet in diameter. All of them are either actually subterranean or, if the exigencies of the site will not permit that, are surrounded by retaining walls, packed about with earth and so put technically at least underground (pl. 28; reference should be had to this plate and to fig. 17 to make clear the details of the following description). It was evidently a strict requirement that kivas should be below the surface, and in essence all of them are merely holes in the ground lined with masonry. Orthodoxy no less stringent is seen in construction. The typical kiva is as nearly round as its builders could make it. At about three feet from the floor the wall is set back a foot or more, thus leaving a narrow bench encircling the room. On this bench are built six masonry pilasters two to three feet high. Their tops come to within two or three feet of the

PLATE 24a. Cliff Palace, Mesa Verde, Colorado. The many round and square towers incorporated in the building are typical of the larger Mesa Verde cliff houses.

PLATE 24b. Cliff Palace, Mesa Verde, Colorado.

PLATE 24C. Cliff Palace, Mesa Verde, Colorado.

surface. The pilasters produce in the upper wall of the chamber six broad recesses. All the recesses are of equal width, but the southernmost is very much deeper than the others. The roof is made by laying short beams from pilaster to pilaster all around the kiva; a second set of beams is then laid across the angles made by the first set. By such cribwork the structure is gradually extended upward, and drawn together into a domed roof, which is completed by horizontal beams laid across the remaining opening, but leaving space for a combined ladder hole and smoke vent.[26]

Just outside the back wall of the deep south recess a small flue leads vertically down. When it reaches the level of the kiva floor it turns inward, runs under the floor of the recess, and opens into the chamber itself. An imaginary line drawn straight across the floor from the mouth of the ventilator bisects the other standard kiva appurtenances. First, and lying two to three feet from the ventilator opening, comes a wall-like erection of masonry or wattlework, two or three feet wide and of about the same height. This evidently acted as a screen or deflector to prevent the draught which is sucked down the flue from blowing too directly upon the fire, as well as to distribute the air more generally through the room. Behind the deflector is the firepit, a round depression, with a coping of adobe which rises a little above the floor level. Lastly, still in the same line, and usually situated about halfway between the firepit and the north wall of the kiva is a carefully made little hole, round, three or four inches in diameter and five or six inches deep. This has been identified with the *sipapu* or symbolical entrance to the underworld found in Hopi kivas.[27] Such is the normal kiva of

26. Fewkes, 1920, figs. 54, 55, gives photographs of models that illustrate very clearly the roofing of Mesa Verde kivas. See also Fewkes, 1908.

27. By Fewkes, who was the first to study intensively the kivas of prehistoric ruins, work out their roofing system and explain the true sig-

the Mesa Verde culture. Minor variations are found, but in general the type is very strictly adhered to even in the smallest details.

Besides living rooms and kivas most large dwellings of the Mesa Verde culture contain one or more towerlike structures (pl. 24). These may be round, oval, D-shaped, or rectangular in ground plan. Their exact function is not understood; many of them were doubtless ceremonial in nature; but from the fact that they are often loopholed in such a way as to command by archery the approaches to the villages, they are usually referred to as watchtowers. Not only do towers occur in the cliff houses and pueblos, but very commonly they are found at a distance from the larger settlements, occupying points easily defended and having a wide outlook over the surrounding country.[28]

As was the case at the Chaco ruins, the cemeteries of the large Mesa Verde dwellings have never been located. Although a few burials have turned up in rubbish heaps, in sealed rooms, and under floors, as well as a few among the rocks of the talus slopes below the houses, not enough have been discovered to account for a hundredth part of the bodies which must have been disposed of. Dr. Fewkes found in Cliff Palace some evidence of cremation,[29] but in view of the rarity of this practice in the San Juan drainage, it does not seem to me conclusive enough to discourage further efforts to locate cemeteries.

The minor arts of the Mesa Verde culture have been well described by Nordenskiold, Fewkes, and Morris.[30] In most ways they do not appear to differ greatly from

nificance of the ventilator and deflector (see Fewkes, 1908 and 1920). Richard Wetherill, however, evidently recognized the purpose of the ventilating apparatus, as he calls the deflector a "wind-wall" (1894, p. 288).

28. For a discussion of the functions of towers, see Fewkes, 1919. Certain isolated ceremonial buildings, of which "Sun Temple" and "Fire Temple" are examples, are described by Fewkes (1916 and 1921).

29. Fewkes, 1910; and 1911, pp. 39 and 77.

30. Nordenskiold, 1893; Fewkes, 1909, 1911a; 1916a; Morris, 1919.

the minor arts of Chaco Canyon, although in general there is less richness of materials, and less perfection of workmanship. The decorated pottery, however, is entirely distinct, even small sherds being easily distinguishable.[31]

The wares are corrugated, black-on-white, and a very small percentage red.

Corrugated vessels are of two sorts: large jars with wide mouths and egg-shaped bodies (fig. 15, b), and small pitcherlike jugs with single handles. The workmanship of

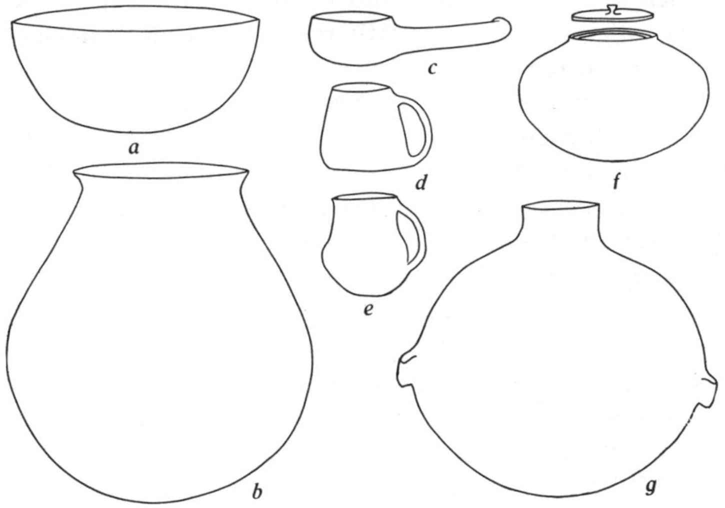


FIG. 15. Mesa Verde vessel shapes.

the large jars is very fine; the walls are thin, the corrugations regular, the indentations evenly spaced, and the proportions remarkably symmetrical.

Mesa Verde black-on-white ware may be recognized by its clear, pearly, grayish-white slip, which seems to have a certain softness and "depth" not found in other groups. The surface of the vessels is carefully polished, so highly

31. Good illustrations of Mesa Verde type pottery are to be found in: Nordenskiold, 1893; Morley, 1908; Fewkes, 1909, 1911a, 1922; Prudden, 1914; Morris, 1915, 1919.

in some cases as to produce a distinct gloss. There are four standard shapes: ollas, bowls, mugs, ladles; less common vessels are kiva-jars, pitchers, seed jars, and canteens.

The Mesa Verde olla (fig. 15, g) is generally twelve to fourteen inches high; it has a full, globular body and short cylindrical neck; at or slightly below the point of greatest diameter is set a pair of horizontally placed loop handles, which almost always tend to rake slightly downwards.

Bowls run from three to four inches up to fourteen or even fifteen inches in diameter. The smaller examples usually have rather flat bottoms and steeply rising sides; the larger pieces, those ten inches or more in diameter, show no distinct change in angle between sides and bottom, there being a very even curve from rim to rim (fig. 15, a; pl. 25). The ware is usually a full quarter of an inch thick, and this thickness of the vessel wall is carried clear to the edge without any thinning or bevelling. Thus a very square, flat rim is produced, which is one of the most characteristic features of Mesa Verde bowls.

Mugs (fig. 15, d) are in shape much like small German beer "steins." They are three to six or seven inches high, have flat bottoms and straight or slightly bulging sides that converge somewhat toward the orifice. The single flat handle with which these mugs are always provided, runs from just above the base to a point a trifle below the rim. The rim is usually square, as in the case of the larger bowls. Mugs range from three and one-half to six inches in height.

Ladles are apparently exclusively of the "bowl-and-handle" variety (fig. 15, c); each one has a small, complete bowl three to four and one-half inches in diameter, to the outside of which is luted a handle six to eight inches long. The handle is usually round and almost always hollow; sometimes it contains tiny pebbles or balls of clay, which act as rattles. I know of no case of the "half-

a

c

e

After Morris

Courtesy Am. Mus. Nat. Hist.

PLATE 25. Black-on-white bowls of the Mesa Verde culture.

gourd" ladle having been found in association with true Mesa Verde ware.

Of the less common forms, the vessel for which I suggest the name kiva-jar is interesting because it seems to occur only in Mesa Verde sites or in sites obviously related to the Mesa Verde culture. Kiva-jars vary greatly in size, running from six to eighteen inches in diameter, but in shape they are very uniform (fig. 15, f). The body is of flattened spherical form, with a round orifice three to three and one-half inches in diameter on the top. The distinguishing feature is a ridge one-fourth to three-fourths of an inch high, which so encircles the orifice as to leave between it and the ridge a narrow ledge for the reception of a cover or lid. Much the same practice is followed in making our modern teapots and sugar bowls. With each jar is usually found its lid, a neatly made pottery disc with a small knob or loop for a handle. The name kiva-jar is applied to these vessels because the great majority of them have been found in ceremonial rooms.

Seed jars are called "heart-shaped bowls" by Holmes,[32] a misleading term, as the objects are not bowls at all. "Seed jar" is, perhaps, little better, but the vessels have often been found containing seeds, and it is possible that this may have been their primary purpose. They average about seven inches in height by eleven inches in diameter, and are characterized by a rounded bottom; they grow gradually larger toward the top, and the greatest diameter is usually near the greatest height. The top is flattish, but not truly flat, and the orifice small. The walls are sometimes depressed to the mouth, sometimes slightly raised, but there is in no case any trace of neck or lip. Some examples show a set of four, six, or eight small holes about the mouth, which seem to have served for suspending the vessels.

The canteen is a small spherical vessel seven or eight

32. Holmes, 1886, p. 306. See pl. 34, c, for an illustration of a seed jar.

inches high, with short, raised neck and very small orifice. Two small loop handles, one on either side of the neck, served for the attachment of a carrying string. In the National Museum there is a specimen from Sprucetree House with a yucca cord still in place.[33]

The decoration of Mesa Verde black-on-white ware is, with the exception of certain zoomorphic figures on bowl exteriors (fig. 16), pretty strictly geometric. It is neverthe-

Fig. 16. Exterior decorations of Mesa Verde bowls.

less bold and free. Large, striking elements are used, and the contrast between them and the clear, pearly-white slip is very pleasing. The earmarks of Mesa Verde design are: the use of balanced sets of framing lines above and below band decorations (pl. 26), the prevalence of patterns, either continuous (pl. 25, c, f) or of repeated units (fig. 16; pl. 25, b), on bowl exteriors, and the common occurrence of large designs in solid black and hatching which cover the entire interiors of bowls (pl. 25, c, e). Mesa

33. Fewkes, 1909, pl. 20, b.

PLATE 26. Designs of Mesa Verde black-on-white ware.

Verde hatching may be distinguished from that of Chaco Canyon by the coarser quality of the component lines, and by the fact that the lines which edge the hatched areas are of approximately the same weight as the hatching lines; whereas in Chaco Canyon work the bordering lines are much heavier than the hatching itself (compare pls. 25, e, and 22, e, h). The normal pattern, however, is the band (pl. 26); it is seldom if ever panelled, but is occupied by a repetition of a single unit or pair of opposed units, these elements being almost always some form of triangle or key figure.

The foregoing description of the Mesa Verde culture is based on the study of the architecture and pottery of the cliff houses and pueblos of the Mesa Verde proper. Similar ruins are found in abundance along the Mancos River and in its eastern tributaries. The Aztec pueblo and the Bloomfield ruin were occupied by Mesa Verde people subsequent to their abandonment by their original Chaco tenants; and Mesa Verde pottery appears in certain rooms of Pueblo Bonito. These seem to mark the eastern and southern limits of the culture, nor was there any extension of it to the north. When we turn to the west, however, we find many Mesa Verde remains.

West of the Mesa Verde and extending as far as the Colorado River, there is a great stretch of upland covered by cedar and pinyon, drained by the following northern tributaries of the San Juan: the McElmo, Montezuma Creek, Recapture, and Cottonwood Canyons, and Grand Gulch. These tributaries and the mesas lying between them are literally crowded with ruins of all sorts; there are probably more archaeological sites to the square mile in this district than in any other equal area in the entire Southwest. Unfortunately the study of the antiquities of the district is still very incomplete; and were it not for the work of Prudden and Fewkes we should know next to nothing about it. A certain number of ruins, however, may safely be classed as of Mesa Verde type, and many others are of a type somewhat less well marked but which may nevertheless be considered as bearing a close relationship to the Mesa Verde culture.

Of the definitely Mesa Verde settlements a good example is the Cannonball pueblo, near the junction of the McElmo and the Yellow Jacket. It occupies a site of a kind very frequently chosen for habitations of late period in the northern San Juan country, namely the rimrock about the head of a steep-walled canyon. The ruins consist of two houses, one on either side of the canyon head, and a square tower perched on the top of a large rock in the canyon itself. One of the two main houses was excavated by Morley, and proved to consist of some thirty ground-floor rooms, a round tower, and seven kivas. In its masonry, its kiva construction, and its pottery the Cannonball pueblo closely resembles the type ruins of the Mesa Verde.[34]

Of the many other sites in the neighborhood of the junction of the McElmo, the Yellow Jacket, and the Hovenweep, very little is actually known. They have often been described, but no investigator has so far paid any attention to their pottery, the best criterion for the classification of unexcavated ruins. Lacking such evidence we must turn to architecture. The most characteristic features of pure Mesa Verde construction are, it seems to me, the block-stone masonry and the use of round, rectangular, or D-shaped towers. I exclude the six-pilastered kiva, for that structure, as will be shown presently, is also found in ruins of slightly different type; kivas, too, can seldom be examined without excavation.

Using block-stone masonry and the presence of towers as criteria, we are led to believe that a number of sites in this district should be classed as of Mesa Verde culture. Among them are the Yellow Jacket spring ruin, ruins in

34. See Morley, 1908.

Hovenweep, Bridge, Holly, and Square Tower Canyons (pl. 27, b), and a large site just below the confluence of the McElmo and the Yellow Jacket. The westernmost example of the type, far as I know, is a pueblo at the head of an unnamed canyon which runs into Montezuma Creek from Alkali Ridge.

*Proto-Mesa Verde ruins.* This term is tentatively used to designate a large and very important class of ruins which are in many ways similar to typical Mesa Verde structures, yet differ from them in being in most respects less highly developed.

These dwellings were first recognized and described by Prudden.[35] The house (fig. 17 and pl. 28) consists of a single or double row of one-story rooms. Sometimes there are also short right-angled wings extending outward from either end. Directly south of the house lies a kiva; and south of the kiva is a rubbish-heap burial mound. Prudden observed that groups of this nature were very abundant in the northern San Juan country between the Mesa Verde in Colorado and Comb Wash in Utah; and that they were normally built in unencumbered situations in open country, as on mesa tops or in broad valleys. He further noticed that the characteristic unit, consisting of a series of living rooms, a kiva, and a burial mound, was employed in the construction of certain very much larger settlements, each of which appeared to be merely a consolidation or grouping together of a number of the villages; and, finally, that the latest and most highly developed structures of the San Juan, such as Cliff Palace and Pueblo Bonito were also laid out on the same general plan as the little mesa-top hamlets. He accordingly called the small houses "unit-type" dwellings, and advanced the theory that they represented the unit or germ of the characteristic pueblo method of house building.

It was natural to suppose that if the unit-type ruins

35. Prudden, 1903, p. 234.

a

b

PLATE 27a. Proto-Mesa Verde pottery. b. Towers in Ruin Canyon, Utah.

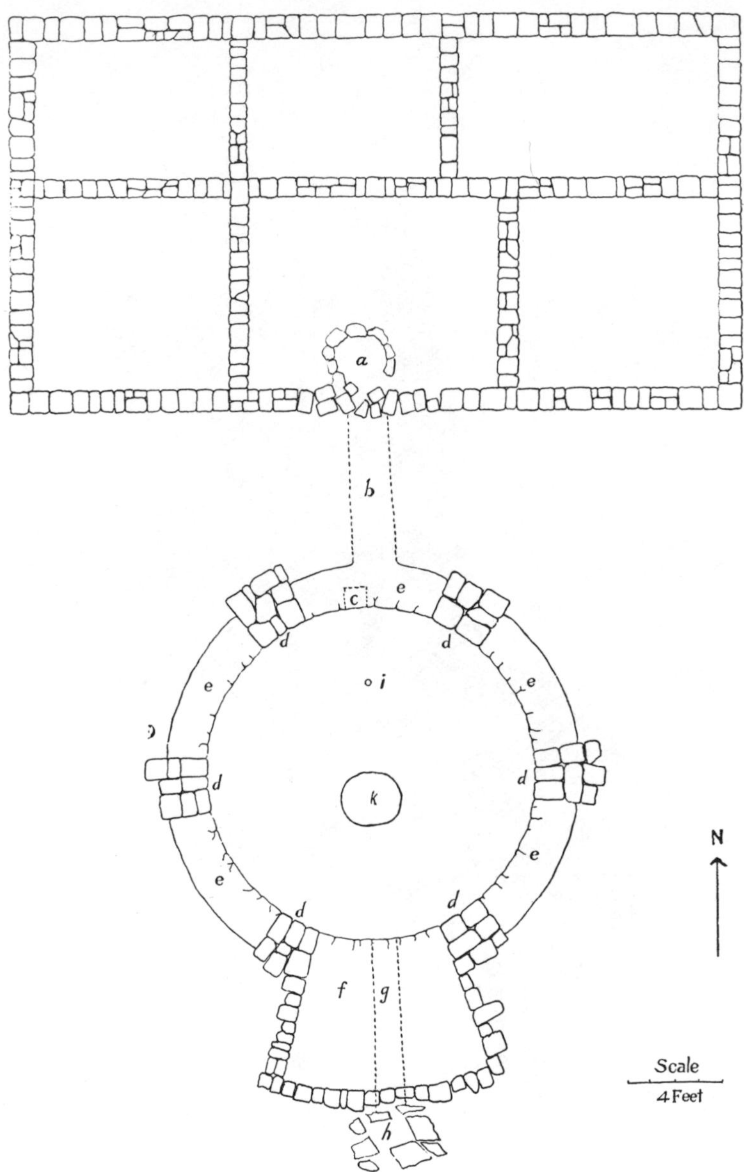


FIG. 17. Ground plan of unit-type dwelling. (After Prudden.)

were at the bottom, so to speak, of the ladder, they would prove to be at least fairly primitive in such important features as kiva construction and pottery. Prudden excavated several unit-type ruins, and from the published results[36] the surprising fact appears that far from being primitive the kivas are as uniform in plan, and as highly specialized in details, as any kivas known; while the pottery bears strong resemblance to that of the great ruins of the Mesa Verde.

This "maturity" of the unit type was to me at first very perplexing, but further consideration leads to the belief that Prudden's original thesis, that the unit-type holds the germ of true Pueblo architecture, is correct. It really serves to explain many hitherto puzzling phenomena and to emphasize the extreme importance of the role that the San Juan has played in the cultural history of the Southwest. We must, however, be ready for the discovery of still more primitive, yet typically Puebloan, villages in the San Juan area. Discussion of this question must be deferred until the rest of the evidence has been presented.

The unit-type ruins excavated by Prudden proved to be built of masonry much less perfect than that seen in the large pueblos and cliff houses of the Mesa Verde and in the canyon-head settlements of the McElmo. The kivas were uniformly six-pilastered, with deep southern recess, ventilator, deflector, firepit, and sipapu (fig. 17 and pl. 28). One feature which is rare in the kivas of the Mesa Verde culture[37] is present in all the unit-type examples excavated by Prudden, namely an underground passageway running back from the north recess and opening upwards through a manhole into one of the adjacent rooms of the dwelling.

The pottery is corrugated and black-on-white, with a

36. Prudden, 1914 and 1918.

37. Seen only in Kiva A of Cliff Palace and Kiva D of Sprucetree House, Fewkes, 1919, p. 42, note 2; absent from Cannonball ruin.

Courtesy American Museum Natural History

PLATE 28. Section of a kiva and dwelling house. Photograph of Dr. Prudden's model of an early unit-type settlement. The cribbed log roof supported by masonry pilasters is found in the Pueblo kivas of the northern San Juan. This particular variety of kiva is typical of the Mesa Verde and proto-Mesa Verde ruins.

very small percentage of red. The black-on-white vessels resemble in shape those of the Mesa Verde; there is the olla with down-raking handles, the bowl-and-handle ladle, and the mug (pl. 27, a). The kiva-jar also occurs. The bowls,. however, tend to have steeper sides, less pronouncedly squared rims, and much less of exterior decoration. The designs are not so involved, and certain typical Mesa Verde elements, such as the split and toothed triangle (pl. 26, f), are rare or absent.

Unit-type sites complying with these general specifications are found, as Prudden says, most commonly from the Mesa Verde to Comb Wash. It is possible that they are present on the Mesa Verde itself, and I have record of a similar ruin on the mesa between White Canyon and Grand Gulch. South of the San Juan the type appears to change, ceramically at least; but the architecture of the small dwellings in the open of that region is very little known, no excavations in them having as yet been published.

Of larger aggregations, formed of several unit-type houses gathered together, there seem to be numbers north of the San Juan. Such settlements are easily distinguishable from the compact Mesa Verde type pueblos that occur in the same range, by the fact that they are usually built in the open country rather than about canyon heads, by their straggling arrangement, mediocre masonry, lack of towers, and particularly by their somewhat less specialized pottery. Excavations have only been carried out in a single instance, at a large ruin on Alkali Ridge, Montezuma Creek, Utah. Here the grouping together of a number of unit types is very clear, the pueblo being made up of sets of living rooms, each set having its own kivas and burial mounds.[38] The kivas are identical with Prudden's, even to the passage running back from the north recess.[39]

38. Kidder, 1910, fig. 2.

39. This feature was not recognized as such during the original excava-

To sum up, in country occupied by typical Mesa Verde sites there occur many small unit-type settlements, and a number of larger ones composed of several unit-types loosely amalgamated. The kivas are very uniform in construction, more so, indeed, than in true Mesa Verde dwellings; the masonry is inferior to that of the Mesa Verde houses and the pottery is somewhat less specialized. It is difficult to escape the conclusion that the three classes: unit type, multiple unit type, Mesa Verde type, are all parts of a single cultural sequence of which the Mesa Verde remains are the culmination. Hence the term proto-Mesa Verde, used to describe the first two stages, is perhaps justifiable; the truth, however, can only be ascertained by more detailed comparative studies, supported if possible by stratigraphic evidence.

There are other ruins in the area which we have been considering that appear to belong to a still earlier period. They are low, inconspicuous mounds, sprinkled with fragments of archaic looking pottery. No excavation has been done in any of them, but in general appearance their wares seem to be allied to those of the small, old sites of the Chaco country.[40]

## Kayenta

South of the San Juan and west of the Chinlee there is a broad stretch of sandy desert. Still further to the west the land rises in a succession of high mesas, finally culminating in the round-topped mass of Navajo Mountain. The country is remarkably rugged, gashed with numberless rock-walled gorges, cut across by great jagged black dykes, and dotted over with buttes carved by erosion into

tion, and is therefore not mentioned in the report; in my field notes I find reference to a "hole in the earth" which is surely such a passage.

40. A preliminary account of such a site, "Pipe Shrine House" on the Mesa Verde, has just appeared (Fewkes, 1923).

the most fantastic forms. These uplands, though comparatively dry, receive more rainfall and contain more springs than do the lower flats along the San Juan.

Near the edge of the mesas lies the trading post of Kayenta, Arizona, and within a distance of fifteen or twenty miles from it are found the large ruins which mark the culmination of the Kayenta culture. The type locality is Sagi Canyon, a tributary of Laguna Creek, which in turn empties, when it has water to empty, into the Chinlee.

The sites are both cliff houses and pueblos, but, as was the case on the Mesa Verde, the cliff houses have been more thoroughly worked, and are better known than the pueblos. The largest are Kietsiel (fig. 18 and pl. 29, b) and Betatakin (pl. 29, a), the former containing about one hundred and fifty, the latter about one hundred ground-floor rooms.

The architectural differences between these dwellings and the ones previously considered are numerous and important. The masonry is inferior in finish, being composed of irregularly shaped stones not very accurately coursed, and laid up with a great deal of adobe mortar (pl. 20, c); wattlework walls, rarely seen on the Mesa Verde and in the Chaco, are relatively common. The round towers, which add so much picturesqueness to the Mesa Verde cliff houses, do not appear.

The greatest difference is seen in the kivas. Those of Kietsiel have not been excavated, but from surface indications seem to be round, semisubterranean rooms without pilasters, and to have a single deep recess with a ventilating shaft opening behind it (see fig. 18). A second type of ceremonial chamber is a square aboveground apartment, entered by a door in one of the short walls, and containing a deflector (to cut off the draft from the door, there being no ventilating apparatus), and a firepit. Fewkes

a

PLATE 29. Kayenta cliff houses. a. A corner of Betatakin.

b

PLATE 29 b. Eastern end of Kietsiel, Sagi Canyon, northern Arizona.

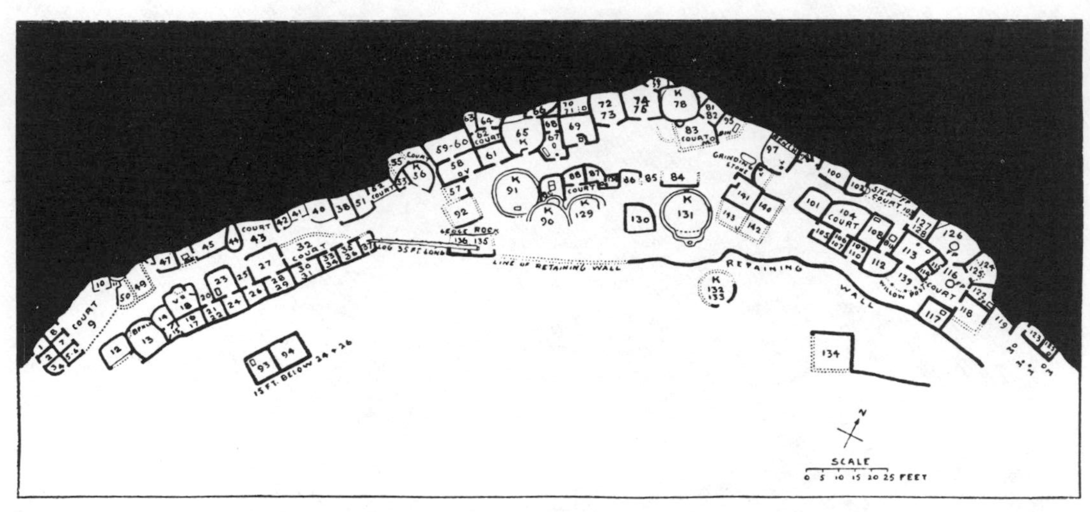


FIG. 18. Ground plan of Kietsiel cliff house, Sagi Canyon, Arizona.

suggests calling such structures "kihus."[41] Kietsiel contains both kivas and kihus; Betatakin, on the other hand, has only kihus, while Bat Woman House has nothing but round kivas. The ceremonial room situation, in the larger Kayenta sites at least, is a difficult one to understand, particularly as the pottery from all these ruins appears to be of exactly the same type.[42]

There also exist large surface sites with pottery that seems to be of normal Kayenta types. Those in Marsh Pass alone have so far been investigated.[43] They are loose aggregations of houses, each house consisting of a block fifty to one hundred feet long, made up of a single or double row of two-story rooms. The masonry, which is superior to that of the cliff houses just described, is composed of large stones, fairly well coursed. The kivas of these surface pueblos are round and subterranean, with firepit, ventilator, and deflector, but without pilasters. They lie near the houses, but unlike the Mesa Verde and Chaco Canyon kivas, are not incorporated in the house clusters.

No burials have been discovered in the large Kayenta cliff houses, but a number of interments of the same period came to light during the writer's excavations at the surface pueblos of Marsh Pass. The bodies were placed in oval grave pits dug in the rubbish deposits near the houses; they were closely flexed, and were usually accompanied by mortuary pottery.[44]

In view of the apparent complexity of the archaeological conditions in these large ruins, and the present dif-

41. Fewkes, 1911, p. 15, note a. No plans or drawings of kihus have been published; the only descriptions are in Fewkes, 1911, pp. 14, 15, 17, and pl. 14; see also Cummings, 1915, p. 277.

42. Professor Cummings has done a great amount of work in this district; the publication of his notes will throw much light on many now obscure problems.

43. Cummings, 1910, p. 28; Fewkes, 1911, p. 10; Kidder-Guernsey, 1919, p. 61.

44. Kidder-Guernsey, 1919, pp. 66–70.

ficulty of recognizing characteristic architectural traits, it is a relief to turn to the pottery, where the types are well-marked, and easily distinguishable from those of any other region in the entire San Juan drainage. The following brief description is based on specimens from Kietsiel, Betatakin, and the surface pueblos of Marsh Pass.[45]

The wares are corrugated, polychrome, and black-on-white.

The corrugated ware is somewhat inferior in execution to that of Mesa Verde and Chaco Canyon. The coils are

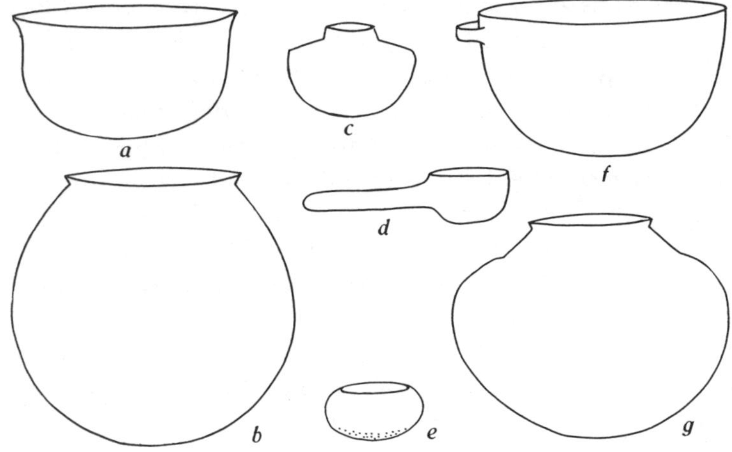


FIG. 19. Kayenta vessel shapes.

less regular in width, and are sometimes not carefully indented. Only one or two whole jars have been recovered; they are fat, round-bodied pots with large apertures (fig. 19, b), quite different in shape from the graceful corrugated vessels of Mesa Verde (fig. 15, b) and of the proto-Kayenta sites.[46]

Black-on-white is characterized by fine, hard paste, clear, white slip, and excellence of decoration. The common

45. So little material from the large Kayenta ruins has found its way into museums that the classification here given is necessarily tentative.

46. Cf. Kidder-Guernsey, 1919, pl. 58, g, h.

PLATE 30. Kayenta black-on-white pottery.

Courtesy Peabody Museum

vessels are ollas, bowls, ladles, and colanders. Much less common forms are small handled jugs similar to those of polychrome ware, and seed-jars. Cylindrical mugs, tall pitchers, and kiva-jars do not, apparently, occur at all except as trade pieces.

The large Kayental olla is exceedingly rare in collections, but from an examination of the sherds at Kietsiel and Betatakin, it is obvious that many such vessels were in use. Our outline (fig. 19, g) is from Holmes.[47] The flattish upper-body appears to be typical. A second variety with more sloping shoulders was also made (pl. 30, g). There are no handles, nor do ever appear, as far as I can discover, on any Kayenta olla. A small flat-topped olla (fig. 19, c) appears to be fairly common.

Bowls are approximately hemispherical, run four or five up to twelve or thirteen inches in diameter, and have either straight (fig. 19, f) or slightly out-curved rims (fig. 19, a). The larger examples tend to be deeper in proportion to width and to lack the outcurved rim. A single horizontally placed loop handle is a common feature of Kayenta bowls (fig. 19, f; pl. 30, d, f), and is never, or almost never, seen on bowls of any other black-on-white group. Decoration is confined to the interior.

Ladles are all of the "bowl-and-handle" variety (fig. 19, d). They average nine inches long. The handle may be either a solid bar, a hollow tube, or, less commonly, an elongated loop of clay.

The colander is a little seed jar-shaped vessel three to six inches in diameter with a fairly large orifice (fig. 19, e; pl. 30, a). Each one has a number of small holes in the bottom (pl. 30, b), evidently fitting it for use as a sifter or strainer. The colander is confined, so far as I know, to the Kayenta culture.

The decoration of Kayenta black-on-white pottery is

47. 1886, fig. 327. The exact provenience of this specimen is unknown, but it is of sound Kayenta type.

PLATE 31. Designs of Kayenta black-on-white ware.

very elaborate. As the illustrations (pls. 30, 31) show, the most marked characteristic is the close-set arrangement of the elements. Little of the white background is allowed to appear, and the drawing of the interlocking frets, keys and spirals is often extraordinarily accurate. The use of an underframework, so to speak, of parallel or cross-hatched lines is the best earmark of this ware. In the finest examples the cross-hatching gives a sort of mosquito-bar effect.

Polychrome pottery is abundant at Kietsiel, Betatakin, and the surface pueblos of March Pass. It occurs in the form of bowls and small, handled jars; polychrome ollas, ladles, or seed jars seem not to have been made. The base color of this ware is yellow or orange, and the decoration is applied in black, red, and white.

Polychrome bowls average about ten inches in diameter, but examples as large as fourteen inches across are occasionally met with. Most bowls have outcurving rims and bear a single horizontal handle on the upper part of the exterior. Exterior ornament is confined to one or two heavy, carelessly drawn lines that encircle the bowls just below the rim. The interior designs (pl. 32) are almost without exception of the "all-over" type; that is to say, they cover, more or less completely, the entire inner surface of the pieces. The framework of all the designs is made up of broad red bands outlined in black, often having a second outlining of chalky white pigment. The simplest figures consist of the bands alone (pl. 32, a, b). In somewhat more elaborate examples the bands bear angular projections or terminal key figures (pl. 32, d). The most ornate and perhaps the most typical specimens have supplementary decoration painted in black over the yellow background between the red bands (pl. 32, c, e, f). This supplementary decoration is characteristic of the group and is generally carried out in the following manner: the spaces to be ornamented are filled with a

PLATE 32. Designs of Kayenta polychrome ware (the shading indicates red).

coarse hachure of parallel lines; while this may completely fill the field, the lines are usually divided into groups of from three to eight or ten, and the small interspaces thus produced are occupied by elements of a different nature, of which by far the most common are stepped lines (pl. 32, c, f).

The range of the Kayenta culture as indicated by the distribution of the above characteristic wares includes, of course, the type localities near Kayenta: Marsh Pass and Sagi Canyon. How far it may have extended to the north and west we do not know, though it is not probable that in these directions it ever overstepped to any great extent the formidable barrier of the Colorado River. There appears to have been little or no eastward spread. To the south a few pieces of Kayenta pottery appear in collections from Canyon de Chelley.[48] To the southwest, however, in the neighborhood of the Hopi towns, there are ruins which produce typical Kayenta black-on-white ware.[49] The same sort of material crops up in the neighborhood of San Francisco Mountain, and on the Little Colorado at Black Falls and above.[50]

*Proto-Kayenta sites.* In the same region which contains the great Kayenta ruins, such as Kietsiel and Betatakin, and also spreading out over a much more extensive sweep of territory, are many sites, mostly small pueblos and cliff houses, obviously allied in some way to the great ruins, but lacking certain of the traits which are most characteristic of them. The strongest likenesses are seen in the mediocre masonry with its copious use of adobe, in the variability and characterlessness of the kivas, and in the prevalence of colored pottery. The differences, aside from the smaller size of the dwellings, lie in the absence of the

48. Peabody Museum, Brooklyn Institute of Arts and Sciences.

49. Ruins along the eastern side of the East Mesa at Polacca and vicinity; a small ruin near Payupki, Middle Mesa (exploration of the author).

50. Colton, 1920; and see Fewkes, 1904, pl. 20.

rectangular ceremonial room, or kihu, and in the less specialized nature of the pottery.

What may be called proto-Kayenta pottery appears in four varieties: corrugated, red, polychrome, and black-on-white. The corrugated vessels are distinctly better made than those of the typically Kayenta sites, the ollas are taller, more gracefully shaped, and the corrugations themselves much sharper, more evenly spaced, and more carefully indented.[51] The redware, which is possibly lacking and certainly less common in the true Kayenta sites, is of a rich dark color. The ornamentation is very uniform, consisting almost entirely of running hachured designs (fig. 20, a). The shapes are small, round-bodied pitchers or

FIG. 20. Proto-Kayenta pottery designs.

jugs, with a few bowls. The polychrome, practically limited to bowls, has a yellowish base color, the decoration being mostly in black hachuring, and the elements filled with red. Bowl exteriors bear broad, carelessly drawn horizontal lines in red. It thus closely resembles the typical Kayenta polychrome, but lacks almost entirely the latter's characteristic white design edgings. The black-on-white vessels are principally ollas and bowls. The ollas are round-bodied and have no handles,[52] the bowls are usually simple in form, with less tendency to outcurving rim and with fewer cases of exterior handles. Colanders and flat-topped ollas

51. See Kidder-Guernsey, 1919, pl. 58, g, h.

52. See Kidder-Guernsey, 1919, pl. 53.

seem to be absent. In decoration, "mosquito barring" and close-set black designs are rare or lacking; the commonest and most characteristic element is shown in Figure 20, c; it is worked into an almost endless number of different patterns.

Sites containing proto-Kayenta pottery of the sorts just described occur in the Kayenta country of Arizona in considerable abundance.[53] The same wares appear, to some extent at least, in the ruins of Grand Gulch and White Canyon; in the Chinlee and Canyon de Chelley; and in sites along the San Juan from Bluff, Utah, nearly to the mouth of the McElmo[54]; I have not seen them in the Hopi country. I have, however, picked up sherds of proto-Kayenta polychrome ware (without white edgings) at Pueblo Bonito and Hungo Pavie in Chaco Canyon, in Cliff Palace on the Mesa Verde, and on Alkali Ridge in the Montezuma Creek drainage.

From the fact that the so-called proto-Kayenta ruins are obviously allied to the Kayenta ruins, but are more abundant, smaller, more widely distributed, and less specialized, it is to be inferred that they are older. As in the case of the proto-Mesa Verde remains, however, definite proof can only be supplied by further studies; but it seems likely from the finds of their typical pottery at Bonito and Cliff Palace that the proto-Kayenta villages were inhabited at the same time as the great dwellings of the Mesa Verde and Chaco Canyon; and that the late Kayenta sites were erected after the Mesa Verde and Chaco Canyon had been abandoned. Thus Kietsiel and Betatakin may well have been the last large communities that existed in the San Juan drainage.

53. Ruins 2, 3, 4, 5, 7, of the Peabody Museum survey of 1914 (see Kidder-Guernsey, 1919).

54. Explorations of the author.

## PRE-PUEBLO
### (Sites with less developed pottery)

Hitherto we have had to deal with dwellings definitely puebloan in structure and room arrangement, and in the possession of one form or another of the kiva. The pottery of each group has been made up largely of two types, the corrugated and the black-on-white. We must now consider a class of remains from which the characteristically puebloan grouping of rectangular rooms built of horizontally coursed masonry is absent; which has no kivas, properly so-called; and whose pottery complex does not contain true corrugated ware.

These remains have been called "slab-house," "early," "pre-Pueblo," etc. The latter term is now the generally accepted one, and properly so, for, as will be shown presently, it is certain that the pre-Pueblo dwellings are earlier, in the San Juan at least, than the mesa villages and cliff houses which we have so far been describing.

There is considerable variety in the pre-Pueblo ruins that have come to light. To summarize, we may say that the houses were constructions with more or less fragile walls, round, oval, or rectangular, built in such a way that the lower parts of the rooms were sunk well into the ground. Each chamber had a semi-subterranean lower third, made by scooping a hole of the requisite size in the earth. If the earth was sufficiently solid to stand alone, it was merely smoothed down, coated with plaster, and made to serve as the lower wall of the room. If it was loose or crumbly it was reinforced with stone slabs set edgeways against it, and often protruding well above the level of the ground. The wall was sometimes carried even higher by building it up with successive courses of large, hand-molded lumps of adobe. In other cases the above-ground or free-standing wall was constructed of upright poles, wattled together with withes and coated inside and out with mud. Nothing definite is known of roof construction, other than that the coverings of the rooms were made of light poles, twigs, bark, and adobe. In some cases at least they were conical or pitched.

Such rooms seldom exceeded ten or twelve feet in diameter. They were normally round, or rectangular with rounded corners, and so could not conveniently be built in the close juxtaposition typical of pueblo room arrangement. Accordingly they are found in loose aggregations of from two or three to several scores, each one-room house being an independent unit in the settlement. The settlements sometimes also contain entirely subterranean round chambers, perhaps prototypes of the Pueblo kivas; they do not, so far as is known, possess any of the specialized features of kivas, such as pilasters, recesses, or deflectors, but were sometimes provided with a ventilating shaft.

Pre-Pueblo house groups are found in caves, in valley bottoms, and on the tops of mesas. The commonest sort of situation appears to be the crest of a slight rise of ground, such as a low ridge between two canyon systems or a swell in the contour of a valley. Considerations of surface drainage rather than of defense evidently led to the selection of these elevated sites, for the small size and scattered nature of the settlements show plainly enough that their inhabitants can not have had much cause to fear the attacks of enemies.

The pre-Pueblo people were agriculturists, growing corn, beans, squashes, and cotton; they also domesticated the turkey. They buried their dead with offerings of mortuary pottery in graves close to the houses. The heads of the babies, like those of most prehistoric Pueblo children, were flattened posteriorly by the pressure of a hard cradleboard, this flattening of course persisting in the adult skull (pl. 33). As to their artifacts in stone, bone, and wood we know very little beyond the fact that they used the bow and arrow. A single well-made basket has

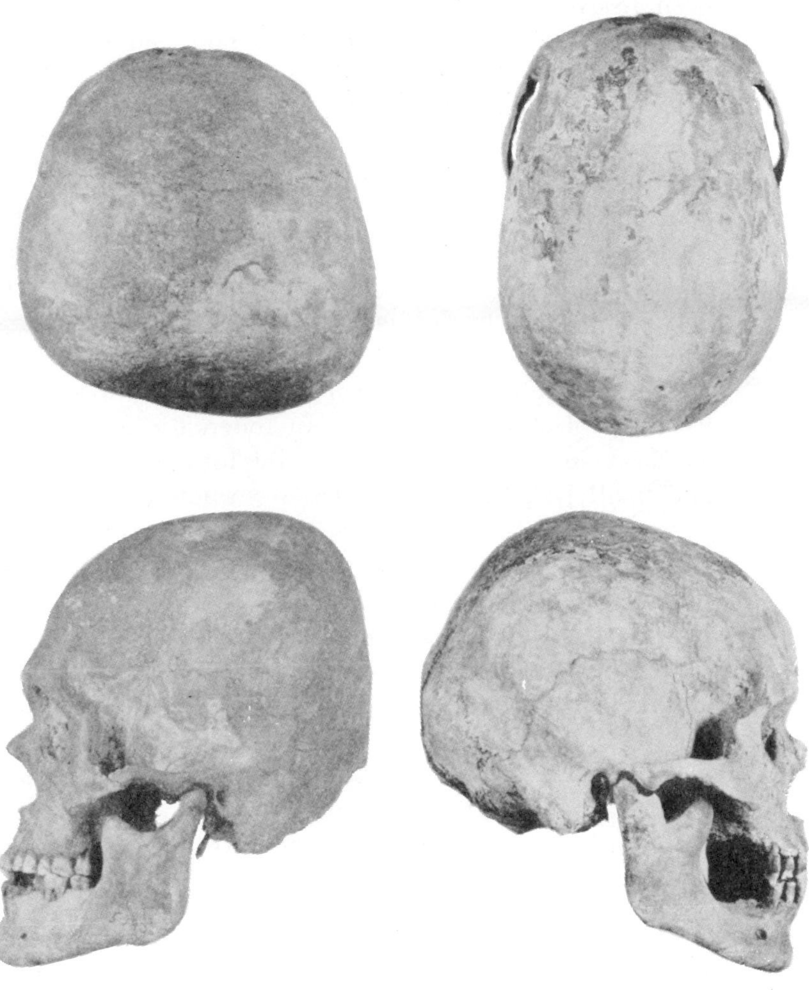

PLATE 33. Deformed and underformed skulls. The lefthand specimen (top and side views) shows the typical posterior flattening of the Pueblo and pre-Pueblo periods; it was produced by the use during infancy of a hard cradleboard. The righthand specimen (top and side views) illustrates the natural or undeformed skull typical of the post-Basket Maker and Basket Maker periods.

been recovered, and a few pieces of cotton and turkey-feather cloth.[55] No sandals have so far been found. Of pottery, however, both mortuary and in the form of sherds from in and about the houses, we have a fairly large amount.

Three wares are represented: black, black-on-white, and red. The black ware corresponds to the corrugated of the pueblos and cliff houses in that it served largely for cooking vessels; but the pots are to be distinguished from true corrugated pieces by the fact that all traces of the structural coils have been obliterated except at the necks of the jars, where they are left in the form of a half-dozen or so broad flat rings of clay entirely without indentations (pl. 34, g, h). Black-on-white ware occurs in the form of bowls, ollas, and small jars. We have as yet few whole pieces, but it is certain that large ollas were made. Bowls (pl. 34, d, e, f) are small, thin rimmed, and decorated only within; pitchers (pl. 34, b), seed jars (pl. 34, c), and small pots with lugs (pl. 34, a) also commonly occur.

The decoration is fairly elaborate, but shows a marked crudity of brushwork; the designs are characterized by dotting of lines and edges, by projections from the angles of key figures, and in particular by sets of widely spaced lines drawn about the edges of triangular or stepped elements (pls. 34, 35). A peculiar and still unexplained resemblance exists between these line edgings and similar work on certain Chaco Canyon vessels (compare pls. 35, d, and 23, a, b). Although red ware is uncommon, a small percentage of sherds seems to turn up at each site. Little can be made out as to shapes, but the prevailing forms are evidently bowls and gourd-shaped vessels; the decoration is in a slightly lustrous but not vitrified blue-black paint.

While all the above wares are well made, they are in-

55. Collected by Guernsey, in Sagi Canyon, Arizona. To be published in the Peabody Museum Papers.

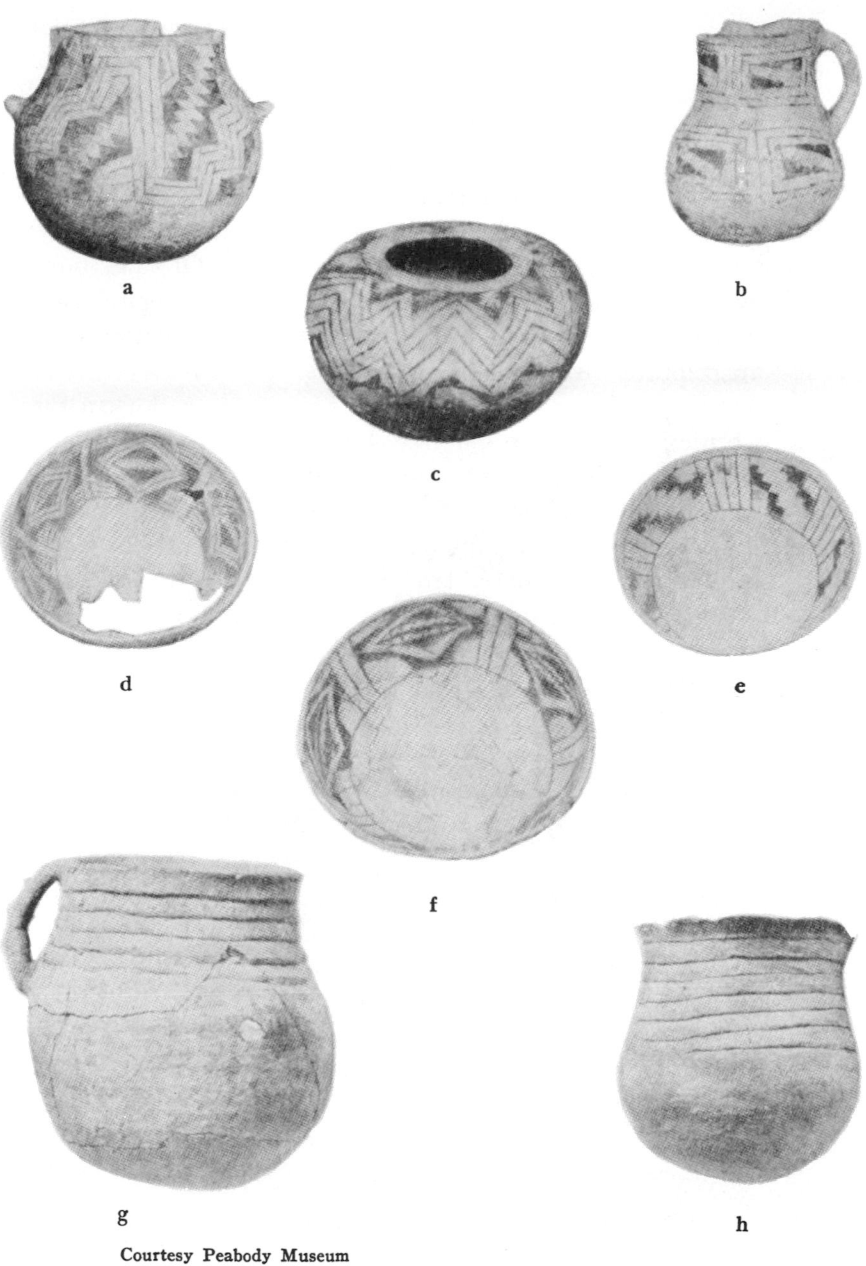


Courtesy Peabody Museum

PLATE 34. Pre-Pueblo pottery.

ferior to the run of Pueblo pottery in finish and in variety of decoration. The crudeness of the coiled technique, as shown by the cooking vessels, is, however, the best indication of lack of development.

Because of their inconspicuousness pre-Pueblo ruins for many years escaped notice and recording. Of late, however, the type has been recognized, and investigators are now on the lookout for it. The result has been that sites are reported in increasing numbers. They are known to occur abundantly in the Kayenta region, as well as in the Chinlee, Canyon de Chelley, Chaco Canyon, the Pagosa country,,on the mesas between the Animas and the Mancos, in the McElmo, and on Recapture Creek.[56] It is probable that further explorations will reveal the presence of many hundreds of pre-Pueblo sites in all parts of the San Juan.

The statement made above, that the pre-Pueblo people antedated the inhabitants of the pueblos and cliff houses, rests on definite stratigraphic evidence. In 1914 Guernsey and I found in a cave in northeastern Arizona a pre-Pueblo ruin overlaid by proto-Kayenta puebloan rubbish.[57] Guernsey's subsequent explorations have resulted in the discovery of several other similar cases.

## POST-BASKET MAKER
### (Sites with crude pottery)

During the early years of my acquaintance with the Southwest it was always puzzling to me that a district which produced so great an amount of fine pottery did not seem to contain any traces of the first crude stages of pottery-making. The fact that the oldest wares then known, the corrugated and the black-on-white, were in many ways the finest of all, made it seem as if the potter's art must

56. The Pagosa ruins have been reported by Jeancon (1922); those of the Animas-Mancos, by Morris (1919); those of Chaco Canyon by Judd (1923); the others were located by Guernsey and the writer.

57. Kidder-Guernsey, 1919, p. 42; in that publication we called the pre-Pueblo remains "Slab-House."

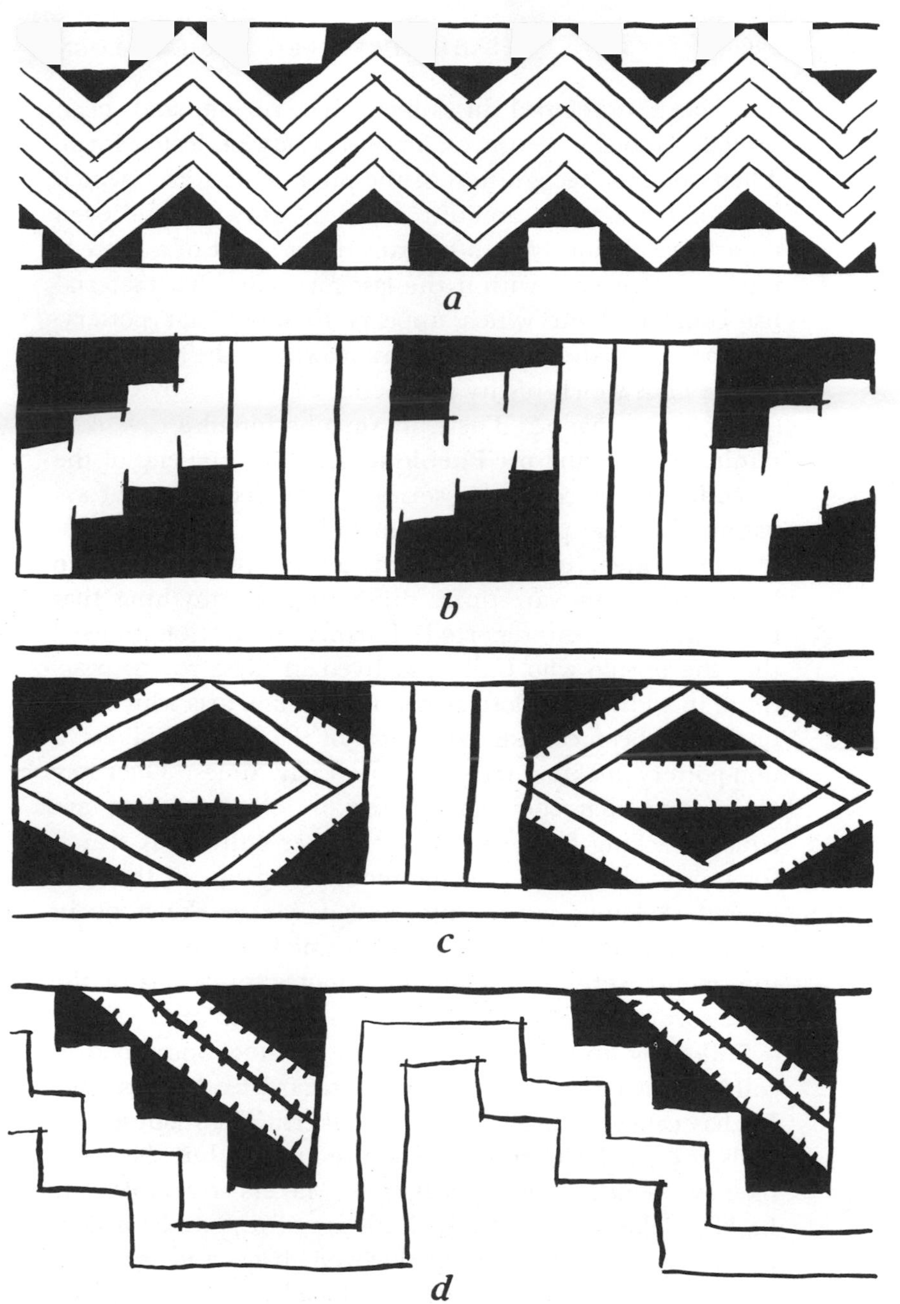


PLATE 35. Designs of pre-Pueblo black-on-white-pottery.

have been developed in some other region, and been brought into the Southwest in an already perfected form. Then came the recognition of the pre-Pueblo wares, which indicated a certain amount of local growth; but even these were obviously by no means the product of a nascent industry. It is only within the last few years that material has come to light which appears to show that pottery-making is actually an indigenous growth in the Southwest.

The finds which justify this belief were made by Guernsey in Sagi Canyon.[58] There in 1920 he found a cave containing Pueblo and pre-Pueblo remains. At one end of the place he also uncovered a series of rounded rooms of apparently normal pre-Pueblo slab-and-adobe workmanship; but the pottery in them proved, to his great surprise, to be a crude gray ware quite different from anything that had hitherto been reported. Further excavation showed that the people who built and lived in these rooms practiced, in addition to pottery-making, certain arts which had until then been considered typical of the Basket Makers, a non-pottery making race of very early times; Guernsey also found that they lacked certain objects which are equally lacking from the Basket Maker culture. A search for burials disclosed in a low mound in front of the cave several skeletons resembling Basket Maker skeletons in the fact that the skulls were undeformed (see pl. 33). The interments were accompanied by mortuary vessels of the same sort as those found in the rooms of the cave.

Following up this lead, Guernsey has since succeeded in collecting a large body of data in regard to these people. He has called them post-Basket Makers. Their houses, he finds, are similar to those of the pre-Pueblo, but there the likeness ceases. The post-Basket Makers resemble the Basket Makers in that their skulls are always undeformed; in the possession of twined-woven bags and furcloth blankets; and in the fact that they had no cotton and no

58. See Kidder-Guernsey, 1921.

a

PLATE 36. Chronological series of sandals. a. Pueblo type; pointed toe with offset on outer edge.

b

PLATE 36b. Pre-Pueblo type sandal: toe broadly scalloped.

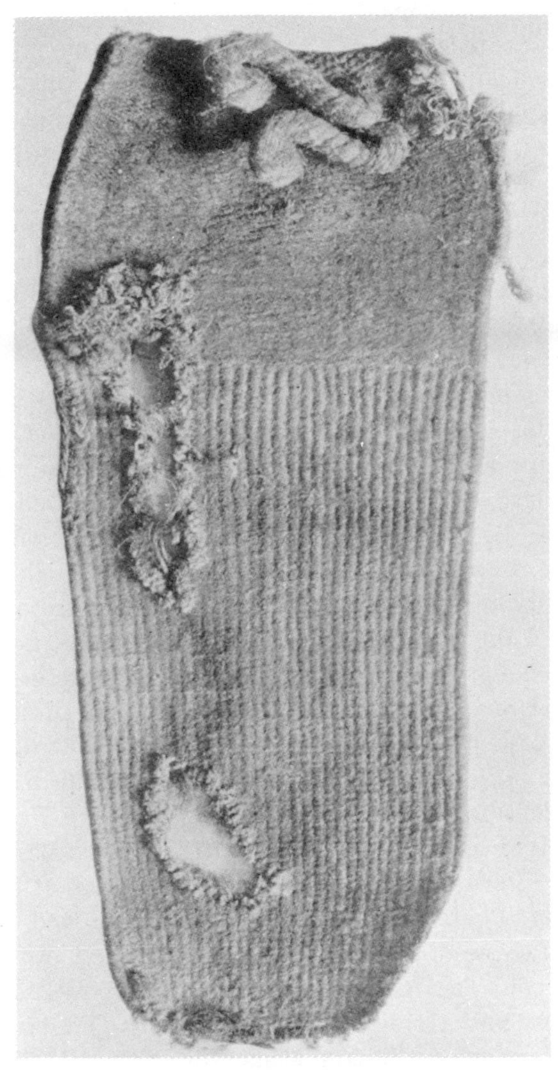

c

PLATE 36c. Basket Maker type sandal: square toe with buckskin or fiber fringe.

domesticated turkeys. At least, no cotton cloth and no turkey-feather blankets have so far turned up. The typical sandal has a single broad scallop at the toe end (pl. 36, b). The pottery is mostly dark gray, but a primitive form of black-on-white ware appears, as well as a few undecorated red pieces. Although Guernsey's material has not yet been published, I have his permission to state that the run of the pottery is inferior to that of the pre-Pueblo and that certain post-Basket Maker sites contain wares of exceeding crudeness.

The present known range of this interesting type of remains is restricted to the Kayenta district, the Hopi country, and the Chinlee Valley of northeastern Arizona; I believe, however, that certain graves opened by Morris on the La Plata will ultimately prove to belong to a late phase of the same culture.[59] It is also possible that the "earth lodges" of the Mesa Verde are of post-Basket Maker origin; the published description of them is, however, not full enough to justify any definite conclusions.[60] Another reason for strongly suspecting the former presence of the post-Basket Makers on the Mesa Verde is furnished by the crude pottery and the scalloped-toed sandal discovered by Nordenskiold in Step House.[61]

It is of course to be inferred that the post-Basket Makers were intermediate in time between the Basket Makers and the pre-Pueblos. This was practically proved during the past two summers, when Guernsey in the Chinlee and the writer in Sagi Canyon found typical post-Basket Maker pottery underlying pre-Pueblo deposits. To date no superposition of post-Basket Maker on Basket Maker remains

59. Morris, 1919, p. 194; Kidder-Guernsey, 1920.

60. Fewkes, 1920, p. 58.

61. Nordenskiold, 1893, pls. 23, 1; 24, 2, 10; 46, 6. Since the above was written, the author has visited the Mesa Verde and found that Step House Cave contained a large post-Basket Maker settlement. Many other sites of this culture were observed on the Mesa.

has come to light; but there can be little doubt that Guernsey's relative dating is correct.

## BASKET MAKER (Sites without pottery)

Although Basket Maker specimens have been known for many years, they have only recently been brought to prominence, and their position at the bottom of the Southwestern cultural sequence firmly established. They were discovered by Richard Wetherill in Grand Gulch, Utah, during the late eighties or early nineties. He recognized the peculiarities of his finds, named them Basket Maker, and also determined, by the first use of stratigraphic evidence ever made in the Southwest, that they belonged to an older period than the cliff houses. Montgomery soon after published notes on certain Basket Maker graves and specimens, but did not believe that they represented a distinct culture.[62] Prudden was the first to give an adequate account of the finds,[63] but it was a matter of ten years after the original discovery before a description of the specimens themselves was published.[64] Students of the Southwest even then paid little or no attention to the chronological position of the Basket Makers, believing that the Grand Gulch remains represented merely a specialized local phase of the general pueblo cliff-house civilization. In 1914, however, Guernsey and the writer hit upon Basket Maker graves in northeastern Arizona, and since that time Guernsey has fully established their antiquity and has gathered a great quantity of data in regard to their culture.

The houses of the Basket Makers have never been identified, which makes it seem probable that they lived in more or less temporary structures, built of perishable materials, and located in the open. Although they did not live in caves, except perhaps during periods of unusually

62. Montgomery, 1894.
63. Prudden, 1897.
64. Pepper, 1902.

severe weather, they habitually availed themselves of the sandy floors of large dry caverns for the storage of their crops and for the burial of their dead. The storage places were slab-walled cists (pl. 37); or, where the earth was firmer, jar-shaped excavations. These were often put to a secondary use as graves. Because of the dryness of the sites picked out for cist-building the contents of the graves are usually excellently preserved, and where subsequent disturbance has not taken place, everything is found in almost perfect condition, the bodies of the dead desiccated to "mummies," the baskets, textiles, and wooden implements as sound and as perfect as if they had been buried yesterday (pl. 38).

The normal Basket Maker grave contains two or three individuals, each tightly flexed, wrapped in blankets, and accompanied by numerous mortuary offerings of foods, tools, weapons, ornaments, and particularly baskets. From a study of the graves we can get an unusually detailed picture of the life and arts of the people. The Basket Makers were long-headed and of medium stature; they did not practice skull deformation (see pl. 33). They were, to a certain extent at least, agricultural, for their caches and graves often contain large amounts of corn. This corn is of special interest because it is of a single and apparently fairly primitive variety, rather than of several distinct varieties as in the case of pueblo and cliff-house corn. Squashes were grown, but no beans or cotton have yet been found among Basket Maker remains. The turkey was evidently not domesticated.

Although they had no cotton and apparently did not use the loom, the Basket Makers were very expert in the making of large and elaborately ornamented twined-woven bags (pl. 38, d, g). Their sandals, too, are twined-woven and are easily distinguishable from later sandals by their square, fringed toes (pl. 36, c). Coiled basketry was made in large quantities in the form of trays (pl. 38, c), bowls, jars (pl. 28, b), and large panniers (pl. 38, f); twilled work in the form of mats and baskets, such as occur commonly in the prehistoric pueblos, is very rare. Fur cloth (pl. 38, a) instead of turkey-feather cloth was used for blankets.

No trace of the use of the bow and arrow has ever been found. The projectiles of the Basket Makers were light darts four or five feet long hurled by means of the spear thrower or atlatl, a device intended to add greater length and therefore greater propulsive force to the arm. The most striking difference between the Basket Maker culture and that of the other people whom we have so far been considering, is seen in the total absence of true pottery. A few unbaked clay dishes of the crudest sort have been found, but no vessel or even sherd of fired pottery assignable to the Basket Makers has ever turned up in the many cists and graves examined.

One might catalogue a dozen more traits in which the Basket Makers differ from the Pueblos, but enough has been said to show the wide cleavage that exists between the two cultures. It was at one time difficult to see any direct connection whatever between them, but the discovery of the post-Basket Maker and pre-Pueblo remains have served in large measure to bridge the gap.

The position of the Basket Makers as the oldest people of whom we have knowledge in the Southwest so far is clearly indicated. Stratigraphic finds have proved that they antedated the Pueblos; and while no Basket Maker remains have yet been found underlying those of the post-Basket Makers or of the pre-Pueblos, the inferential evidence for greater antiquity is so strong as practically to amount to proof.

The known range of the Basket Makers has been considerably enlarged since the first discoveries in Grand Gulch, Utah. It now includes all the northern tributaries of the San Juan from Comb Wash to the Colorado; it covers the Chinlee Valley, and the entire drainage of its largest affluent, Laguna Creek; recently it has been extended to the Kanab district north of the Colorado River (fig. 28, p. 327).[65] Outside these limits no surely Basket Maker remains have yet come to light, but certain specimens taken by Hough from caves in the Tularosa country of southern New Mexico have a Basket Maker look.[66]

Thus the known range of the Basket Maker culture is a fairly restricted one; but I feel sure that it, or cultures closely allied to it, will ultimately be found to have covered a vastly more extensive territory, embracing, perhaps, all the arid lands drained by the Colorado River and running south along the central plateau well into Mexico.

## NORTHERN PERIPHERAL DISTRICT

Although they are not in the San Juan drainage, it is convenient to mention here the ruins that occur in the country to the north and northwest of the San Juan. To the northeast the high Rockies contain no traces of Pueblo occupation; but in the lower arid and semi-arid regions of Utah, from the Colorado line westward to the Great American Desert and northward to Salt Lake, are the remains of numerous settlements. The archaeological data for most of this vast territory are unsatisfactorily vague, and were it not for the recent work of Judd in western Utah we should have little idea as to the nature of the sites.

The accompanying map (fig. 21) shows the general location of such remains as have been reported. In the drainages of the Green and Grand Rivers are a few sites briefly described by Newberry, Montgomery, and Fewkes.[67] All these are small groups of rooms and towers, built of rough masonry on pinnacles, juts of mesas, and other places easy of defense and commanding wide outlooks.

65. Nussbaum, 1922.

66. Hough, 1914, p. 21, and pl. 20, fig. 2, a spear thrower.

67. Newberry, 1876; Montgomery, 1894; Fewkes, 1917a.

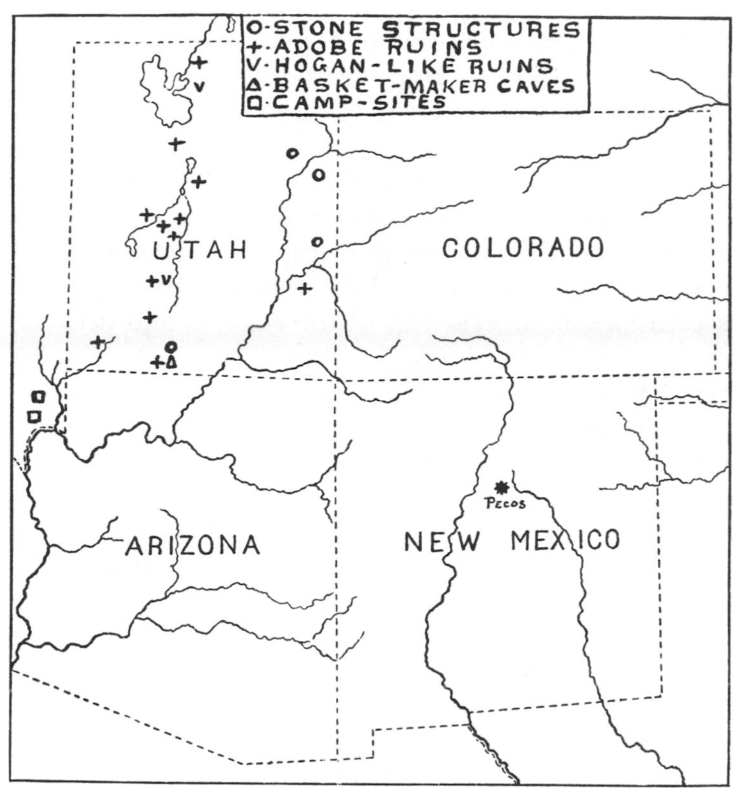


FIG. 21. Distribution of the several types of remains in the Northern Peripheral district.

The ruins visited by Fewkes contained no pottery, but both Newberry and Montgomery state that painted wares are to be found at the sites they examined. They give no information, however, which allows us to judge of the type of vessels encountered.

The ruins of central and southwestern Utah are better known. As the map shows, they extend in an almost continuous line from the northern shore of Great Salt Lake to the extreme southwestern corner of the state. Throughout this whole region there are, or rather there were before repeated plowings resulted in their destruction, great numbers of low adobe mounds. Excavations have been made by many investigators, mostly treasure seekers, but the only adequate published accounts are those of Montgomery and Judd.

The mounds consist of adobe from the disintegrated walls of houses, and of rubbish deposits that grew up about the dwellings while they were still in use. The sites would seem to have been occupied for relatively long periods, as each one shows evidence of the erection and decay of many successive structures. No differences, either in architecture or in artifacts, is, according to Judd, to be observed between the oldest levels and those above. The villages were more or less loosely grouped assemblages of rectangular one-story rooms, built singly or placed end-to-end in sets of three or four, and all arranged about an open central space or plaza.[68] The walls of the rooms were of adobe laid up in lumps or "gobs" and worked to an even surface with the hands. Entrance must normally have been through the pole-and-adobe roofs, as lateral doorways are exceedingly rare.

In the courtyards of the villages are found remains of round chambers so sunk into older rubbish deposits as to be wholly subterranean. Each one has a central firepit, and although no ventilating device has been recorded, there can be little doubt that Judd is correct in considering them closely allied to the kivas of more southerly ruins.

Of the mortuary customs practically nothing is known, but Montgomery notes the finding of a few burials in a mound at Paragonah. They lay deep in the deposit, well below house floors; but from the fact that there was always so much rebuilding at these sites it is not certain that the original interments were made under floors. One skull was strongly flattened posteriorly, the others all undeformed.

Among the minor antiquities recovered from the Utah mounds are fragments of coiled basketry, great numbers

68. See Judd, 1919, pl. 1.

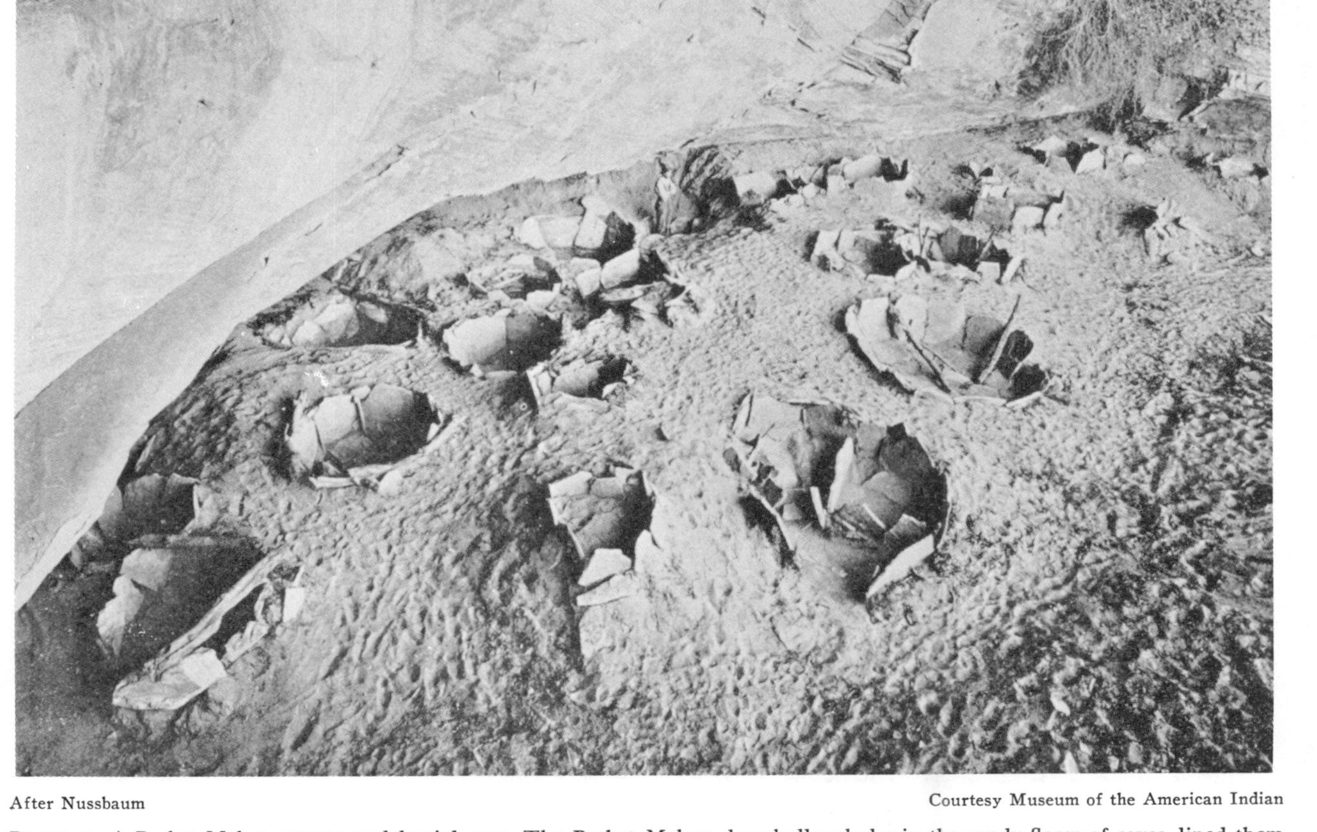

After Nussbaum | Courtesy Museum of the American Indian

PLATE 37. A Basket Maker storage and burial cave. The Basket Makers dug shallow holes in the sandy floors of caves, lined them with stone slabs, and roofed them with poles and bark. Such cists were used primarily for the storage of crops, but burials were often made in them. The round, slab-walled rooms of the post-Basket Maker and pre-Pueblo periods doubtless developed from the Basket Maker cist.

of bone implements, as well as manos and metates for grinding corn. Charred corn, also, has been found in considerable quantities. The grooved stone axe is not represented in any collection. The pottery is of particular interest. There is much crude undecorated gray ware, but with it there always occur a number of pieces of very well-made corrugated vessels, and a certain percentage of black-on-white sherds. The latter are usually from bowls, decorated only on the inside, and bearing geometric ornamentation. Judd's pottery has not yet been illustrated, but a number of decorated pieces from St. George, Utah, are figured by Holmes.[69] They bear a rather generalized type of ornament, not definitely to be associated with any of the specialized design systems of the San Juan. One peculiarity is mentioned by Judd, the interlineal use of red paint, superficially applied after the bowls had been fired.[70]

Such are the common mound ruins of central and southwestern Utah. There is also a different kind of site. Near Willard, on the northeastern shore of Great Salt Lake, Judd opened a mound which covered the remains

> of a structure which must have resembled, more or less closely, the well-known winter hogan of the Navaho Indians. The central and most prominent feature was a fireplace, two feet seven inches in diameter and three and one-half inches deep. Surrounding this, and nearly four feet from each other, were four post holes, marking the former position of as many upright supports. Since the floor of this dwelling could not be traced beyond a diameter of fifteen feet, and as the ease with which it could be traced decreased with the distance from the firepit, it may be assumed that the hut had been circular in

69. Holmes, 1886, figs. 258–71.
70. Judd, 1919, p. 19.

> form, and that its roof and walls were of heavy timbers which rested upon the ground and leaned against crosspieces supported by the four posts surrounding the fireplace. Fragments of charred wood, and large quantities of baked clay bearing impressions of logs, willows, and grass, furnished material evidence respecting the nature of the roof construction.[71]

The potsherds in this mound were of coarse plain ware, and corrugated ware. Black-on-white had been reported from the vicinity but Judd was unable to find any specimens.

At Beaver City, about forty-five miles southeast of Sevier Lake, Judd found further examples of the hogan-like houses, and in these were the same sorts of pottery, besides many fragments of black-on-white. The Beaver City round houses lay *above* the disintegrated walls of a typical rectangular-roomed adobe village. Special emphasis should be laid on this find, for although we cannot yet decide what its exact significance may be, it illustrates very clearly how vitally important it is to excavate carefully and to be constantly on the lookout for any case of superposition. Had Judd been less keenly observant, he might easily have missed this particular bit of evidence, and might well have considered the primitive-looking Willard houses as belonging to a stage of development earlier than that represented by the adobe ruins, and so have gained an entirely wrong impression of the archaeological problems of the area.

We have not as yet enough data to allow us to draw final conclusions as to the place of the Utah ruins in the general scheme of Southwestern archaeology. They are, however, surely Puebloan, as is proved by the evident permanence of the settlements, the pottery, the corn and the use of the metate. Their age, relative to that of more

71. Judd, 1917b, p. 119.

Courtesy Peabody Museum

PLATE 38. Basket Maker specimens. a. Blanket of fur-cloth. b, c, f. Baskets. d, g. Bags of fiber-string with colored designs. e. Cradle originally covered with mountain-sheep hide.

southern ruins, is hard to estimate. The simple nature of the houses, and the primitive appearance of the kiva-like structures, might seem to indicate that they were actually pre-Puebloan; but the black-on-white and corrugated pottery is certainly of Pueblo types. This would appear to show that they were built during the first part of the Pueblo period, when the vigorous early culture of the San Juan was spreading out and exerting its influence far and wide, but before the highly specialized subcultures of that region (the Chaco Canyon, Mesa Verde, and Kayenta) had yet come into being. How long the inhabitants of these Utah settlements managed to hold their country we have as yet no means of knowing, but eventually they disappeared entirely. Their end, it is to be supposed, came suddenly, because nowhere in this district do we find that they gathered together into large communities, as Pueblos normally did when in difficulties. That the end came early is indicated by the fact that pottery of early types was made to the very last, and that no sherd of late southern wares, Little Colorado, Gila, or Tularosa, has turned up in any of the mounds excavated.

No pre-Pueblo remains have yet been found in Utah outside the San Juan drainage, although one small neck-coiled jar from St. George has a suspiciously pre-Pueblo look.[72] A very interesting Basket Maker cave, however, was recently discovered in the southern part of the state by Nussbaum.[73] This greatly enlarges the previously known range of the Basket Maker culture, but whether it penetrated still farther to the north and northwest is not known.

72. Holmes, 1886, fig. 242.
73. Nussbaum, 1922.

## BIBLIOGRAPHY OF THE SAN JUAN


### General

Prudden, 1903.*
Hewett, 1908, chap. 6.
Cummings, 1910.
Kidder, 1917.
Morris, 1921.*

### Pueblo Remains by Districts

**Pagosa District**

Jeancon, 1922.*
Roberts, 1922.

**La Plata—Animas District**

Newberry, 1876, pp. 79–80.
Holmes, 1878, pp. 387–88.
Birnie, 1875.
Morgan, 1880; 1881, pp. 172–88.
Moorehead and Gunckel, 1892
Moorehead, 1902, chaps. 13–16; 1908.
Morris, 1915*; 1917a; 1917b; 1918; 1919, pt. II; 1919a*; 1921a.*
Nelson, 1917a.

**Mesa Verde—Mancos Canyon District**

Jackson, 1876, pp. 369–77.
Holmes, 1878, pp. 388–98.*
Chapin, 1890; 1892.
Nordenskiold, 1893.*
Fewkes, 1908; 1909*; 1910; 1910a; 1911a*; 1916*; 1916a; 1916b; 1916d; 1916e; 1917; 1917a; 1917b*; 1920; 1922; 1923.
Morris, 1919, pt. 1.*

**Montezuma Valley—McElmo District**

Jackson, 1876, pp. 377–81; 1878, pp. 411–15.
Holmes, 1878, pp. 398–400.
Morgan, 1881, pp. 188–93.
Wetherill, 1894.
Gunckel, 1897.
Crotensburg, 1900.
Prudden, 1903, pp. 257–67*; 1914.*
Morley, 1908.
Morley and Kidder, 1917.
Fewkes, 1918*; 1919*; 1923b.

**Montezuma Creek—Grand Gulch District**

Jackson, 1878, pp. 425–30.
Moorehead and Gunckel, 1892.
Montgomery, 1894, pp. 227–34.
"H," 1894.
Prudden, 1903, pp. 267–76*; 1918.*
Kidder, 1910.

**Kayenta District**

Prudden, 1903, pp. 282–85.
Cummings, 1910*; 1915.
Fewkes, 1911.*


* Major contribution.

Judd, 1918.
Kidder and Guernsey, 1919*; 1921.

CANYON DE CHELLEY—CHINLEE DISTRICT
Simpson, 1850, pp. 102–05.
Jackson, 1878, pp. 415–25.
Putnam, 1879, pp. 372–73.
Stevenson, 1886.
Bickford, 1890.
Mindeleff, C., 1895; 1897.*
Fewkes, 1906.
Prudden, 1903, pp. 279–82.
Kidder and Guernsey, 1919, pp. 71–74.

CHACO CANYON DISTRICT
Simpson, 1850, pp. 75–86.
Jackson, 1878, chap. 2.*
Morrison in Putnam, 1879, pp. 366–69.
Loew, 1875.
Hoffman, 1878.
Morgan, 1881, chap. 7.
Bickford, 1890.
Pepper, 1899; 1905; 1906; 1909; 1920.*
Hewett, 1905a; 1921a; 1922.
Huntington, 1914, pp. 75–82.*
Chapman, 1921.
Bradfield, 1921.
Judd, 1922*; 1922a; 1923.
Wetherill and Cummings, 1922.
Wissler, 1922.

NORTHERN PERIPHERAL DISTRICT
Newberry, 1876.
Palmer, 1876; 1880.
Holmes, 1886, pp. 287–88.
Montgomery, 1894.*
Duffield, 1904.
Judd, 1917; 1917a; 1917b*; 1918; 1919*; 1920.

PRE-PUEBLO REMAINS
Morris, 1917b, p. 462; 1919, pp. 182–94.*
Kidder and Guernsey, 1919, pp. 41–45, 152–54.*
Jeancon, 1922, pp. 5–11.*

POST-BASKET MAKER REMAINS
Nordenskiold, 1893, pp. 37–43.
Morris, 1919, pp. 194–95.
Kidder and Guernsey, 1920; 1921.

BASKET MAKER REMAINS
Montgomery, 1894, pp. 227–34.
"H," 1894.
Prudden, 1897.
Pepper, 1902*; 1905a.
Kidder and Guernsey, 1919, pp. 74–90, 154–92; 1921.
Guernsey and Kidder, 1921.*
Nussbaum, 1922.*

* Major contribution.

# The Rio Grande

The sources of the Rio Grande are in the same high mountains of southern Colorado which give birth to the San Juan. Thence the river turns eastward, enters New Mexico, and flows practically due south through the entire length of that state (fig. 22). Its western tributaries head against the continental divide, on the other side of which lie the upper tributaries of the Little Colorado and the Gila. The Rio Grande drainage in New Mexico comprises every sort of land, from lofty mountain ranges to bleak, sandy desert; a large part of it, however, is typical Southwestern country, arid, yet not hopelessly dry; its mesas covered with cedars and pinyons, its lower stretches overgrown with sagebrush, cactus, and other semidesert vegetation. Such parts of this great area as are between 3,000 and 7,000 feet in elevation, and as are not absolute desert, usually contain the relics of former sedentary inhabitants in the form of house ruins great and small. Below the Texas line there seem to be no ruins.

Archaeologically, the Rio Grande is like all other parts of the Southwest in that certain sections of it have been carefully explored and their antiquities more or less fully studied; while other areas, much larger in extent and equally prolific in ruins, still await adequate investigation. It differs, however, from all other parts of the Southwest, with the exception of the Little Colorado drainage, in that it is still occupied by living tribes of Pueblo Indians, who to this day carry on most of the arts and customs of their prehistoric ancestors. Thus we have an invaluable starting point for our researches, and can work back from the known to the unknown without meeting any very serious obstacles.

The most carefully studied part of the Rio Grande country is what may be called Santa Fe region, viz., the Rio Grande Valley from San Juan to Santo Domingo, with the Pajarito plateau on the west and the Galisteo basin and the upper Pecos Valley on the east. In this area prior to 1912 much exploration had been done by Bandelier, Hewett, and others, a great number of ruins had been mapped, and several had been excavated.[1] Little progress, however, had been made toward the relative dating of the numerous prehistoric remains; and few convincing results of a correlative nature were attained until N. C. Nelson began his studies in the Galisteo basin. Here, as has been said in a previous section, he dug in the hitherto neglected early historic ruins and made himself familiar with the styles of pottery in vogue in the sixteenth and seventeenth centuries. Then, by working in the rubbish heaps of sites whose occupancy had lasted back into prehistoric times, he was able by stratigraphic methods to recognize the pottery types of the late prehistoric period. By an extension of the same stratigraphic methods, and by using pottery as a criterion, he succeeded in determining the outline of culture growth in his area from a very early period down to the time of the Pueblo revolt of 1680. The writer's excavations at Pecos have served to amplify these data and to extend our knowledge well past the beginning of the last century; from which point studies at the still-inhabited pueblos carry it to the present day.

To summarize the knowledge gained from these investigations, we may say that the earliest remains of which we so far have knowledge are certain small settlements, apparently of pre-Pueblo type, observed by Nelson but as yet undescribed.[2] Such settlements seem to be rare in the Pajarito plateau and in the Galisteo basin and have so far entirely eluded search in the Pecos Valley. The next stage

1. See bibliography of the Rio Grande at the end of this section.

2. Nelson, 1916, p. 171, footnote, and table, p. 179.

that we can recognize is marked by small houses scattered in considerable abundance over the whole region; they consist of from three or four to twenty or thirty rooms, were probably not over one story high, and may or may not have contained kivas. Their small size and the nature of

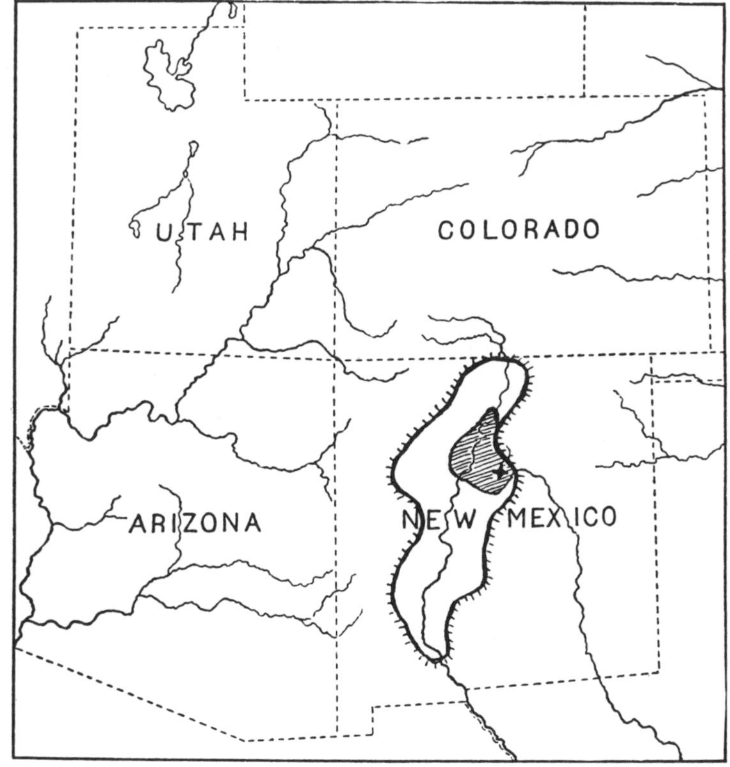


FIG. 22. The Rio Grande area (outlined), the Santa Fe region (shaded), and Pecos (star).

the sites upon which they were built show plainly enough that their inhabitants were in little fear of attack by enemies. The pottery of these ruins is black-on-white and corrugated, with a very small percentage of black-on-red. The black-on-white is of a generalized style not closely identifiable with any of the specialized types of the San

Juan or other regions. The corrugated ware is distinctly poor, the coiling uneven and the indentation work slipshod.

Following these small ruins in time are much larger structures, definitely puebloan in form, the rooms being built about courtyards and terraced to a height of at least two stories.[3] They contain round subterranean kivas with a central firepit, and a ventilator opening to the east, but have no recesses or pilasters.[4] The pottery (pls. 39, a; 40, a) is similar to that of the small ruins, but a number of the black-on-white bowls have flaring rims. A few red bowlsherds appear bearing interior decoration in dull black and exterior designs in white.

The next step in ceramic evolution was the introduction of glaze paints (pls. 39, b; 40, b). These first occur on red, shortly afterward on light-colored vessels; black-on-white ware dies out and is replaced by a thick gray pottery called biscuitware. The ruins at which this first glaze (Glaze 1 of the Pecos series) occurs are large; indeed, from Glaze 1 times onward, the settlements become greater in size, more compact in ground plan, and fewer in number.

The continued development in pottery-making brought in the use of dull red paints to add to the beauty of the glazed designs (Nelson's "three-color glazed and painted wares"; Glazes 2, 3, 4, 5, of the Pecos series; see pls. 39, c-f; 40, c-f); biscuitware gradually declined, and corrugated gave place to plain black for cooking pottery. The ruins of this general period are well exemplified by the large pueblos of the Pajarito such as Puyé and Tyuonyi, great quadrangular or circular villages surrounding courts

3. Examples in the Pecos Valley are at Rowe and on the Pecos mesa (North Terrace and underlying main plaza); for an account of the Rowe ruin see Guthe, 1917. The same type evidently occurs in the Galisteo basin; as Nelson says: "the large quadrangular village was fully developed before the black-on-white pottery went out of style" (1916, p. 171).

4. This description is of the only kiva of the period so far excavated. It lies in the plaza of the north quadrangle at Pecos (see p. 118).

PLATE 39. Pecos pottery. Chronological series arranged to illustrate the sequence of types from the Black-on-white ware of early prehistoric times (a), to Modern ware made during the first part of the nineteenth century (h).

PLATE 40. Pecos pottery. Chronological series of bowl designs: a. Black-on-white; b. Glaze 1; c. Glaze 2; d. Glaze 3; e. Glaze 4; f. Glaze 5; g. Glaze 6; h. Modern.

(pl. 41, a). Their kivas are round subterranean rooms with plain unrecessed walls, central firepits, and ventilators opening to the east.

Toward the close of the glazed-ware period, and after many of its most flourishing sites had already been abandoned, came the discovery of the Southwest by the Spaniards. Glazing held on for a hundred years or so, becoming more and more degenerate (Nelson's "historic two-color glazes"; Pecos Glaze 6; pls. 39, g; 40, g); until at or about the time of the revolt of 1680 it was finally abandoned and the Rio Grande potters began to produce light-colored wares ornamented with dull black and red paints (Nelson's "modern painted"; Pecos "Modern"; pls. 39, h; 40, h), closely resembling the present-day pottery of San Ildefonso, Cochiti, and Santo Domingo.

The above sketch of the archaeology of the Santa Fe region has been made very brief because papers on the general problems of this area, as well as detailed studies of the different periods, will appear in the later reports of the present series.

We have, as has just been shown, a fairly good knowledge of the Santa Fe district, but there are many other parts of the Rio Grande drainage as to which we have so far very little information. Of these the Jemez area, the country about Acoma, the region of the Salines, and the lower valley of the river itself are the most notable examples. What little we do know, however, indicates that throughout the whole central Rio Grande drainage in New Mexico the course of development was analogous to that in the Santa Fe district; i.e., there was an early period in which the people lived in small communities and made black-on-white and corrugated pottery, a later time when they gathered together into larger villages, and a still later time when they became concentrated in a few great pueblos, discontinued the more archaic types of pottery, and turned to the use of colored wares decorated with glaze paint. With the increase in concentration ensued a tendency to draw in toward the centre of the area and toward the valley of the river, and when the Spaniards arrived, the country held by the Pueblos was far less extensive than it had been in the Black-on-white and earlier Glaze periods.

When we come to consider the archaeology of the Rio Grande as a whole, we are struck by the paucity of pre-Pueblo remains and by the entire absence, so far as we know, of any sign of the post-Basket Maker and Basket Maker. As to the pre-Pueblo, I feel certain that further reconnaissance will result in the finding of many more sites, but I should expect them to occur in the northern and western parts of the Rio Grande rather than in the eastern and southern. If evidence of the post-Basket Maker and Basket Maker cultures ever turns up, it will be found, I think, in the same districts. In other words, it is my opinion that the eastern and southern parts of the Rio Grande drainage in New Mexico were not occupied by agricultural people prior to the early Pueblo period. This feeling is based on the general lateness of development in the Rio Grande as compared to that in the San Juan.

There are not many data to correlate chronologically the Rio Grande with the San Juan, for the latter country had been deserted for an unknown length of time before the arrival of the Spanish in 1540. We do have, however, a few scraps of evidence. At Bandelier Bend, a late archaic Black-on-white site in the Pecos Valley, there have turned up several undoubted Mesa Verde bowl sherds; thus, the late archaic Black-on-white period in the Pecos Valley appears to have corresponded in time to the epoch of greatest development in the San Juan. Furthermore, the entire life of the glaze-paint stages seems surely to have been later than the abandonment of the San Juan, for no scrap of glazed ware or of the contemporary biscuitware

a

b

PLATE 41. Rio Grande habitations. a. Large circular pueblo, Tyuonyi. b. Artificial caves used as dwellings near Tyuonyi.

has ever been found in any San Juan ruin. It would seem, therefore, that all the more sizeable villages of the Rio Grande were built subsequent to the abandonment of the San Juan; and that at the time of the great towns of the Chaco and the Mesa Verde, which represented the culmination of San Juan civilization, the Rio Grande people, although they were already definitely puebloan in culture, were only just beginning to gather together into large communities.

The chronological correlation between the Rio Grande ruins and those of the Little Colorado will be taken up after the discussion of that area.

## EASTERN PERIPHERAL DISTRICT

The country lying east of the Rio Grande drainage in New Mexico has not been explored by archaeologists. It is not known, therefore, just how far in that direction ruins of pueblo type extend. I have been told by ranchers that there are sites almost to the Texas border. From the descriptions and from the few potsherds I have seen, the villages would all appear to have been small and to have belonged to the early part of the Black-on-white period. The limits indicated on the map (fig. 9, p. 141) show the extent, so far as we can determine it at present, of such sites in eastern and southeastern New Mexico. The ruin in Scott County, Kansas, described by Williston and Martin[5] was undoubtedly built during the historic period by Pueblos seeking to escape from Spanish rule.

## BIBLIOGRAPHY OF THE RIO GRANDE

Chama-Taos District

Cope, 1875.

Holmes, 1878, p. 401.

Yarrow in Putnam, 1879, pp. 362–65.

Bandelier, 1892, chap. 1.

5. Williston, 1899; Martin, 1909.

Hewett, 1906, pp. 33–44.*
Jeancon, 1911; 1912; 1919; 1921; 1923.*
Harrington, 1916, pp. 107–205.

PAJARITO PLATEAU DISTRICT
Stevenson, 1883a, pp. 430–32.
Bandelier, 1892, chaps. 1 and 4.*
Starr, 1900.
Hewett, 1904a; 1906, pp. 16–32*; 1908, chap. 9; 1909*; 1909a*; 1909b; 1920.
Bierbower, 1905.
Beam, 1909.
Morley, 1910.
Hewett, Henderson, and Robbins, 1913.*
Huntington, 1914, pp. 82–85.
Kidder, 1915.
Harrington, 1916, pp. 205–390.
Wilson, 1916; 1916a; 1918.

JEMEZ DISTRICT
Loew, 1875, pp. 176–77.
Bandelier, 1892, chap. 5.
Holmes, 1905.
Hewett, 1906, pp. 44–51.
Reagan, 1917; 1922.
Bloom, 1922; 1923.

PECOS DISTRICT
Bandelier, 1881*; 1892, chap. 3.
Hewett, 1904.*
Kidder, 1916a; 1916b; 1917a; 1917b.
Kidder, M. A. and A. V., 1917.*
Guthe, 1917.

GALISTEO DISTRICT
Bandelier, 1892, chap. 2.
Nelson, 1913; 1914*; 1916*; 1917.

RIO PUERCO DISTRICT
Lummis, 1889.
Bandelier, 1892, pp. 305–26.
Hodge, 1897; 1897a; 1914.

LOWER RIO GRANDE—MANZANO DISTRICT
Bandelier, 1892, chap. 6.
Huntington, 1914, pp. 72–74.
Walter, 1916.

* Major contribution.

# The Little Colorado

The Little Colorado River rises in the highlands of western New Mexico and flows a little north of west to empty into the Colorado (fig. 23). Its course roughly parallels that of the San Juan, but unlike the San Juan its sources are not in high, snow-covered mountains, so that the actual amount of water it carries is not great. It often runs dry in midsummer, and much of the country along its lower reaches is practically uninhabitable desert. The upper tributaries, however, particularly those of the east and southeast, traverse some of the most beautiful hill and mesa land of the Southwest, well watered and often heavily forested.

The ruins of the Little Colorado drainage are for the most part reduced to low, inconspicuous mounds. This is evidently due to poor construction, and perhaps in some degree to climatic conditions, rather than to great antiquity. The result of it, however, is that a classification based on architectural features is impossible without house excavation, very little of which has ever been done, almost all investigators having contented themselves with digging in the easily found and extremely prolific burial grounds. Hence we know almost nothing of the details of room arrangement, masonry, or kiva construction; in most cases, indeed, we are even ignorant as to whether or not kivas are present. Accordingly, in attempting a classification, one is forced to rely upon the evidence of pottery to an even greater degree than elsewhere. Here again difficulties are encountered, for the pottery situation in the Little Colorado is evidently a very complex one and no comprehensive classification of the wares has yet been made. The trouble is that most work in the Little Colorado, particularly in the very important central regions along the river itself, has been carried on by explorers who have placed more reliance upon the clan-migration legends of the Hopi and Zuñi, than upon the empirical evidence offered by the ruins and their contents. Hence

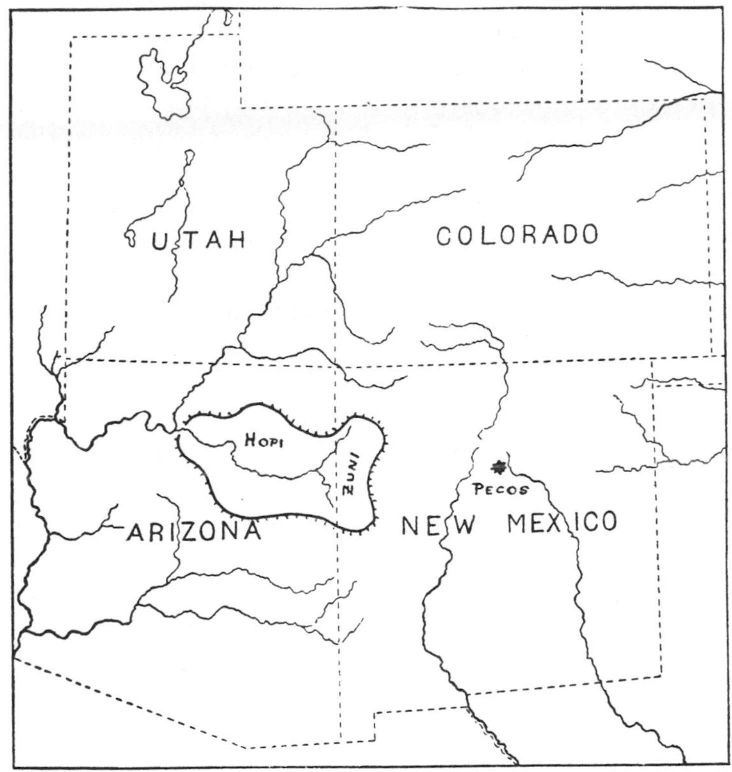


FIG. 23. The Little Colorado area.

the strictly archaeological aspects of the problem have been to a large extent disregarded.

To make a start, therefore, we are forced to turn to the Zuñi district at the extreme eastern end of the drainage, where recent studies by Kroeber, Nelson, and Spier of the Archer M. Huntington Survey of the American Museum of Natural History, have achieved clear-cut and satisfactory results.

This region contains a single inhabited town, the pueblo of Zuñi, and the ruins of a great number of other villages, large and small. Certain of the sites had been identified by previous students as the "Seven Cities of Cibola," which were visited and described by the Spanish explorers of the sixteenth and seventeenth centuries; most of them, however, are obviously prehistoric. Spier, who carried on most of the investigation, paid particular attention to the pottery, and was able, by a combination of stratigraphic, comparative, and statistical methods, to work back from the wares of the historic ruins, and eventually to arrange many sites in a chronological sequence which is without much doubt correct.[1] By relying upon empirical evidence rather than upon native legendary testimony Spier proved that one ruin, Hallonawa, hitherto considered historic, is in reality prehistoric; and that Zuñi, long thought to have been founded since the conquest, was actually settled prior to 1540.

The process of development, as determined by Spier, may be summarized as follows. The earliest sites were little buildings with pottery identical with that of the pre-Pueblo ruins in the San Juan. Then came somewhat larger houses whose pottery is preponderantly corrugated and black-on-white (pl. 42, c); then began a decline in black-on-white ware, accompanied by a rise of redware with decoration first in black paint (pl. 42, a), later in both black and white paint (pl. 42, b). During the earlier phases of this period the structures were still small, and lacked the compact grouping and terraced arrangement of the later pueblo. After the introduction of three-color (i.e., black-and-white-on-red) painted decoration, there came into use the true pueblo form of architecture. Painted

1. For the details of this important contribution to archaeological method, see Spier, 1917, and review by the writer (Kidder, 1919).

PLATE 42. Little Colorado pottery.

decoration soon gave way to decoration in black glaze, the three-color scheme still obtaining (i.e., black glaze and white paint on red, pl. 42, d, f). After a considerable time glaze painting and red backgrounds declined more or less together, and were replaced by light backgrounds (buff or white). Glaze paint, although it lingered upon the white backgrounds for a while, was steadily losing ground. This period saw the arrival of the Spaniards. During historic times dull paint finally triumphed over glaze, and the wares gradually changed, and grew into the styles which are made at Zuñi today.[2] From the time of the introduction of the pueblo form of architecture the tendency was always toward a reduction in the number of towns and an increase in their size.

Spier's sequence of pottery types is undoubtedly correct in its main outlines. Its correctness, however, will be thoroughly tested, and much valuable information will surely be added, by the excavations now being carried on by Hodge for the Museum of the American Indian, Heye Foundation, at the large Zuñi ruin of Hawikuh, an historic pueblo founded in prehistoric times, whose rubbish heaps contain a splendid stratification of several of the more important wares in Spier's chronological series.

Hodge has, indeed, just published the following preliminary chronological classification of Hawikuh pottery, which in general confirms Spier's results:

A. Black-on-gray; black-on-red; finely corrugated. Pre-Hawikuh period.

B. Black or green glaze on red or orange-red. Corrugated much cruder. Earliest Hawikuh (prehistoric).

C. Black, green, or purplish glaze on white or creamy slip. Early Hawikuh (prehistoric).

2. Whole vessels of some of these wares are not at present available for illustration, but Spier (1917, 1918, 1919) figures a representative series of sherds; and Fewkes (1909b) gives some excellent color plates of early glazed ware from Zuñi sites.

D. Black or green glaze on white or cream, with non-glaze colors introduced. This was the first step toward a pure mat polychrome. Prehistoric.

E. Polychrome. Various colors were used and life forms became much more common. The glaze decoration has disappeared. The range of decorative designs indicates two periods, one merging into the other, the first prehistoric, the second prehistoric but extending into the historic period.

F. Recent glaze. The glaze, especially black, and green of varying shades, was revived, but the glaze was crudely applied. This style of ornamentation seems to have been gradually superseding the polychrome when Hawikuh was abandoned.[3]

Of the kivas of the Zuñi area we have so far little information. Hodge states that the ceremonial rooms of Hawikuh, both prehistoric and historic, are rectangular.[4] At a pre-Hawikuh site in the vicinity, which was built during Hodge's period A, there were found by the Museum of the American Indian expedition two circular kivas. The excavation of these was so carefully done and the publication of the results is so full and clear that they may well serve as models for future work of the sort.[5] The two kivas lay side by side with remains of a house structure to the north of them. They were round and subterranean, the larger seventeen feet, the smaller a trifle over fifteen feet in diameter. Each one was encircled by a low inner wall without roof-support pilasters; and each one contained a ventilating shaft opening in the floor, a deflector, and a rectangular firepit. In both kivas there was sunk into the floor west of the firepit a rectangular, stone-lined vault. No traces of roofing were discovered.

These two kivas show strong Chaco Canyon influence,

3. Hodge, 1923, p. 29.
4. Hodge, 1923, p. 10.
5. Hodge, 1923.

but they appear to represent a sort of cross between the great kiva and the small kiva types. They resemble the great kivas in possessing an unpilastered encircling bench, and a rectangular firepit; the small kivas in having a subfloor ventilating shaft, a deflector, and a single rectangular vault west of the firepit.

The pottery found by Hodge in the undisturbed lower portions of the kivas was black-on-white, black-and-white-on-red, and corrugated. The black-on-white is not, to my mind, of the typical Chaco style, but belongs to what I believe we shall eventually be able to recognize as a distinctive Little Colorado group influenced by Chaco ware and by the black-on-white of the Upper Gila (see p. 284 below). Contemporaneousness of these kivas with the upper Gila culture is indicated by Hodge's discovery in the original undisturbed fill in one of them of an Upper Gila type corrugated bowl.[6] In view of finds made in the upper layers of the kivas this becomes a fact of great importance. The finds just mentioned consisted of the remains of two rudely made chambers built in the kivas, but well above their floors. They were obviously constructed after the kivas had been abandoned and had fallen into decay. They were identified by Hodge as of the Hawikuh period, for they contained pottery of several definitely Hawikuh types. Associated with these later rooms were several skeletons accompanied by mortuary pottery, also of Hawikuh types. With skeleton no. 1, was a bowl of Lower Gila polychrome ware, and a Hawikuh Type C or D canteen with purplish glaze on a white slip.[7] The significance of the Upper Gila corrugated bowl from the kiva proper and the Lower Gila bowl in a later grave and associated with a Hawikuh Type C or D vessel, will be reverted to in a subsequent section. Here I wish merely to call the facts to the reader's attention, and to emphasize, as I did in the case of Judd's ob-

6. Hodge, 1923, pl. 22, a; and see p. 283 below.
7. Hodge, 1923, p 31 and pls. 28, c; 29, c.

servations on the Beaver City mounds (see p. 252), the great importance of careful observation and recording, particularly where there is the least suspicion of a superposition of the remains of different periods. Had Hodge merely dug out his kivas and burials, allowed the sherds from different levels to become mixed, and failed to note the small details of depth and position which allowed him to state positively that the burials belonged with the later rooms rather than with the earlier kivas, all these most valuable data would have been lost. Consideration of this particular case makes it seem likely that the strange mixtures of pottery types recorded by other students from some of the ruins of the Little Colorado valley were due to like reoccupations of sites, and that the evidence of such reoccupations was not recognized by the excavators.

We must now turn to the Hopi district in the extreme northern part of the Little Colorado drainage. Here no stratigraphic work such as that of Hodge has been done; nor have any comparative and statistical studies of the pottery been made comparable to those of Spier in the Zuñi country. We have, however, thanks to Fewkes, an intimate knowledge of one very characteristic ware, and the writer has made brief reconnaissances at a number of sites at and near the East Mesa.

The general conditions duplicate those in the Zuñi country; that is to say, there are inhabited pueblos (pl. 43), a few early historic towns, and many prehistoric ruins. The recent wares of the Hopi[8] are light colored, with decorations in brownish blacks and reds (see pl. 18, a); the light backgrounds are a dirty white, the slip being thickly seamed with fine cracks. A surface examination of the rubbish heaps below Walpi and Sichomovi seems to show

8. Pottery making is now extensively carried on only at Walpi and Hano. By recent wares I mean those produced prior to 1897; at that time the Hopi potters began to copy the fine old vessels unearthed by Fewkes at Sikyatki, and this archaistic style has now practically superseded the nineteenth-century pottery.

PLATE 43. Typical terraced pueblo. Hopi town of Oraibi.

that this ware has been made for a long time. It must, however, have come into use after 1700, for the surface pottery at the nearby ruin of Awatobi, which was destroyed at about that date, is dissimilar to it. The latest Awatobi ware is much yellower in tone, its slip lacks the characteristic modern Hopi crackling, and the decoration in browns and reds is more skillfully applied. This ware, although better than modern Hopi, is much less fine than a third style which is also found at Awatobi and at various other sites, but which is best known as Sikyatki ware. The beautiful plates in Fewkes' monograph on Sikyatki[9] have made this pottery well known. Its surface color ranges from creamy white through the yellows to shades of flushed orange; the elaborate designs are executed with marvellous sureness and accuracy in brown-blacks and reds (pl. 42, g, h). The best pieces of the Sikyatki type are technically and artistically the finest ceramic products of the Southwest, ancient or modern.

Sikyatki, the type site for this ware, is believed by Fewkes to be prehistoric.[10] Finds of Sikyatki pottery at Pecos seem to show that it was contemporaneous with Rio Grande late Glaze 4 and early Glaze 5, which would place it in the late prehistoric period; this supposition is further borne out by its obvious family resemblance to the seventeenth-century wares at Awatobi.

Sikyatki pottery is found well under the surface at Awatobi, and also occurs at a site below the mesa near Walpi, at Old Shumopovi, and at several other ruins. What preceded the Sikyatki wares in the Hopi district has only just been determined. During the past summer I made a series of stratigraphic tests in the deep rubbish heaps of Old Shumopovi and the Jeddito Valley ruins of Awatobi, Neshepatanga, and Kokopnyama.[11] At each of

9. Fewkes, 1898.
10. Fewkes, 1898, p. 636.
11. For the location of these sites, see Hough, 1903, pl. 82.

these sites I found underlying the Sikyatki wares similar but easily distinguishable pottery which I have tentatively called Jeddito yellow (pl. 42, e). It is decorated with brown-black paint alone, rather than with brown-black and red, and the vessel shapes and the ornamentation show plainly enough that it is directly ancestral to Sikyatki ware. Beneath the Jeddito yellow there occurred still older pottery of an orange-red shade, the ancestry of which is still unknown, but which may prove to be allied both to the Kayenta polychrome and to the early dull-black-and-white-on-red of the Zuñi series. These data show that the latest prehistoric Hopi pottery, the Sikyatki, is a local growth from local prototypes, and not, as had formerly been supposed, an importation by clans from the Rio Grande. These local prototypes, first the orange-red and then the Jeddito yellow, were evidently contemporaneous with the early glazed wares of the Zuñi district.

The still older steps in the Hopi series are to be found at many almost obliterated ruins which contain only black-on-white and corrugated ware; some of this is a sort of amorphous stuff like generalized San Juan, some is quite distinctly proto-Kayenta and Kayenta. There are also in the Jeddito Valley and at the East Mesa a number of unmistakable pre-Pueblo ruins, little slab-walled structures with characteristic black-on-white and neck-coiled black pottery. Finally, at two places on the East Mesa are small sites marked by a few scattered stones and containing sherds of typical rough, gray, unornamented post-Basket Maker vessels.

To sum up, we have in the Hopi country the post-Basket Maker, pre-Pueblo, prehistoric Pueblo, and modern Pueblo cultures. The prehistoric Pueblo culture probably passed through, first a generalized, and later a more specialized, black-on-white stage. Then came a period when both degenerate black-on-white and a new orange-red style were in vogue. Black-on-white eventually disappeared and the Jeddito yellow ware became the predominating type. Toward the close of prehistoric times there developed from it the beautiful black-paint-on-yellow Sikyatki wares, whose influence certainly extended down into the Little Colorado. The early modern ware surely, and the late modern ware probably, grew from this.

From the foregoing it will be seen that the general course of development in the Hopi and Zuñi countries was virtually the same, particularly during the earlier phases. In the later prehistoric periods, however, specializations set in which became more and more pronounced, until at the time of the discovery in 1540 the two regions were marked by cultures which, ceramically at least, were quite distinct.

I am not able to throw much light on the problems presented by the numerous and important ruins in the river valley of the Little Colorado and in its southern tributaries. An examination of the plates in the works of Fewkes and Hough[12] shows that the situation is by no means simple; there are vessels of all sorts, black-on-white, black-and-white-on-red, glazed, Jeddito yellow, and Sikyatki, as well as pieces of Kayenta, Tularosa, and Lower Gila types. This very complexity, however, is encouraging, for it shows that the Little Colorado has been a meeting and mixing ground of several cultures. The discovery of stratified sites or, if such cannot be located, further work along the lines developed by Spier, will not only surely result in the solution of local problems, but will also give us invaluable data as to the time-relations of many other Southwestern groups.

As to time correlations between the Little Colorado and the Rio Grande, we are provided with a good starting point by the fact that the upper ends of both series run into historic times and are therefore contemporaneous. Dropping to the bottom, we find each series beginning

12. Fewkes, 1904; Hough, 1903.

with more or less similar types of generalized black-on-white ware; this would also seem to imply approximately equal age for the beginnings of puebloan development in the two areas. The Black-on-white period, however, appears to have lasted somewhat longer in the Rio Grande than in the Little Colorado, for fragments of the dull paint redware with white exterior decoration which succeeded the black-on-white in the latter region, have been found in otherwise pure black-on-white sites in the Rio Grande. The next stage, that of glaze painting, began at about the same time in both areas, though it may perhaps have started a trifle earlier in the Little Colorado.[13] Evidence for these statements is provided by the finding of sherds of Little Colorado glaze-paint wares of Hodge's Type B (see p. 270) in Glaze 1 strata at Pecos, and, indeed, in some very late black-on-white deposits at Pecos and at Rowe.

The above correlation between these two regions, while by no means detailed or complete, is reasonably convincing. It depends in large measure upon the evidence of cross-finds of fragments of non-local pottery. Such fragments of vessels belonging to types not standard in a region, but which *are* characteristic of another region, are of the greatest importance for determining chronological relationships. It is immaterial whether the vessels were actually traded from one district to another, whether they were made by women married or captured into a tribe, or whether they were produced locally in imitation of foreign styles; their significance in showing contemporaneity is the same. I wish to lay particular stress upon this method of correlation as it is one which has proved very useful in the past, and may be depended upon to help us greatly in the future. To take full advantage of it, however, the field archaeologist must be a close student of ceramic types, and must be constantly on the lookout for

13. See Kidder, M. A. and A. V., 1917, p. 354.

fragments, no matter how small, which differ in any way from the run of material in the site that he is excavating.

## BIBLIOGRAPHY OF THE LITTLE COLORADO


ZUÑI DISTRICT

Simpson, 1850, pp. 117–33.
Cushing, 1886.
Mindeleff, 1891, chap. 3.*
Fewkes, 1891*; 1909b.
Bandelier, 1892, pp. 326–45; 1892a.
Hodge, 1895; 1918; 1920; 1921; 1922; 1923.*
Kroeber, 1916; 1916a.
Spier, 1917.*
Anonymous, 1918.
Wissler, 1919.

HOPI DISTRICT

Mooney, 1893.
Mindeleff, 1891, chaps. 1, 2.*
Bandelier, 1892, chap. 9.
Fewkes, 1893; 1896a; 1896c; 1896d; 1898, pp. 577–742,* 1898a; 1904, pp. 111–34; 1919a.
Hodge, 1904.
Hough, 1903, pp. 326–52.*

RIVER VALLEY AND SOUTHERN TRIBUTARIES

Nelson, E. W., 1884.
Hough, 1902; 1903, pp. 289–325; 1920.
Fewkes, 1896b; 1898b; 1900; 1904, pp. 20–111, 134–68.*
Palmer, F. M., 1905.
Spier, 1918; 1919.
Colton, M. R. F. and H. S., 1918.
Colton, 1920.


* Major contribution.

# The Upper Gila

This district comprises the headwaters of the Gila in southeastern Arizona and southwestern New Mexico (fig. 24). The Gila River forks near the interstate border, one branch (still called the Gila) draining the high land north of Silver City, New Mexico, the other, the San Francisco, swinging northward to head in the mountains of northern Socorro county, New Mexico, just west of the barren San Augustin plains. Both these main tributaries run through rough, broken country, abundantly watered and for the most part heavily forested.

Of the archaeology of the southern branch, the Gila proper, nothing, or next to nothing, is known. Bandelier states that there are numerous ruins, both surface sites and cliff houses, and that the former are similar to the ruins of the Upper Mimbres. He also describes a small cliff house on Diamond Creek.[1] As to the pottery of the district we are entirely ignorant.

The northern fork, the Rio San Francisco, and its tributaries, the Blue and the Tularosa, are, thanks to the explorations of Hough,[2] much better known. This river system drains a high, broken, and in general well-forested region, with abundant water supply but with rather limited amounts of land easily available for primitive agriculture. Because of this the ruins are confined, apparently, to the immediate vicinity of the watercourses, where there are stretches of alluvial bottoms suitable for growing corn. It would seem, from Hough's accounts, that nearly every locality of this sort contains vestiges of former occupation.

1. Bandelier, 1892, pp. 359–62.
2. Hough, 1907, 1914.

The dwellings are situated on the crests of low ridges overlooking the flats, and although most of them have been reduced to more or less inconspicuous mounds, enough remains to show that they were fairly compact aggregations of living rooms enclosing courts or plazas. The rooms

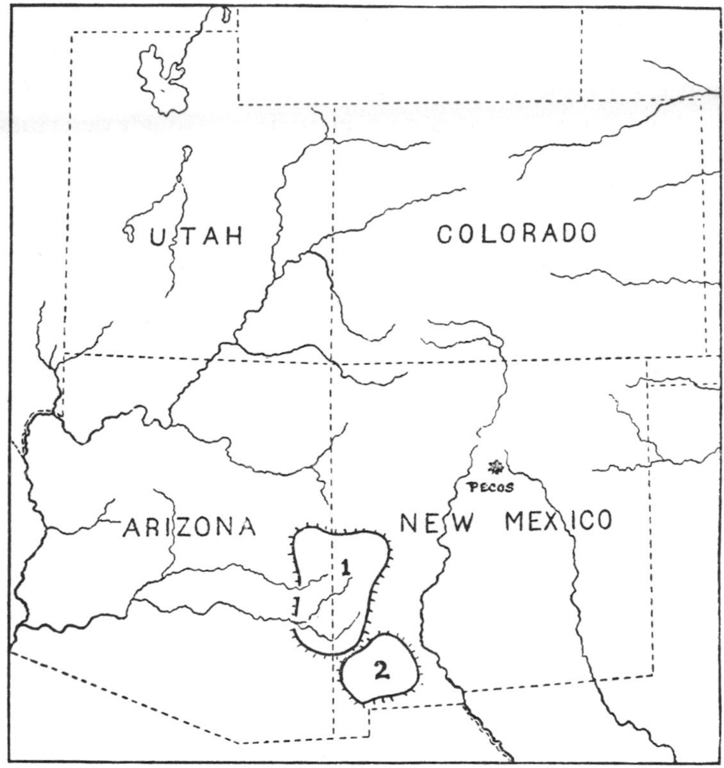


Fig. 24. The Upper Gila area (1) and the Mimbres area (2).

are built of horizontally coursed masonry, but not enough excavation has been done to allow of any generalizations as to the details of arrangement or of architecture; nor do we know whether or not the buildings were more than one story high. Hough believes that there are kivas in these ruins, as, indeed, seems probable from the occurrence in them of round and square depressions. None, however, have been cleared for examination.

The cemeteries usually adjoin the buildings, but burials are also encountered below the floors of rooms.[3] Interments were both at length and flexed; cremation was apparently not practiced except in the lower reaches of the San Francisco near its junction with the Gila.[4]

One very striking feature of the culture under consideration is the abundance of offertory shrines. These occur on mountain tops, in caves, and at springs. Hough describes a large number of such shrines, the most important being the Bear Creek and Tularosa Caves, in each of which were found large deposits of offerings such as miniature pottery vessels and effigies, miniature bows and arrows, cane cigarettes, carved wooden sticks, and many other objects plainly ceremonial in nature. In cleaning out springs great numbers of small pots, chipped implements, and stone beads have been discovered.

So little digging has been done in the San Francisco-Tularosa region that we cannot further characterize the culture as exemplified by the house ruins. The pottery, however, of this district is very characteristic, and differs from that of any other part of the Southwest. Large lots of it are to be found in several museums, but they are unfortunately for the most part commercial collections, accompanied by few or no data, so that we know nothing as to the circumstances of discovery or of the exact provenience of the specimens. It seems certain, however, that the bulk of the material came from ruins in the San Francisco drainage.

There are three wares: corrugated, black-on-white, and red. The corrugated appears in the form of large ollas of fairly good workmanship, but as I have never seen a whole vessel I can say nothing as to the shape. Another type of

3. Hales, 1893, p. 537.
4. Hough, 1907, p. 44.

corrugated ware is, however, very abundant in collections. It is made of a high grade paste which allows the production of very fine work. The commonest forms are rather flat-bottomed bowls eight to ten inches in diameter. The interiors of these bowls are of a deep black color and highly polished (pl. 44, m-p). The black gloss was evidently obtained by the process in vogue today among the potters of Santa Clara pueblo, by smothering the fire toward the end of the burning with an application of pulverized fuel. The blacking, however, in the case of the Tularosa bowls was only produced on the interior, the exterior surfaces being brown or red-brown. In rare instances the exteriors are smooth, but usually they are wholly or partly covered with exceedingly fine corrugation, often tastefully patterned with decorative indentations (pl. 44, m-p). The coils in most Southwestern corrugated ware are relatively broad, running three to five to the inch; in the Tularosa bowls there are often as many as twelve to the inch. This fine corrugation may extend over the entire outside of the specimen, or may be confined to a narrow, fillet-like band just under the rim.

Black-on-white pottery is well-made, the slip bright, and the paint a sharp, clear black. Ollas have not been recovered, the only forms that appear in collections being pitchers, bowls, ladles, and eccentrically shaped pots. By far the commonest type is the pitcher, a round-bodied vessel with cylindrical neck and with a handle which extends from below the rim to the upper side of the body (pl. 44, i-l). A common feature of Upper Gila pitchers, occurring in forty to fifty per cent of all specimens, is the modification of the handle into the crudely modelled form of a small animal. The entire body of the animal may be shown (pl. 44, j), or the handle may be reduced to a small protuberance representing the head and neck (pl. 44, c, d, f).

Black-on-white bowls (pl. 44, a, b) are relatively rare,

their place having been taken, apparently, by the fine corrugated bowls. The few specimens that I have seen are decorated only in the inside, have rather steeply rising sides, and plain rims. Ladles, also, are uncommon; they are all of the bowl-and-handle variety. Bird-shaped, double-lobed, doughnut-like, and other small vessels of eccentric form occur in considerable numbers.

The decoration of the black-on-white ware is elaborate and in most cases well painted. The most typical design is an involved interlocking device in contrasted black and hatching that is applied very skillfully to the rounded bodies of pitchers. It may be either angled (pl. 44, k, l) or curvilinear (pl. 44, i, j). The necks of pitchers are usually ornamented with interlocking key figures in solid black (pl. 44, d-f, i, j, l). Other characteristic motifs are close-set small key figures so arranged as to cover large areas (pl. 44, c), and fine herringbone work in black lines (pl. 44, e, f).

Redware is so rare in collections that I cannot give any adequate description of it. It seems, however, to appear in the form of bowls and pitchers, decorated with dull black paint.

Pottery of the above types is commonly known as "Tularosa," from the fact that most of the collections have come from the ruins in the valley of that river. While its headquarters was doubtless there and in the other tributaries of the Upper Gila, it had a considerably greater range, and trade pieces are found in ruins at great distances from the home area.

Ruins producing nothing but Tularosa pottery occur on the San Francisco from mouth to source, and on its tributaries, the Blue and the Tularosa. The numerous sites that are presumably to be found on the Upper Gila proper, north of Silver City, may also be expected to contain the same wares. I have been told by cattlemen that there are many ruins in the vicinity of Magdalena, New Mexico, and from their descriptions of the pottery it would seem to belong to the Tularosa type, which may thus be expected to occur as far east as the Rio Grande and to extend along that stream from Socorro south to Elephant Butte. I have no evidence of its extension east of the Rio Grande.

To the south Tularosa ware appears not to have penetrated the valley of the Mimbres; nor to the southwest is it found, as far as I know, on the Gila below Solomonsville.[5] In the northwest and north, however, the conditions are different. The White Mountain country, the Zuñi district, and the Little Colorado contain, according to Spier, ruins which show an admixture of Tularosa wares. This admixture is strong in the Black-on-white ruins, may last into the early Glaze period, but disappears in later times.[6] Tularosa polished black bowls have been found by Morris at Aztec,[7] and Nelson has recorded fragments of the same sort of vessels from the upper layers of the Pueblo Bonito refuse heap.[8]

The chronological relation between the Upper Gila culture and the groups to the north and west of it is fairly clear. It was contemporaneous with the later Black-on-white periods in the San Juan and Little Colorado and may even have lasted long enough to be coexistent with the early Glaze period in the latter district. How it compares in age with the Mimbres, Chihuahua, and Lower Gila cultures is not known, but the fact that bowls with polished black interiors are found only in the Upper Gila and Lower Gila cultures seem to show some connection

5. Fewkes figures some corrugated ware from Solomonsville that shows strong Upper Gila influence (1904, pl. 67).

6. Spier, 1919, p. 372. One site has only Tularosa pottery. See also Hodge, 1923, pl. 22, a, showing a Tularosa bowl from a Black-on-white site in Zuñi Valley.

7. Morris, 1919, p. 73.

8. In Pepper, 1920, p. 384.

a
b
c
d
e
f
g
h

PLATE 44. Black-on-white and corrugated wares of Upper Gila type.

between the two. My guess would be that the Upper Gila antedated the Lower Gila, and passed on to it certain elements of pottery technique.[9]

Of remains earlier than the Tularosa in the Upper Gila district we have but one definite instance. In the vicinity of Luna, in the San Francisco Valley, Hough discovered a group of about one hundred pit houses. Upon excavation these proved to be circular structures about fourteen feet in diameter by five feet deep, and apparently to have had conical roofs of logs and earth supported by low, wattled sidewalls.[10] The pottery was neck-coiled dark ware and black-on-white of a sort quite different from the Tularosa type and somewhat resembling the pre-Pueblo black-on-white of the San Juan. The primitive nature of these pit houses and of the artifacts found in them would alone be quite sufficient to indicate that they antedate the true pueblo ruins of the neighborhood, but this was proved beyond question by Hough's discovery of similar pit dwellings underlying a rectangular pueblo in the Los Lentes Valley.[11] Although the still older Basket Maker culture has not been certainly identified in this region, a number of Hough's cave specimens have a suspiciously Basket Maker look.[12]

## BIBLIOGRAPHY OF THE UPPER GILA

Bandelier, 1892, pp. 359–65.
Hales, 1893.
Heister, 1894.
Duff, 1897.
Lyon, 1906.
Hough, 1907*; 1914*; 1917; 1918; 1919*; 1923.

* Major contribution.

9. Since the above was written this guess has been practically confirmed by Hodge's find of a Lower Gila polychrome bowl in a grave that lay *above* rubbish containing an Upper Gila corrugated vessel (Hodge, 1923; and see p. 272).

10. Hough, 1919.

11. Hough, 1907, p. 63 and fig. 28; and Hough 1919, p. 409.

12. For example, an atlatl; see Hough, 1914, pl. 20, fig. 2.

# The Mimbres

The Mimbres River rises in the Black Mountains of southeastern New Mexico and flows southward toward the Mexican border (fig. 24). Although it is tributary to the inland drainage system of northern Chihuahua, its waters sink into the sand on emerging from the mountains, and its lower course consists, except in times of exceptional flood, of an underflow which only appears here and there in the form of seep springs. The upper river, however, is a fine running stream bordered by willows and cottonwoods. Its narrow valley contains many patches of easily irrigable and very fertile land; lower down toward the city of Deming, New Mexico, the country opens out into great barren flats and much of it is practically desert.

Both Bandelier and Hough[1] mention ruins in the Mimbres Valley, but no adequate descriptions of them were published until the appearance of a series of articles by Webster in the *Archaeological Bulletin*.[2] The very extraordinary pottery of this district was brought to the knowledge of students by Fewkes less than ten years ago.[3]

Ruins in the Mimbres extend from an unknown distance below Deming to the headwaters of the river, and also occur in its western tributaries which drain the country about Silver City and Fort Bayard. Passing over for the present certain ruins that belong to another culture, we may say that the typical Mimbres sites are small stone-built pueblos of from five or six to forty or fifty rooms. They are situated, as are those of the Tularosa region, on ridges, or knolls, or slight swells in the valley bottoms,

1. Bandelier, 1892, p. 350; Hough, 1907, p. 83.
2. Webster, 1912a.
3. Fewkes, 1914.

and show no particular desire on the part of their builders for defensive locations. The houses are in all cases badly preserved, but from the ground plan of the Swarts ruin given by Webster,[4] and from a hasty personal examination of several others, it seems to me that these dwellings are typically puebloan, for they are composed of closely set rectangular rooms grouped about courts, and both Webster and Duff believe that some of the houses were more than one story high.[5] Further relationship to the northern pueblos is to be seen in the presence of the underground kiva. The important discovery that the kiva was in use by the ancient Mimbreños was made by Mr. and Mrs. C. B. Cosgrove of Silver City. Ardent archaeologists, the Cosgroves have done everything in their power to preserve the fast disappearing ruins of their neighborhood; and have purchased and themselves carefully excavated a site near their home. In it they found a sunken rectangular room with firepit and ventilator, an undoubted kiva, by far the southernmost example of such a structure yet recorded.[6]

The burial customs of the Mimbreños were peculiar. The bodies were placed, closely flexed, in excavations under the floors of living rooms. Over the head in almost every case was put a pottery bowl so inverted as to cover the skull closely. In the bottom of each such bowl a small round hole was broken in order to "kill" it ceremonially.

Because so little excavation has been done the details of the Mimbres culture are practically unknown.[7] We are accordingly forced, as so often elsewhere in the Southwest,

4. 1912a, pl. 25.

5. Webster, 1912a, p. 113; Duff, 1902, p. 397.

6. Cosgrove, 1923.

7. An expedition sponsored by the Chino Copper Co., and directed by W. Bradfield of the New Mexico State Museum, has begun excavations in the Mimbres. A brief preliminary report indicating the great importance of the work has been issued (Bradfield, 1923). When Mr. Bradfield's complete results are published, they will throw much light on this interesting culture.

to rely upon the evidence of pottery for our knowledge of distribution and exterior relationships. Of Mimbres pottery there is fortunately a large amount in our museums, but the collections, having been made in all cases by commercial diggers, are inadequately labelled and few or no data accompany them.

The wares are of two sorts, black-on-white and corrugated. Decorated red ware very seldom occurs in pure Mimbres sites. The corrugated ware appears in the form of small pitchers and large full-bodied ollas with slightly flaring rims. The corrugations are narrow and therefore close-set; they are never, so far as I can tell from the sherds that I collected in 1922 from Mimbres sites, sharply notched or indented, being merely waved or roughly punched. Even this amount of decoration is uncommon. Before the pots were sun-dried, the corrugation was usually more or less worked over with some sort of smoothing tool which has given the surfaces a "wiped" appearance.

The standard black-on-white ware form is the bowl, ollas being unusual to judge by the sherds. A few small, narrow-mouthed vessels were made,[8] but apparently no pitchers resembling those of Tularosa, or ladles of any sort. The bowls are relatively deep, run up to as much as fourteen or fifteen inches in diameter, and have rather steeply rising sides. The rim is usually straight (i.e., with no in- or out-curve), square topped, and well finished. Some bowls are slipped with white on both exterior and interior, but the majority have slip only within. The slip is a clear chalky white in most specimens, but it is very often overfired (?) to a yellowish shade. In these cases the normally black paint of the decoration has turned to a bright red.[9] The paint when not so affected is a sharp, clear black.

8. Fewkes, 1914, pl. 8.

9. That this flushing to yellow of the slip and to red of the paint is due to some peculiarity in firing seems proved by the fact that it often occurs on certain parts of pieces the rest of whose surfaces are normal black-on-white.

In bowls the ornamentation is confined to the interior. The rim is usually painted black. Below the rim comes a series of framers, either one or two wide lines, or a set of several very fine lines drawn close together. Under the framers there is often a band of geometric decoration which leaves according to its width a larger or smaller open space in the bottom.

The geometric decorations are extraordinarily well executed, with a delicacy of line and an accuracy of spacing unequalled in Southwestern ceramic art. Only a limited use is made of the key figure, the bulk of the patterns being based on opposed dentate elements in contrasted hatching and solid black. The nature of the geometric designs alone would be sufficient to distinguish Mimbres ware from all others, but it is further characterized by a most amazing profusion of naturalistic drawings. These range from strange composite creatures, evidently mythical, to figures of animals, birds, fishes, insects, and human beings; and there are also many cases of true narrative depiction, such as hunting and trapping scenes, dances, and ceremonial observances. The figures are sometimes interwoven to a certain extent with the geometrical patterns under the bowl rims, but are more commonly set clear in the large round spaces left in the bottoms of the bowls. A few examples are here shown (pl. 45), but to get a true idea of the richness and variety of the work one should consult the excellent pictures in Fewkes's publications on Mimbres pottery.[10]

True naturalism is so rare a phenomenon in all Southwestern pottery decoration, particularly in the early phases marked by black-on-white wares, that its very high development here is most puzzling. When one takes into consideration the superlative excellence of the geometrical work on the same pieces, it must be granted that the ancient Mimbreños were the most remarkable artists of

10. Fewkes, 1914; 1916c; 1922; 1923a; 1923c.

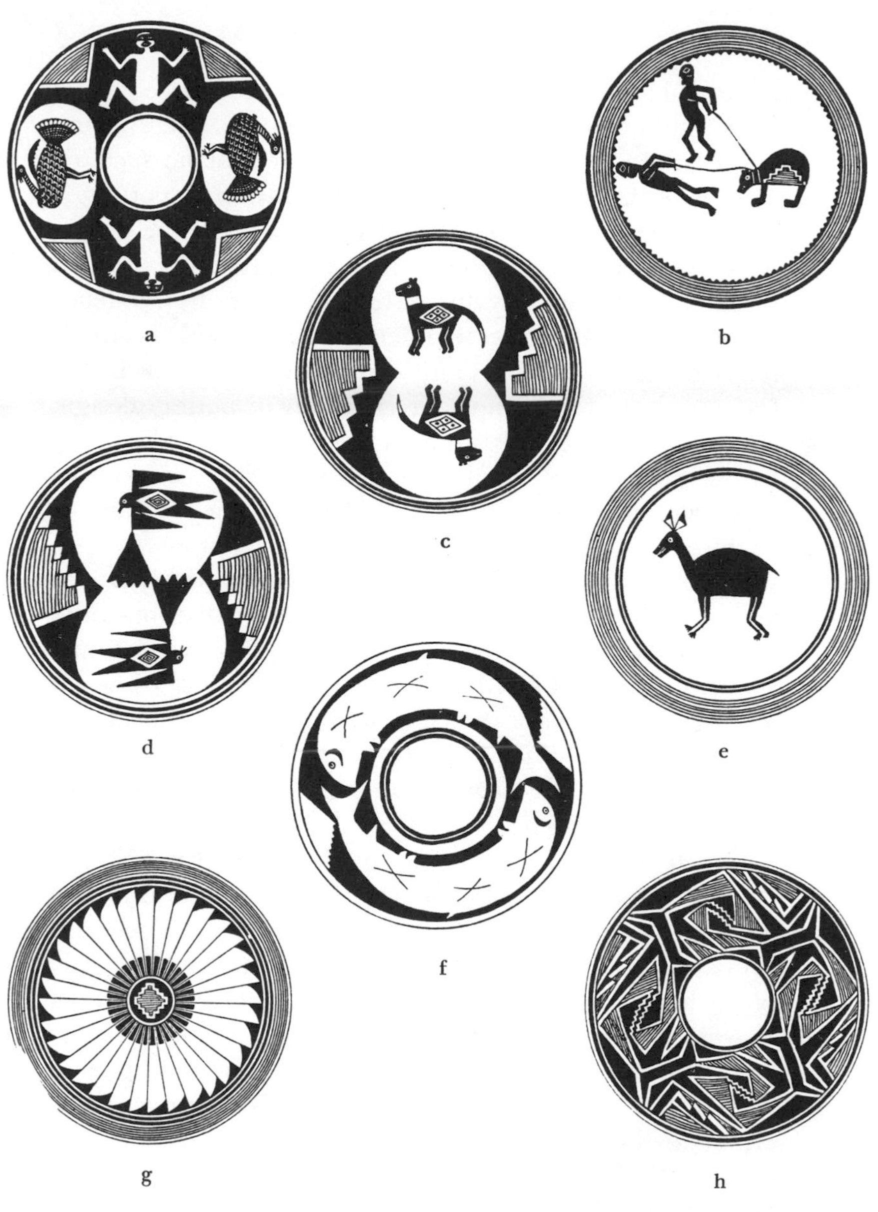
a b c d e f g h

After Fewkes Courtesy Smithsonian Institution

PLATE 45. Mimbres pottery. Interior designs of black-on-white bowls.

the Pueblo area, not even excepting the yellow-ware potters of Sikyatki. In the case of the Mimbres, there is no question of the intrusion of a foreign art, for no such art exists elsewhere; and furthermore the Mimbres pottery is surely a development of the old stock wares of the Southwest, the black-on-white and the corrugated. In such an instance as this one is almost forced to see the influence of some forgotten individual genius, whose work so stimulated her contemporaries and successors as to result in the founding of a local school or tradition in pottery design.

As the Mimbres culture is at present known to us only by its pottery, we cannot as yet say what its exterior affiliations may be in other respects; but the appearance of the ruins (and the general nature of the pottery as well) would lead us to identify it with the Pueblo civilization, and to place it chronologically in middle Black-on-white times. It does not seem to have been exactly contemporaneous with the Tularosa culture, for, so far as I know, no Mimbres specimens have turned up in Tularosa collections, or vice versa, in spite of the fact that the two districts lie close together.[11] We have so far but a few bits of relative chronological evidence.

It will be remembered that in the third paragraph of this section certain ruins in the Mimbres country were mentioned that belonged to another culture. These are sites about Deming (the Black Mountain ruin is the only one which I have visited) that without question are of Lower Gila affiliation, the pottery being preponderantly of Lower Gila types.[12] Now at the Black Mountain pueblo there is also a very strong admixture of Chihuahua (Casas Grandes) sherds, but no Mimbres ware at all, although typical Mimbres ruins lie within a few miles of the place. Some sixty miles northwest, on Duck Creek, a tributary

11. Mr. Cosgrove informs me that he has never found Tularosa sherds at any of the Mimbres ruins he has examined.

12. See Fewkes, 1914, p. 13.

After Fewkes — Courtesy Bureau of Ethnology

PLATE 46. The Casa Grande ruin.

of the Gila, is an unnamed ruin, one or two rooms of which had at the time of my visit been recently partly cleared out. The sherds on the slopes below this site were a mixture of Lower Gila and Mimbres wares. On examining the excavated rooms, however, it was seen that the sherds protruding from the earth still left in them were mostly Lower Gila with a few Chihuahua specimens, but those embedded *in the adobe of the walls* were straight Mimbres. All of which of course indicates that the houses were built by Mimbreños and later occupied by people of Lower Gila culture. Lower Gila and Chihuahua being approximately contemporaneous, these data practically prove that Mimbres preceded them both.

The pottery of the Mimbres has, as I pointed out several years ago,[13] certain points of resemblance to that of Chihuahua; the likeness is to be seen in the use, by artists of both areas, of negative drawing, and in the forms of certain bird and serpent heads. As the Mimbres ware is without much doubt earlier than the Chihuahua, the above similarities must be accounted for, I think, by Mimbres influence on the formative stages of the Chihuahua culture, which, as will be shown below, appears to be a mixture of Pueblo and Mexican elements.

I have gone into these matters at length in order to bring out the fragmentary nature of our present knowledge and the need of careful stratigraphic and analytical studies. Data to settle these questions positively are to be had; it is merely necessary to do more field work and to keep the problems constantly in mind.

We have as yet no evidence as to the presence of antecedent cultures, pre-Pueblo or earlier, from the Mimbres.

13. Kidder, 1916, p. 268.

## BIBLIOGRAPHY OF THE MIMBRES

Henshaw in Putnam, 1879, pp. 370–71.
Bandelier, 1892, pp. 350–58.
Taylor, 1898.
Duff, 1902.
Hough, 1907, pp. 83–89.
Webster, 1912; 1912a*.
Fewkes, 1914*; 1915; 1916b; 1916c; 1922; 1923a*; 1923c*.
Bradfield, 1923*.
Cosgrove, 1923.

* Major contribution.

# The Lower Gila

The country we are about to consider comprises the valley of the Gila from Solomonsville, Arizona, west to Gila Bend; it also includes the lower valley of the Gila's great northern tributary, the Salt, and that of its southern affluents, the Santa Cruz and the San Pedro (fig. 25). This is a very large stretch of territory and is in many respects different from any which we have so far taken up. The average elevation of the land is much less, there is little rainfall, the winters are mild and the summers exceedingly hot. Vegetation is correspondingly scanty, and many southern desert growths appear. In spite of the general barrenness of the country much of the soil along the rivers is very rich, and where water can be got upon it is of amazing fertility.

The archaeological remains are also unlike those of any of our other districts, and are in some ways so aberrant that, were it not for the pottery, we should be forced to consider that we had overstepped the limits of the Southwestern culture area. Although little is known of the ruins, they all seem to have certain features in common. It is wisest, therefore, to consider first one of the few sites that has been carefully studied. The best known ruin of the Lower Gila region is Casa Grande (pl. 46), a site discovered in the early historic period, frequently described by explorers and archaeologists, and recently excavated by Fewkes.[1] It consists of a large five-room central structure forty feet long by sixty feet wide. The massive walls are of adobe and formerly extended to a height of at least three stories. About it are lower buildings, also of adobe, made up of large but not uniformly sized rectangular

1. For early accounts of Casa Grande, see Fewkes, 1912, pp. 53–81.

rooms. The whole is surrounded by a heavy adobe wall probably once seven or eight feet high; this forms a rectangular enclosure some 420 feet long by 230 feet wide (pl. 47). Fewkes has very aptly termed groups of this sort "compounds." There are several others in the immediate

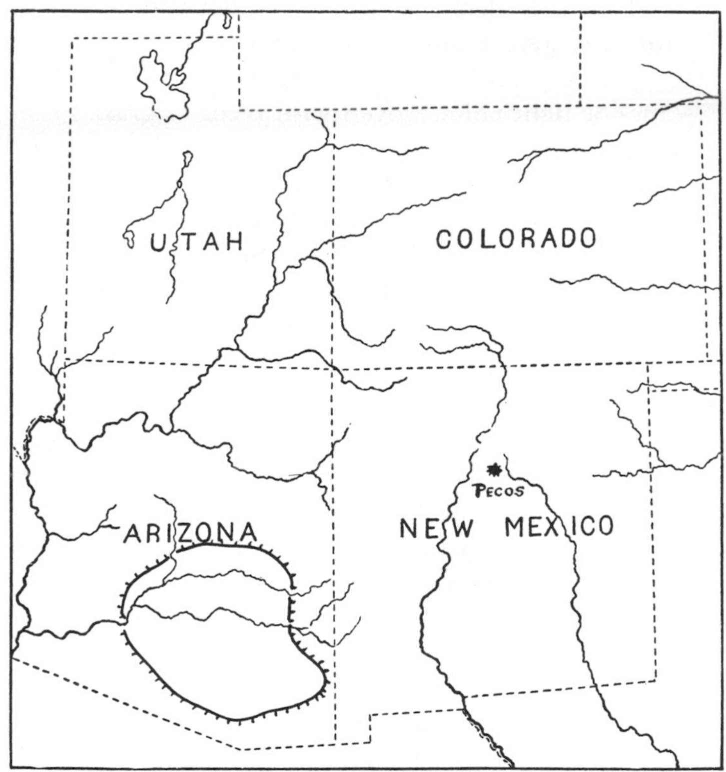


FIG. 25. The Lower Gila area.

vicinity, smaller than Casa Grande, but closely similar to it. In one of them, "Compound B," are both adobe buildings and the remains of less solidly made houses, the walls of which consisted of upright stakes covered with mud.[2] Some of these houses were congregated on large, low,

2. Fewkes, 1912, pl. 26.

pyramidal substructures. The method of erecting adobe walls in the various Casa Grande buildings much resembles modern concrete work. To quote Mindeleff:

> The walls are composed of huge blocks of earth, three to five feet long, two feet high, and three to four feet thick. These blocks were not molded and placed in situ, but were manufactured in place. The method adopted was probably the erection of a framework of canes or light poles, woven with reeds or grass, forming two parallel surfaces or planes, some three or four feet apart and about five feet long. Into this open box or trough was rammed clayey earth obtained from the immediate vicinity and mixed with water to a heavy paste. When the mass was sufficiently dry, the framework was removed along the wall and the operation repeated.[3]

The rectangular compound as seen at Casa Grande is evidently the unit of Lower Gila architecture. A village might have consisted of one or several compounds, each having a large central building, a number of smaller houses, and a heavy surrounding wall. The exact function of the different elements is unknown, but it seems likely that the large central structure was a sort of temple. The smaller houses may have been ceremonial in nature, residences of priests, or, less probably, the dwellings of the people. Most observers, however, seem to believe that the commoners lived in more perishable quarters, perhaps such log-walled houses as were found in Fewkes's Compound B. In any case the whole conception of a Lower Gila community of the Casa Grande type is radically unlike that of a Southwestern pueblo, which has no single dominating structure, either religious or residential, and in which the living rooms of all the people are identical in size and construction. The Casa Grande groups seem to

3. Mindeleff, 1896a, p. 310.

have been laid out on lines very similar to those of Central Mexican communities, and the resemblance is still further heightened by the pyramidal substructure seen in Compound B.

Sociological conditions are always strongly reflected in architecture and village planning; hence it is to be inferred that the people of the Lower Gila were organized on a different and probably a less democratic basis than were the true Pueblos. The result of this may perhaps be seen also in the extraordinarily elaborate irrigation works executed in the district, works so extensive as to hint at the existence of a strongly centralized form of government.[4]

In such of the Lower Gila ruins as have been excavated evidence of two kinds of mortuary customs have come to light: cremation and inhumation. Cremation would appear to have been the commoner method. The bodies were burned on large "pyral mounds," and what fragments of bones were left unconsumed were enclosed in jars and buried in the edges of the mounds. Offerings of ceremonially broken ("killed") pottery were frequently placed about the cinerary urns.[5] Inhumation seems to have been less regularly practiced; in most such cases the body was placed in a hole dug in the floor, or even in the wall, of a house or temple structure and carefully mudded in, thus occupying a sort of adobe sarcophagus. Mortuary pottery with such burials was seldom "killed." Cushing believed that these two methods of disposal indicated a difference in the rank of the dead; the common people being cremated, the priestly class interred.[6] Although this is, of course, quite possible, and indeed the general layout of the Lower Gila settlements seems to suggest that a sociologic system involving strong differentiation between

4. See Hodge, 1893.
5. Cushing, 1890, p. 172.
6. Cushing, 1890, p. 174.

classes and masses was in force in that district, yet it is perhaps even more likely that the two sorts of mortuary customs represent a change in culture, and accordingly a more or less considerable lapse of time. As will be brought out in the discussion of the pottery, two distinct groups of wares come from the Lower Gila ruins, wares so unlike as to raise the suspicion that they may even have been manufactured at different periods. The accounts of both Cushing and Fewkes, the only investigators who have done any excavation in these sites, indicate that there are large deposits of refuse at and about the ruins, and it is unfortunate that neither of them were able to make any stratigraphic studies. It is certain that important chronological information could be obtained from the Lower Gila.

Although the architectural remains of the Lower Gila communities present many non-Southwestern features, the culture of the district is in certain respects surely allied to that of the Pueblos. This is illustrated most clearly by the pottery. Lower Gila vessels, although aberrant in certain respects, are in shape and in technology very similar to those of the country to the north and east; and in the decoration many typical Southwestern elements are to be recognized.

There are three principal wares: plain red, polychrome red, and red-on-gray. Very little corrugated pottery appears in collections from these ruins; and when it does, it is in the form of small sherds.

The plain red pottery occurs in three varieties: (1) unslipped pieces of a light brick-red color; (2) slipped pieces of a richer red with black firing clouds; (3) large-mouthed pieces (bowls, dippers, etc.) with polished black interiors.

The base clay of all these is reddish gray and of rather coarse texture, thickly but not grossly tempered with finely ground particles of quarts or some other silicious rock. The second and third classes differ from the first only in the

After Fewkes

Courtesy Bureau of Ethnology

PLATE 47. The Casa Grande ruin excavated. Photograph of a model showing the main structure, the groups of smaller rooms, and the enclosing wall. The whole forms a typical Lower Gila "compound."

addition of a slip, which in both of them is rich turkey red and often contains a considerable amount of powdered mica. The surfaces of both are well smoothed and in some cases made glossy by means of the rubbing stone.

The most interesting specimens are the bowls and dippers with polished black interiors, as they remind us of like wares from the Upper Gila, the Chihuahua basin, and modern Santa Clara. The exteriors are always red, some with and some without firing clouds; the interiors are a deep jet black, often bluish or greenish in certain lights.

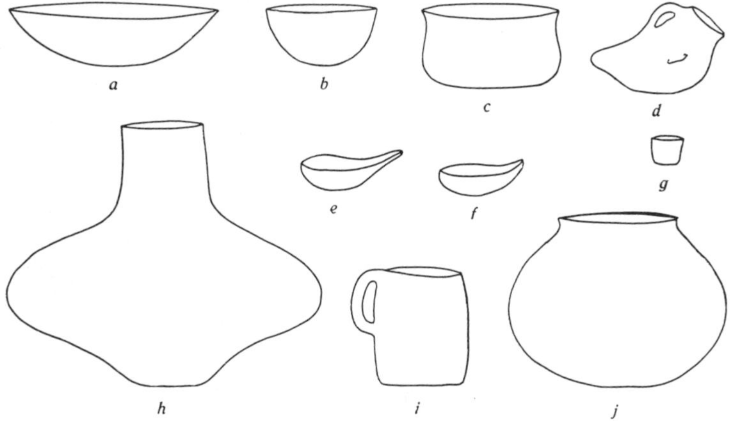


FIG. 26. Lower Gila vessel shapes.

The surface is very highly polished, smooth, even, and glossy (pl. 48, b).

Bowls are all straight rimmed; there is never any in- or out-curve, bevel, or thickening. The largest examples are shallow, with a flat base and flaring sides (fig. 26, a). From this they shade gradually off into smaller and relatively deeper types (pl. 48, b; fig. 26, b), and so pass into tiny handleless cups (fig. 26, g).

Cups and mugs (pl. 48, a; fig. 26, i) occur in great variety both of size and shape. Apart from the difference in color they are quite unlike the mug form of Mesa Verde black-on-white ware in that the handle never runs to the bottom of the side. Some of them are not over one and one-half inches high by two inches in diameter, and are shaped almost exactly like modern teacups. From this form they run up through larger replicas of the same to mugs (fig. 26, i), the biggest examples being ten inches to twelve inches high. None of them have constricted necks like the pitchers of other regions. The handles are heavy, being composed of a solid round bar of clay. They run from just below the rim to a point about halfway down the side. A few examples of the taller types are not provided with handles.

Dippers (fig. 26, e, f) are so called to distinguish them from the ladles of other regions, although they doubtless served the same functions. They have no true handles and are thus really bowls, modified by having part of one side somewhat elongated and bent outward and made into a sort of "tab" by which the piece can be lifted. A few of them distantly resemble the "half-gourd" ladle, but the shape of the majority is very distinctive. The inner surface of these dippers is almost always polished black. Bird- or foot-shaped pots are very common (fig. 26, d).

Ollas vary a great deal, but there seem to be two main types with a number of intermediate examples between them. The first may be called the "high-necked" olla (fig. 26, h). It has a rounded, sometimes recurved, underbody, a very wide and sharp shoulder, and a straight cylindrical neck, which is usually between one-third and one-half of the total height of the vessel. Most of these ollas are from fifteen to twenty inches high.

The second class, "round-bodied" ollas (fig. 26, j), are less uniform in shape, the variations being produced by the raising or lowering of the point of greatest diameter. In general these ollas are smaller than the "high-necked" variety, but in the Peabody Museum collection fragments are preserved of a vessel of this form which was apparently about six feet in circumference and two and a half feet high. Some modern storage jars reach proportions comparable to this, but I know of nothing in ancient pottery to approach it.

Polychrome redware is the typical pottery of the Lower Gila. The base clay and general technology are exactly the same as in the plain red, but the pieces are more carefully finished. The black firing clouds, which in the plain red seem not to have been guarded against, or perhaps even to have been intentionally produced for their decorative qualities, are rarely seen on the polychrome. The visible surfaces bear a clear red slip, well polished, and upon this are applied bands and other fields of white slip, upon which, in turn, are painted the decorations in black. The majority of designs are in black alone, but red is occasionally introduced to set off or complement some element of the main black device (pl. 49, c). It is never used, I think, in producing independent figures.

Polychrome bowls fall into two classes: (1) those with rounded sides (fig. 26, b); (2) those with sides more or less vertical, with outcurving (fig. 26, c) or straight lip. In both cases the whole interior is slipped with white, and the black, or black and red, design applied over it. The decoration usually takes the form of an "all-over" figure (pls. 48, d, e; 49, d, e); less commonly it is a band leaving a round empty space in the bottom. Bowls of Class 1 are plain red on the exterior. Class 2 bowls, however, bear an encircling band of white slip about the upper half or two thirds of the exterior, and this space is further elaborated with decoration in black, or black and red. The rims of both classes are generally left red, although in a few cases they are slipped with white (either wholly or in sections) and ticked with black.

Cups, mugs, dippers, and bird-shaped pots do not differ greatly in shape from the like forms in plain red ware described above. Polychrome dippers are much rarer than plain red ones, there being no perfect examples in the Pea-

Courtesy Peabody Museum

PLATE 48. Lower Gila pottery.

body Museum collection. All these pieces have decorated zones of white slip.

Ollas (pl. 48, f, g) are the handsomest examples of the polychrome technique. In shape they form a somewhat less sharply defined type than do the high-necked plain red ollas; the shoulder is rounder, the neck lower and less cylindrical, and the underbody is not so flat.

The bottom is uniformly red, and is cut off from the main decorative band by a broad black line, broken as a rule by an "exit space" (pl. 48, g). The two zones of ornamentation are, as usual, white with black, or black and red, figures. One encircles the body, another the neck. The two are almost always separated from each other by a band of red.

The decoration is usually in black, but, as was stated above, red counterelements are sometimes introduced. The designs are strictly geometric; life forms, either plant, animal, or symbolic are entirely wanting. While curvilinear elements are common (pls. 48, d, f; 49, b, c), angled patterns predominate, and chief among these are various modifications of the ubiquitous key figure (pls. 48, e, g; 49, e). Bands consist of a series of repeated units, often worked into a current design by means of decorative connections between the units; interlocking scrolls with toothed backs occur again and again (pl. 49, c). A characteristic feature of Lower Gila art is the use of small triangles set along lines or on the margins of painted areas to produce a sawtooth edge (pls. 48, e; 49, d).

In the case of bowl interiors where an all-over decoration is applied, it often takes the form of a dual balanced design in black or in black opposed to hatching (pls. 48, d, e; 49, d, e).

We now come to the red-on-gray pottery. Judging from the small number of whole pieces of this ware in the Peabody Museum collections, it might seem to have been rather uncommon, but an examination of the sherds from the ruins excavated shows that this was not the case. The base clay is reddish yellow, containing a moderate amount of tempering material, some of which is crushed quartz and some a substance which may be either ground-up potsherds or tiny bits of tufaceous rock. The visible surfaces are treated with a grayish or buff-colored slip so thin as to be almost a wash. In it can be made out small particles of mica. The surfaces are well smoothed but are never polished, the finishing was done with an implement that has left numerous faint scratches and striations in the slip. The rubbing stone was obviously never used.

The paint of the ornamentation is usually a sort of faded chocolate-red; it is dark crimson in certain examples that seem to have been particularly thoroughly fired. This pigment does not stand out sharply from the surface of the ware, but appears to have sunk into it, giving a flat, dull look to the designs. This is due, probably, both to the porosity of the ware and to the thinness and lack of body of the paint itself.

Little can be said of the shapes of red-on-gray pottery, as so few whole pieces are available. A sort of globular cup with a single handle seems to have been a common form, and small ollas with very flat bases also occur. There are sherds of bowls and larger ollas in the collection. The former were apparently dish-like, with flat bases and flaring sides (a type not seen elsewhere among ancient Southwestern pottery); the latter seem to have been more round in the body than polychrome or plain red examples. Scoops or dippers are not represented.

In decoration red-on-gray ware is strikingly different, not only from the polychrome of this region, but also from all other groups of pottery in the Southwest. The principal difference lies in the fact that the designs, instead of consisting of repetitions of bold geometric units, coherently arranged in bands, squares, or other definite zones and areas, are made up of series of tiny independent units, most of them evidently produced by a single stroke or "quirk" of the brush, and these are used as fillers of zones, or to give a sort of "texture" to the zone, rather than as elements of a coherent ornament. I give a selection of these little elements (fig. 27). All of them are seen again and again on the sherds, arranged in series of lines, horizontal, vertical, and oblique. There are simple dots and dashes, crosses, an infinite variety of squiggles of all sorts, little crude swastika-like figures, and, most singular of all, numerous

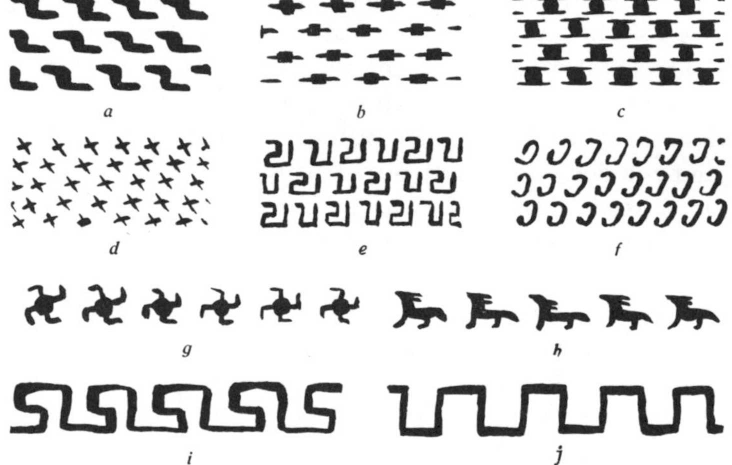


FIG. 27. Lower Gila red-on-gray designs.

sets of small animal-like things (fig. 27, h) that pursue each other around and around the sides of bowls, ollas, and globular cups.

All of these units are characterized by hasty, offhand brush work; they appear to have been scribbled on the pots with an eye more to general textural effect than to the achievement of true designs. They represent the impressionist school in ancient Southwestern art, and break very radically from the rigid formality that in general characterizes it.

The same dash and lack of convention characterize also

PLATE 49. Designs of Lower Gila polychrome ware.

a rarer category of red-on-gray designs, some examples of which are shown (fig. 27, i, j). These consist of meanders, current motifs, interlocking units, and waved and stepped lines. The circle and the spiral are of very common occurrence; but terraced elements in general and the key figure in particular seem to be entirely absent.

I have gone to this great length in considering the wares of the Lower Gila, because no adequate description of them has been published, nor are illustrations of representative pieces available in any book. The red-on-gray ware is especially interesting because, as was said above, it is so radically unlike the polychrome and, indeed, so unlike all other Southwestern pottery, that it gives rise to the suspicion that it may be the result of an intrusion from some hitherto unlocated centre; or may represent an early or a late period of local work. Careful excavation can be counted upon to clear up these points.

In the minor arts the people of the Lower Gila turned out a number of objects not made, or at least not commonly found, in other areas. Their stone axes, for example, are of a peculiar type, with straight back, and three-quarter groove; they are fashioned from hard black stone, and are beautifully shaped. Another peculiar class of objects are miniature effigies of frogs, birds. and animals cut from shell or from thin flakes of stone. Shell was much used for bracelets, finger rings, and pendants.[7] Flat, rectangular slate palettes with decorated borders are also found at Lower Gila sites; never, as far as I am aware, in other parts of the Southwest.

The Lower Gila culture had an extensive range. The easternmost ruin of which I have knowledge is in the Mimbres Valley, at Black Mountain near Deming, N. M.[8] The pottery of this site is typical of the Gila, as Fewkes

7. Axes are well illustrated by Fewkes (1912, pls. 49–56); effigies (ibid., pl. 75, b; and Moorehead, 1906, fig. 47); bracelets (Fewkes, 1912, fig. 48); rings (ibid., pl. 75, a, and fig. 49).

8. Fewkes, 1914, p. 13; and p. 294 above.

points out; but the building itself, as far as I could tell from surface indications, was a rectangular adobe structure made up of a double or triple tier of cell-like rooms surrounding a large plaza; I could not make out, nor does Fewkes mention, any large central "temple." Hence this ruin seems to be more like a pueblo than a true Gila compound. No red-on-gray ware appeared on the mounds, but I noticed a considerable admixture of sherds of Chihuahua (Casas Grandes) type.

Some seventy-five miles to the west, however, in the Pueblo Viejo Valley near Solomonsville, Arizona, on the Gila, there are evidently real compounds. The ruins mentioned here by Fewkes are large, are enclosed by walls, and contain great central structures; they produce typical Lower Gila polychrome ware, but seem to contain no red-on-gray. Both cremation and inhumation occur.[9] For the next seventy-five miles downstream we have no data for the Gila, but from a little east of Florence, Arizona, and thence almost if not quite to Gila Bend, the valley contains a considerable number of typical compounds, including the famous Casa Grande ruin itself. In the San Pedro Valley, which enters the Gila from the south between Solomonsville and Florence, are ruins apparently of compound type, and there are many others in the Santa Cruz drainings, notably near Tucson.[10] Lastly, the great group of ruins investigated by the Hemenway Expedition under Cushing lies in the valley of the Salt, fifteen to twenty miles above its junction with the Gila.[11]

The culture represented by these enormous adobe constructions, and by the easily recognizable types of pottery that seem always to accompany them, is a most interesting one, and it is a pity that we know so little in detail with regard to it. Fewkes's work at Casa Grande was hampered

9. Fewkes, 1904, pp. 168–87.

10. The Gila, San Pedro, and Santa Cruz sites are described by Fewkes, 1909a.

11. Baxter, 1888; Cushing, 1890.

by the necessity of repairing the buildings, so that he was unable to devote himself to the purely archaeological problems encountered; and Cushing's excavations were very inadequately published. The pressing need is for stratigraphic research, to determine whether or not there is any chronological distinction between the polychrome wares and the remarkable red-on-gray group. Reconnaissance should also be carried out in the Gila country, in order to ascertain if it was ever occupied by makers of black-on-white pottery. At present there is no evidence that this ware, so typical of the earlier phases of Southwestern development, occurs in the Lower Gila.

As to the age of the compounds we have some hints. We know that the characteristic polychrome pottery is later than that of the Mimbres (see p. 296), and we suspect the Mimbres wares to have been made in the middle Black-on-white times. Lower Gila polychrome vessels have been found in Little Colorado sites, as at Stone Axe ruin, where was also found buffware of probably late prehistoric date; but Tularosa type vessels also came from this ruin or group of ruins, as well as red vessels with white exterior decoration, which appear to be earlier than the buffware, so that it is uncertain just where the Gila pieces fit into the Little Colorado series.[12] Hodge, however, has discovered Gila ware at Hawikuh, in the Zuñi country, in association with pottery of his Class C, a fairly late prehistoric ware (see p. 272).

The chronological relation between the Lower Gila and the Chihuahua (Casas Grandes) culture is clear enough. Their contemporaneity is established by many cross-finds of pottery,[13] and by the mixture of the characteristic wares of the two cultures at several sites in southern New Mexico, for example, at the Black Mountain ruin.

While neither the Lower Gila nor the Chihuahua

12. Hough, 1903, pls. 57–64.
13. Kidder, 1916, p. 267.

cultures can yet be positively correlated in time with any of the groups we have previously considered, I feel sure that they were in their prime toward the end of the prehistoric period, perhaps at about Glaze 1 times in the Rio Grande, and after most if not all of the pure Black-on-white cultures had passed away.

Belonging geographically to the Gila drainage are the many ruins of pueblos, cliff houses, and caveate lodges that occur in the Verde Valley. I have never had the opportunity of visiting these sites, and the descriptions given by Mindeleff and Fewkes[14] are derived almost exclusively from surface observations. For this reason they contain so little information as to the details of Verde archaeology (the pottery, for example, is nowhere properly described) that it seems wiser not to attempt to classify these sites at present. The pottery, according to Fewkes,[15] is principally black-on-white and corrugated. This would appear to indicate early occupancy and northern, possibly Kayenta, affinities.

## BIBLIOGRAPHY OF THE LOWER GILA[16]

Bartlett, 1854, vol. 2, pp. 272–77.
Burr, 1880.
Baxter, 1888.
Cushing, 1890.*
Bandelier, 1892, chaps. 10, 11.*
Fewkes, 1892; 1904, pp. 168–92; 1909a*; 1912.*
Hodge, 1893.
Matthews, 1894.
Mindeleff, 1896a.*
Moorhead, 1898; 1906.
Patrick, 1903.
Huntington, 1914, chap. 7.

VERDE DISTRICT

Mearns, 1890.
Hall, 1895.
Mindeleff, 1896.*
Fewkes, 1896; 1898, pp. 536–76*; 1912a.
Spier, 1919.

* Major contribution.

14. Mindeleff, 1896; Fewkes, 1898, pp. 536–76.
15. 1898, p. 70.
16. For early accounts of Casa Grande, see Fewkes, 1912, pp. 53–81.

# The Chihuahua Basin

This, the last great area of specialization definitely associable with the Southwestern culture, lies in the northern part of the Mexican state of Chihuahua (fig. 11, p. 163). Bounded on the west by the high chain of the Sierra Madre, and on the east by lower mountain ranges, is a long, wide valley. The waters which drain into it from the Sierra Madre have no outlet to the sea, but flow into a series of salt lakes, such as the Lago de Guzman and the Lago de Santa Maria; the Mimbres also, geographically speaking, empties into this basin; but actually goes dry far to the north of it. The eastern and northeastern part of the plateau is largely desert, but its southern and western slopes are beautiful rolling uplands, covered with long grass, well watered, and forming one of the finest cattle ranges to be found anywhere.

The archaeological remains are situated for the most part in the western side of the basin. They consist of mound ruins and cliff houses. The mound ruins extend from about the American border to an undetermined distance southward. The majority of them have become reduced to low, inconspicuous piles of adobe, and only one survived into the last century in anything approaching a good state of preservation. This ruin is the so-called Casas Grandes group, which lies on the Casas Grandes River, a southern tributary of the Ascension.[1] Although Casas Grandes was in fair condition when it was examined by Bartlett in the early 1850's, as well as when Bandelier saw it some thirty-five years later, it has recently been so badly destroyed

1. There is a confusing similarity in the names of the principal ruin groups of the Lower Gila and Chihuahua areas. Casa Grande is the Lower Gila ruin, Casas Grandes the Chihuahua site.

that when I visited it in 1922 only a few fragments of wall remained standing. The outlines, however, of the structures described by the earlier writers could still be made out, and the ground plans of certain rooms were plainly discernible.

Casas Grandes was a massive adobe building standing to a height of at least three stories. The walls were built of puddled adobe blocks cast in place in movable frames by the same method that was employed at Casa Grande on the Gila. The rooms were large and rectangular, and were grouped together to form a great central structure with lower buildings about it. Were it not for the absence of a surrounding wall, the ruin would closely resemble a Lower Gila compound.

The other mound sites in the Chihuahua basin are, as was said above, so reduced by decay that little can be learned from a surface examination of them, and none have so far been thoroughly excavated. From Lumholtz's descriptions, however, and from the few observations I was able to make on the sides of pothunters' diggings, it appears that the buildings which once occupied these sites were much less massive and less extensive than Casas Grandes. The walls of all of them are of adobe, but they are generally not more than a foot in thickness, as against three or four feet in some of the Casas Grandes walls. The rooms, too, are smaller, and seem to have been built in rows about square or rectangular courtyards, thus approximating the pueblo arrangement.

It would seem, then, that the practice of "great house" building was less developed in the Chihuahua basin than on the Lower Gila, and that Casas Grandes was an exceptional rather than a typical structure.[2] That it was at least approximately contemporaneous with the smaller settlements is proved by the fact that the pottery from

2. Blackiston, however, mentions some larger ruins which may possibly have been great houses (1906b).

Casas Grandes and from the small sites is about the same. I say "about" advisedly, for there do appear to be slight differences in wares from Casas Grandes and from some of the less conspicuous sites, and in one mound near Corralitos I found evidence in an old pothunter's hole, of a cruder style underlying the later and finer wares of the upper levels. The data, however, are insufficient.

The burial customs of this region were apparently very uniform. Cremation was not practiced. The bodies were flexed tightly and disposed of in holes under the hard adobe floors of the rooms, usually in the corners and often four or five together. With the dead were placed offerings of shell and turquoise beads, as well as the beautiful pottery vessels that have caused the mounds to be so thoroughly ransacked.

Chihuahua pottery or, as it is more commonly called, Casas Grandes pottery, is represented by large collections in several museums, but unfortunately it is mostly unlocated, as the bulk of it was dug by Mexican peons and sold to traders and ranchers. It is very fine, harmonious in color, and in accuracy of line work is not surpassed by any other class of Southwestern ceramics. There are five styles: rough darkware, corrugated ware, polished blackware, redware, and polychrome painted ware.

Of the rough darkware only sherds are known. They indicate olla-shaped vessels of considerable size. Corrugated ware also is only represented by fragments. The bulk of the pieces are of reddish paste, poorly coiled and with the indentations wiped over and nearly obliterated while the clay was still soft.[3] Polished blackware occurs in the form of bowls and small jars. It is excellently made and the glossy black surfaces are as fine as those of the best old Santa Clara pieces. Redware was used for a great variety of

3. Corrugated is not mentioned in my paper on Casas Grandes pottery (Kidder, 1916), as no specimens were in the collections then available for study.

vessels, such as little bowls, medium-sized jars, and many odd-shaped pieces. The redware is occasionally painted with large fret designs in black, but is more commonly decorated by incision, gouging, scraping, or some other sort of surface texturing.[4]

The typical Casas Grandes pottery is the polychrome painted ware. It is a warm yellow color with decoration in black and red. The standard form is the jar (pl. 50), a gracefully shaped vessel seven or eight inches high. There are also many effigy pots made by adding animal, bird, or human heads to the sides and rims of jars (pl. 50, nos. 5, 7, 8, 9); and a few effigies of more realistic type.[5]

While the decoration is elaborate, only a few design elements are used, and of these a considerable number are non-Southwestern in appearance. The ubiquitous key-figure, however, is present, as well as the triangle and the scroll (pl. 50). "Negative," or background, drawing is much used to produce life designs such as birds and human figures. Altogether, Casas Grandes decoration is less Puebloan than is any other class with which we have had to deal. It has obviously assimilated a number of Mexican elements, but its basic structure is nevertheless Southwestern.

Aside from the pottery we have little knowledge of the minor arts of the builders of the adobe mound ruins. They produced large quantities of fine shell beads and bracelets, but did not apparently make the little shell and stone carvings that were turned out so commonly on the Lower Gila. The metate, according to Lumholtz,[6] was provided with four legs, thus differing from all other Southwestern metates and recalling the Mexican type. The stone axe is common, and is beautifully made. It has the same

4. For illustrations of the above wares, see Kidder, 1916.

5. See Kidder, 1916, pl. 3; and Lumholtz, 1902, p. 89.

6. Lumholtz, 1902, vol. 1, p. 88; Bartlett illustrates one (1854, vol. 1, p. 362).

Courtesy Peabody Museum

PLATE 50. Pottery of the Chihuahua basin.

straight back and three-quarter groove possessed by Lower Gila axes. This kind of axe is not found elsewhere in the Pueblo region, except sporadically on the Little Colorado, where its presence is probably to be ascribed to Gila influence.

As to the range of the Chihuahua basin culture we have no precise information. It extended northward to the American border and perhaps even a short way into New Mexico. On the west it only here and there managed to work through the barrier of the Sierra Madre into Sonora.[7] For the east we have no data at all, and for the south little more, although Hewett states that there are no "pueblos" south of the Babicora plains.[8]

Something may be gleaned as to the exterior relationships of the culture. In architecture it is surely allied to the civilization of the Lower Gila, and that the two were at least approximately contemporaneous is proved by cross-finds of traded pottery. It is connected in some way with the Mimbres, as is shown by similarities in design elements, and the use of negative painting; but the finds at the Duck Creek ruin (see pp. 294–95) seem to show that the Mimbres culture was the older. There is need for much more work in this most interesting area: first, reconnaissance to determine the range of the sites; secondly, excavation to find out whether or not there is evidence of a succession of types in the district; and thirdly, analytical studies of the remains, to enable us to ascertain which elements are Southwestern and which are Mexican.

Another important question that should be investigated is the relation between the cliff houses that occur in the Sierra Madre west and southwest of Casas Grandes, and the mound ruins of the open country. These houses are built in caves, are constructed of adobe, and bear a super-

7. What appears to be Chihuahua-type pottery is described by Bandelier from Huachinera (1892, p. 517).

8. Hewett, 1908, p. 76.

ficial likeness to the cliff dwellings of the north. At present we have no idea whether they are earlier or later than the mound ruins; or, indeed, whether they were made by the same people at all. Of their pottery we know nothing, but Blackiston states that it is different from that of Casas Grandes.[9]

## BIBLIOGRAPHY OF THE CHIHUAHUA BASIN

Bartlett, 1854, vol. 2, chap. 35.
Bandelier, 1892, chap. 14.*
Lumholtz, 1891; 1891a; 1902, vol. 1.*
Saville, 1894.
Hewett, 1908, chap. 8.
Blackiston, 1905; 1906; 1906a; 1906b; 1908; 1909.
Kidder, 1916.

* Major contribution.

9. Blackiston, 1905, p. 361. The cliff houses are described in that paper; also in Lumholtz, 1902, vol. 1, chap. 5; and in Blackiston, 1906, 1909.

# Conclusions

The data, so far as we can summarize them at present, are now before us. It remains to combine them into some sort of coherent whole. This can best be done in the form of an historical reconstruction, but it must be remembered that such a reconstruction is merely a working hypothesis, designed to correlate our information, and to indicate more clearly the needs of future study. We must have no hesitation in abandoning our conclusions, partly or *in toto,* if contradictory evidence appears.

To begin with, it is safe enough to postulate the former presence in the Southwest of a more or less nomadic people, thinly scattered over the country, ignorant of agriculture and of pottery-making. Their life must have resembled closely that of the modern Digger tribes of the Plateau; that is to say, they dwelt in more or less makeshift houses, and subsisted principally on small game: rabbits, prairie dogs, and doves; and on such wild vegetable products as grass seeds, berries, and roots. As to their language, it is less safe to speculate; but from the fact that peoples of Uto-Aztecan speech seem to have formed the basic population of the highlands from Montana far south into Mexico, it is quite likely that they belonged to that group.[1] Whoever they were, there could not have been many of them, for the natural food resources of the Southwest were probably, even in those ancient times, not sufficient to support more than a very small population. Remains of these aborigines have not yet been discovered, nor will they be easy to distinguish from those of such modern nomads as the Apache and Paiute, unless they are found buried below the relics of later cultures.

1. See Goddard, 1920.

These supposedly original Southwesterners eventually acquired the knowledge of corn-growing; they took up farming in a more or less haphazard way, but its practice did not at first react very strongly upon their way of life; for the Basket Makers, as we call the earliest agriculturists, apparently had no permanent houses, nor did they make pottery. As to the date of the introduction of corn we are still ignorant, but it is possible to make certain deductions.

Corn was originally brought under cultivation in the highlands of Mexico or Central America. This general locality is indicated by the identification of the probable wild ancestor of corn, a heavy-seeded grass which grows only in that region.[2] How long ago Mexican agriculture began is unknown; the remains indeed, of the first farmers, the Mexican Basket Makers so to speak, still await discovery. Corn, however, is a very highly specialized cereal, a fact which would seem to indicate great antiquity. Be that as it may, corn-growing was without any question the factor which made possible the development of all the higher American civilizations, and so the discovery of agriculture must have long antedated their rise. Now the Maya, apparently the oldest and certainly the most brilliant of these civilizations, was at its zenith during the sixth century of the Christian era; and its complex calendar system, which we must suppose to have taken several centuries to develop, had undoubtedly been perfected by the year 1 A.D.[3] It is, therefore, not rash to guess that the Maya began to differentiate themselves from the other archaic corn-growing peoples as long ago as 1000 B.C. Judging by the rate of progress made by nascent civilizations elsewhere in the world, it seems safe to allow at least two thousand years more for the period that elapsed be-

2. Harshberger, 1893.

3. Since the above was written Spinden has announced in the press the discovery that the Maya calendar was in use as early as the seventh century before Christ.

tween the time of the first cultivation of corn (say at about 3000 B.C.) and the beginnings of the Maya culture.[4] During these two millenniums we must allow for the early, localized practice of agriculture in the highlands; and the subsequent very extensive diffusion of the primitive corn-growing, pottery-making complex known as the Archaic Mexican culture.[5]

All this somewhat speculative time reckoning does not help us directly in our attempt to arrive at an approximate date for the introduction of farming in the Southwest, and the consequent springing up there of the Basket Maker culture; but it does give us a certain sense of perspective, and makes it seem quite possible that the Basket Makers as we know them lived as long ago as fifteen hundred or two thousand years before Christ. I believe, indeed, because of the simple and undifferentiated nature of Basket Maker corn, that the practice of corn-growing may have spread into the Southwest in the pre-Archaic period of Mexico, and that the influence of the developed Archaic is perhaps to be seen in the pottery and crude figurines of the post-Basket Makers.

There is still another set of considerations which bear on the question of chronology, namely, the problem of whether the entire development of the Pueblo civilization was an autochthonous one, or whether it consisted of a series of cultural leaps stimulated from without. If the second supposition be true, the post-Basket Maker stage might have grown up elsewhere and imposed itself directly on the antecedent Basket Maker, the pre-Pueblo on the post-Basket Maker, and the true Pueblo on the pre-Pueblo. Such a process would not necessarily have required a great stretch of time, for the long developmental stages of each culture might have taken place in other areas.

When our knowledge of Southwestern archaeology was

4. In this connection see Wissler, 1919, p. viii.

5. For a valuable discussion of the Archaic, see Spinden, 1922, chap. 1.

less full than it is today, transition stages between the main periods were not recognizable, and a theory of development by jumps or influxes seemed necessary to account for the observed facts. Now that transitions are beginning to be found, it is becoming increasingly evident that the Southwest owes to outside sources little more than the germs of its culture, and that its development from those germs has been a local and almost wholly an independent one. This being the case, the time required must have been long, and the postulated date of Basket Maker origin of 1500 to 2000 B.C. does not seem at all improbable.

At some early time, then, the Southwestern nomads took up the practice of corn-growing; but at first their agriculture sat lightly upon them; their crops were not of sufficient importance, nor had their methods of cultivation become intensive enough, to tie them very closely to their fields. Eventually, however, better care brought fuller harvests, and it became necessary to provide storage places for the garnered grain. Where caves were available they were used, holes being dug in the floors for caches. The population undoubtedly increased, and the leisure acquired from the possession of surplus foodstuffs, and the consequent partial release from the exacting requirements of the chase, allowed the people to work at, and to perfect, their arts, and to lavish time upon elaborate sandal weaves, fine basketry, and carefully made implements. But they were as yet ignorant of pottery.

Such were the Basket Makers. Their range is known to have covered south-central and southeastern Utah and northeastern Arizona (fig. 28); but from the fact that the knowledge of agriculture and the seeds of corn reached them from the south, it is probable that tribes of similar culture occupied parts of New Mexico and southern Arizona, and stretched southward well into Mexico. It seems likely, however, that Basket Maker culture reached its highest and most characteristic development in the San

Juan, for the cultures which appear to have developed from it, and which ultimately spread out and gave rise to the later Pueblo civilization, had their origin, as will be shown presently, in that country.

In the course of time the Basket Makers, becoming more

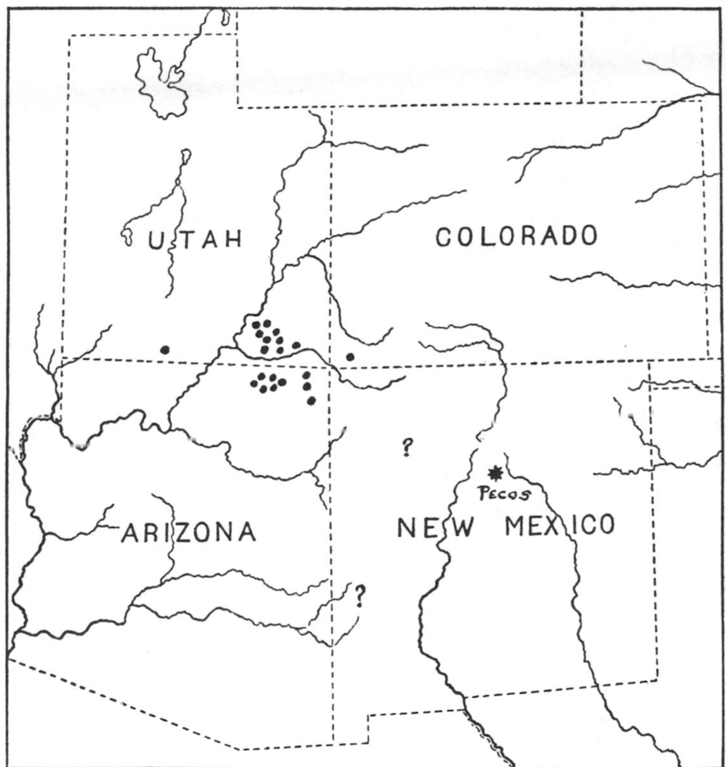


FIG. 28. Distribution of Basket Maker sites as known at the present time.

and more dependent upon their crops, and correspondingly more sedentary in habit, either discovered for themselves, or (more probably) learned from tribes to the south, that vessels fashioned from clay, dried in the sun, and finally fired, were easier to make, and more suitable for holding water and for cooking, than the baskets that had hitherto served these purposes. At about the same period they began to enlarge their storage cists into dwellings, to wall them higher with slabs, and to provide them with pole-and-brush roofs. These two great advances mark the opening of the post-Basket Maker period. That its culture

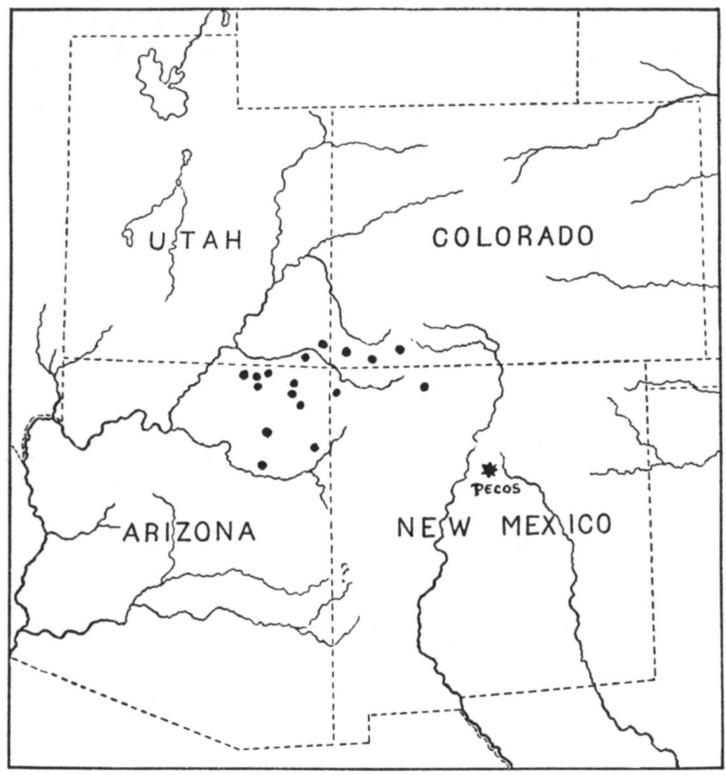


FIG. 29. Distribution of post-Basket Maker sites as known at the present time.

was merely a developed phase of the Basket Maker there can be little doubt, the headform of the people remained the same, several old Basket Maker arts, such as twined-woven bag making, held on in degenerate form, and the territory occupied includes most of the known Basket Maker country. Post-Basket Maker remains occur throughout the whole San Juan drainage and also appear in the northern parts of the Little Colorado watershed (fig. 29).

Guernsey has found indications that the pottery of certain post-Basket Maker sites is much cruder than that of others, and Morris's Long Hollow settlements with their well-decorated black-on-white ware would seem to represent a late phase of the culture little inferior to the pre-Pueblo.[6] Thus we have a hint that the post-Basket Maker period was a long one, during which a steady evolution in all the arts went on.

There now comes one of the apparent breaks in continuity which formerly made it seem that Southwestern growth must have advanced in leaps stimulated from without the area. To be explicit: the pre-Pueblo, the next stage of which we have knowledge, shows a population with an entirely different headform. Furthermore, the houses began to be grouped into more or less compact communities.

It must be remembered that pre-Pueblo remains were known long before the discovery of the post-Basket Maker stage, and the gap between pre-Pueblo and Basket Maker was accordingly so very wide that it was hard to see any relationship between the two. With the post-Basket Maker culture now becoming understood, however, the break is being narrowed; we have the post-Basket Maker slab-walled house standing between the Basket Maker cist and the pre-Pueblo dwelling, and the crude and advanced styles of post-Basket Maker pottery to indicate a local growth in that art. The new and so far unexplained elements in the pre-Pueblo complex are the presence of the bow and arrow, the use of cotton, and particularly the practice of skull deformation.

The skulls of the Basket Makers and post-Basket Makers are dolichocephalic and undeformed; those of the pre-Pueblo are, as far as we know, always artificially flattened

6. Morris, 1919, p. 194, and review of same by Kidder and Guernsey (1920).

posteriorly (pl. 33). This flattening renders it difficult to tell what the natural form of the head might have been, and it is possible that the mere introduction of hard-bedded cradles (a not very radical cultural change) might have caused this effect, and that the pre-Pueblos were really as long-headed as their predecessors. My feeling is, however, that the pre-Pueblo were actually of a different physical type, naturally brachycephalic, and that their broad-headedness was merely accentuated by deformation.[7]

It seems, therefore, that we must recognize the arrival in the Southwest of a new race, which eventually became the preponderating one, to the submergence of the old dolichocephalic strain. But (and this point deserves emphasis) the new people, if such they were, introduced no new cultural elements except cotton and perhaps the bow and arrow. The really vital traits, agriculture, pottery, and semipermanent houses, were already in the possession of the post-Basket Makers. The broad-heads, then, merely took over the old way of life and added certain improvements; but in general carried it on in a perfectly normal course of development.

The pre-Pueblo period saw some increase in the agricultural population of the Southwest and a considerable enlargement in the territory occupied. Pre-Pueblo sites are found throughout the entire San Juan country, as well as in parts of the Rio Grande, the Little Colorado, and the Upper Gila (fig. 30). Wherever this culture penetrated it resulted in the introduction of more or less permanent settlements and in the manufacture of black-on-white and neck-coiled pottery. It is probable that as the houses became more solidly built, more drawn together, and more commonly above ground, there was evolved a rudimentary type of kiva, a ceremonial survival of the subterranean and

7. For a discussion of the relation between skull deformation and head-form, see Hooton, Peabody Museum Papers, vol. 8, no. 1, pp. 85–89.

semisubterranean dwellings of former days. Such rooms have been found in association with pre-Pueblo ruins in northeastern Arizona and southwestern Colorado,[8] both sites in the San Juan drainage. The San Juan, indeed, appears to have been the breeding ground and place of

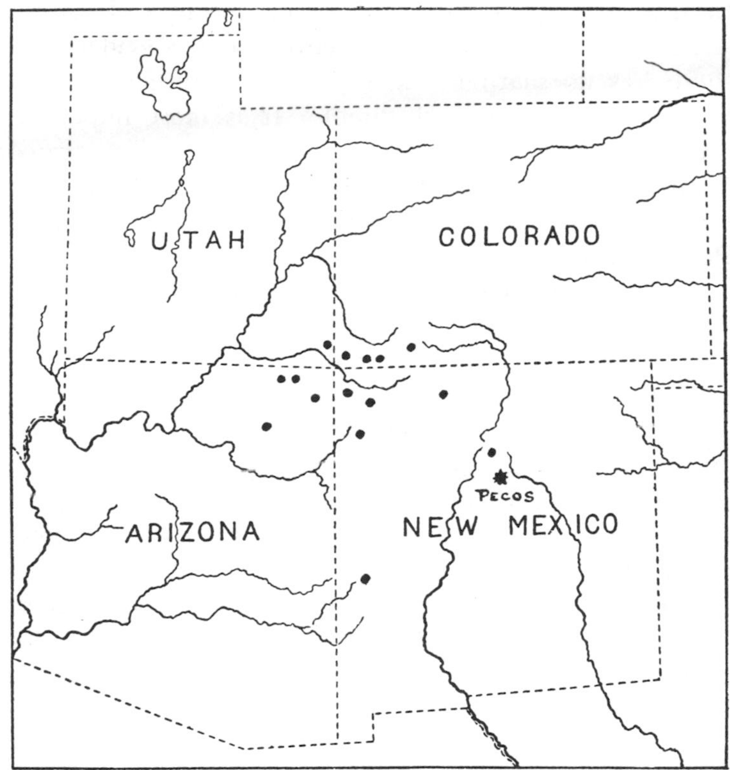


FIG. 30. Distribution of pre-Pueblo sites as known at the present time.

dissemination of all the traits typical of the pre-Pueblo culture, for it is there that the remains are most abundant and most highly specialized; and as one goes out from the San Juan one seems to find the pre-Pueblo culture considerably less advanced.

8. Kidder-Guernsey, 1919, p. 43; Morris, 1919, p. 186.

At the present time we possess enough data as to pre-Pueblo ruins to enable us to characterize them fairly accurately. We also have abundant data as to the developed Pueblo culture. But the small pueblo-like ruins that presumably were built during the transition period between the two are, as Morris observes,[9] practically unknown. I use the term "transition" advisedly, for it is evident that there was no sharp break, either in culture or in race between pre-Pueblo and Pueblo. It is most important, then, that these small ruins be sought out and excavated, because in them we should find the germs of all the traits that were later developed and combined to form the classic Pueblo culture.

Lacking these data, we are forced to proceed with our reconstruction on the basis of very scanty information. All we know is that scattered over almost the entire Southwest are little ruins built of horizontally coursed masonry, or of adobe, with closely grouped rectangular rooms and containing corrugated and black-on-white pottery. All such sites I class together as belonging to the early Pueblo period, for wherever they are even cursorily investigated they prove to have antedated the larger pueblos. The limits of their enormous range (fig. 31) extend from southern Nevada east and north to Great Salt Lake in Utah, east again to Colorado, down the edge of the Rockies to the headwaters of the Rio Grande, east again around the southern end of the Rockies practically to the Texas border, thence southwest across New Mexico to the neighborhood of El Paso, along the southern border of New Mexico, south of the headwaters of the Gila and Salt, along the southern base of the Mogollons, thence across to the edge of the western Arizona desert and so northwest to southern Nevada. The only parts of the Southwest in which so far no remains of the small-house, black-on-white

9. Morris, 1921.

pottery people of the early Pueblo period have been found, are the Lower Gila and the Chihuahua basin.

Thus it appears that the early Pueblo culture spread far and wide over country which had not previously been occupied by pre-Pueblos. I speak of it with considerable confidence as a spreading, for it is virtually out of the question that so uniform a culture could have sprung up simultaneously and independently in several districts. We must, therefore, search, for the point of origin, and all the information we now have points toward the San Juan drainage.

It may, of course, be due to the fact that the San Juan has been more thoroughly worked than other areas, but it is nevertheless very suggestive, that the most abundant and most highly developed exemplifications of the early cultures (the Basket Maker, post-Basket Maker, and pre-Pueblo) have been found in or near that country. And when we consider the early Pueblo remains we seem to see the same state of affairs. Early Pueblo ruins are very abundant in the San Juan, and they possess the traits most characteristic of Pueblo culture in greater perfection than do the early ruins in any other area. To be explicit: corrugated ware is at this period of marked excellence in the San Juan, and becomes progressively cruder as we proceed outward; the same is true, though perhaps to a less extent, in the case of black-on-white; the kiva also reaches an early high specialization in the San Juan, and becomes less common and less specialized the further away we get. As to other architectural traits we cannot yet speak, our data being still too scanty, but as will be shown in the consideration of a later period, the typical pueblo style of building also seems to have worked outward from the San Juan.

Somewhere, then, in the San Juan, probably in the northern tributaries, the pre-Puebloans had begun to build their houses of horizontally coursed masonry and to work their rooms into rectangular form. In so doing they were faced by the necessity of keeping certain round chambers, already used for ceremonies, separate from the house clusters. These took on more and more the aspect of places apart, became specialized in construction and in function, and so finally developed into what we call kivas. At the same time the methods of pottery-making were improved; the neck coils of the pre-Pueblo water jars and cooking pots were found to be pleasing, and possibly also of practical value in increasing evaporation or the conduction of heat; they were accordingly extended to cover the entire bodies of the vessels. Black-on-white decoration became more varied. The above improvements in architecture and ceramics were taken over by neighboring groups, and having, so to speak, a head start over most of pre-Pueblo culture, did not encounter the resistance of competition by other localized improvements. They accordingly spread very easily. How rapidly they spread we have at present no means of knowing, but from the fact that great territorial expansion involved very little change, it would seem that the process must have been a relatively quick one.[10] At all events the early Pueblo culture ultimately diffused itself well beyond the former range of the pre-Pueblo, and became planted, as has been said, in territory not hitherto occupied by sedentary peoples. I think that this was not due to actual migration, but rather to a taking over of the culture by tribes who were already semi-agricultural, and therefore ready to embrace the manifest advantages of the new form of life. A certain increase in population, however, must have been brought about by the greater ease of existence and security of food supply; and this increase would naturally have been most rapid at the original point of diffusion, and so would have caused more or less outward pressure therefrom.

10. A parallel phenomenon is seen in the wide and uniform extension of the Archaic culture in middle America (see Spinden, 1922, chap. 1).

I have tentatively located the center of diffusion in the San Juan, and believe that because of the early advantage thus gained by the inhabitants of the San Juan, they continued for a long time to be the leaders in the development of Southwestern culture. They seem to have evolved, late in this period, the unit-type dwelling, a compact and eminently practical home for a small farming community, and one which, as Prudden originally suggested, appears to have had a very important influence on the form of all later pueblo structures.

In assigning all small ruins containing true corrugated ware and more or less unspecialized black-on-white pottery to the early Pueblo period, I may of course be in error, it is wholly possible that some of the examples in the outlying regions may be peripheral survivals into much later times; but, as will be shown presently, the forces that tended to break up this early widespread population, and to concentrate it into more compact groups, would have been particularly unfavorable for the persistence of small isolated settlements along the borders.

The small sites show, as a general rule, little provision for defense against enemies. The villages are seldom large, nor do they often occupy protective sites. Gradually, however, we begin to see the working of the forces mentioned in the last paragraph which were ultimately to bring about the concentrations typical of the later prehistoric and the historic Pueblo periods. To what this integration may have been due cannot be stated definitely, but I am inclined to see in it the result of hostile pressure from without rather than the effect of climatic change. To begin with, many of the districts which were shortly to be abandoned are still among the most favorable as to water supply in the entire Southwest; secondly, many peripheral ruins (as in western Utah and eastern New Mexico) were seemingly deserted at an early time; lastly, the more recent villages are larger, and stronger, and occupy more easily defensible sites, than the older ones.

From the very beginning of agricultural life in the Southwest there must have been strife between the farmers and the hunting tribes. Even the Basket Makers probably had their difficulties with wilder neighbors. But, as has been said before, the Southwest is a land too poor in game to have supported a large nonagricultural population, and the first sedentary people presumably had few foes to trouble them. As the early Pueblos, however, increased in prosperity, and began to extend their sphere of influence outward from the point of origin, they presumably came in contact with the more powerful hunting tribes of the Great Plains, of the Rocky Mountains, and of the northern Plateau. Attacks by these hunters brought the latter rich stores of garnered corn, and they soon came to realize that by raiding the practically defenseless small towns they could supplement their food supply and so maintain themselves in territory not hitherto open to them because of lack of game.

It is not necessary to postulate any great incursion of nomads. A few bands working in here and there and adopting a semiparasitic existence might well have been sufficient to bring about the observed results. But when such a process was started, even in a small way, it must have had the most far-reaching consequences. The parasite ultimately destroys its host, and is then forced to seek new prey; and the nomad once blooded, so to speak, by the sack of frontier settlements, had to push farther in to gratify his new tastes. Ruined farmers, too, their crops destroyed or stolen, might themselves have turned hunter-raiders and so increased the inward pressure. Wars between village and village, or between stock and stock, may also have occurred, but as yet we have little evidence of such feuds.

There is reason to believe that the region north of the

Colorado River was first given up, although some settlements evidently held out for a time along the Grand Canyon and in the Virgin Valley. In the northern San Juan the unit-type villages began to bunch together to form somewhat larger aggregations; the same thing appears to have gone on in the Mesa Verde country and south of the San Juan. In the Kayenta region there seems at first to have been less trouble. In the Rio Grande, the Little Colorado, and the Upper Gila and Salt there was also little or no change from the easy, small-village life of earlier times.

Until this stage the danger from the postulated nomads seems to have come from the north, and the outlying Pueblos were pushed in, or destroyed. Now, however, wild tribes appear to have infiltrated from all sides. They spread out over the San Juan basin, and carried their incursions well to the south. The result was that the small towns of the San Juan had to be abandoned; but instead of giving up the struggle, their inhabitants gathered together in large communities, and these large communities became more or less isolated from each other. Thus their enemies seem to have forced the Pueblos into that very form of life which, by fostering communal effort, was to permit them to attain their highest cultural achievements.

I stress here, as before, the influence of the nomadic enemy; for this appears to me best to explain the observed facts of Pueblo history. The same facts, however, may also be, and indeed have been, explained in accordance with the theory of a progressive desiccation of the Southwest.[11] During the discussion of the Chaco Canyon certain arguments opposed to the desiccation theory were presented, and these apply equally well to the situation in other parts of our area. Although the question is still an open one, the bulk of the evidence now available seems to me to indicate that as far back as the time of the Basket Makers

11. Hewett, Henderson, and Robbins, 1913; Huntington, 1914.

the climate was much the same as it is today; and that aridity, comparable to that of the present, has from the very beginning been one of the most vital factors in shaping Southwestern culture. I find it, therefore, hard to believe in a progressive drying up of the country during the period of its occupancy by man.

Whatever the causes may have been, whether aridity, the attacks of savage enemies, or a combination of the two; the Pueblos gave up great stretches of outlying territory, began to congregate into large communities, and entered that stage of their history which we may call the Great Period, or the Period of Specialization (see fig. 31).

In the San Juan it was indeed a Great Period, for it saw the building of the Chaco Canyon towns, the Mesa Verde cliff houses and canyon-head fortresses, as well as the imposing cliff dwellings of the Kayenta country. In the south, compact pueblos sprang up on the Rio Grande, on the Little Colorado, and even on the Upper Gila and Salt. Still further to the south in northern Chihuahua, and to the southwest on the Lower Gila, there were coming into being the great adobe "casas grandes." The archaeology of the latter regions is too little understood to permit much speculation as to the origin and growth of their cultures; but though their peculiar architecture has no recognized prototype in the Southwest, their pottery is definitely puebloan in style. My feeling is that these two related and contemporaneous civilizations were rather rapidly achieved results of an amalgamation of Mexican Indians, forced northward, with Pueblos forced or strayed south. At all events it is probable that the Chihuahua-Gila cultures were just beginning to get under way at the time that the maximum development was taking place in the Chaco and on the Mesa Verde.

The underlying causes for the Great Period are not hard to discern. Pressure of one sort or another had forced the Pueblos to draw together into large aggregations, where community of interest stimulated community of effort. The difficulties confronting them were sufficient to spur them to their best endeavors, but not great enough to stunt their progress. Life was not too easy, nor yet too hard. They

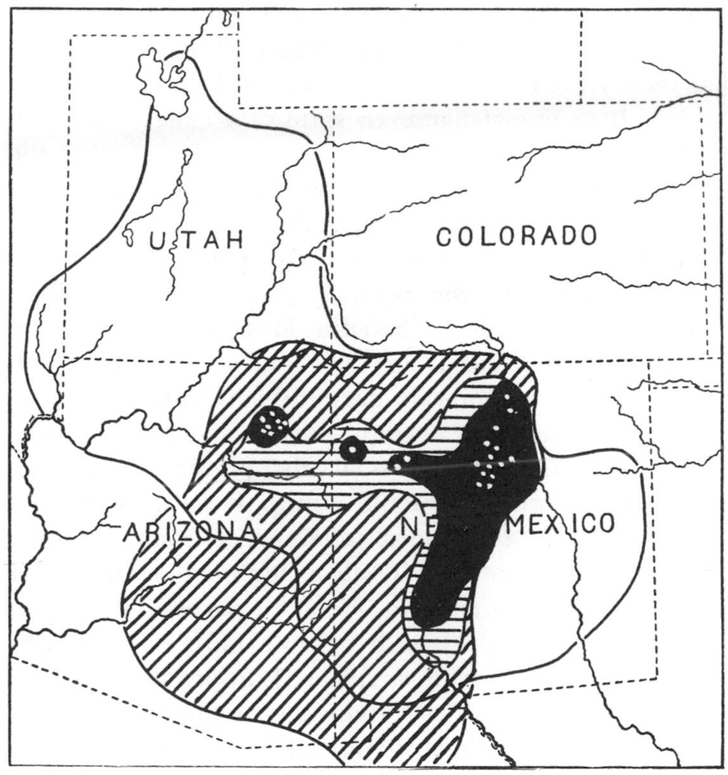


FIG. 31. Distribution of population during the various periods of Pueblo history. Early Period (unshaded). Great Period (oblique shading). Late Prehistoric Period (horizontal shading). Period of the Conquest (black). Present-day Pueblo villages (white dots).

had reached that vital moment in their history when opportunity and necessity were evenly balanced. And, as before, the San Juan was the seat of the highest development; the achievements of its people in architecture, in the arts, and probably also in social and religious organization, were obviously of great importance in determining the development of the peoples to the south of them. This is most clearly seen in the spread of the massed-terraced style of building which during the Great Period began to come into vogue in the Rio Grande and the Little Colorado.

It was fortunate for the persistence of Pueblo culture that these tendencies did work southward, for the time of the San Juan was at hand. In spite of all they could do, the people of this region were finally forced to give up the struggle; but that they made a hard fight of it is witnessed by the strongly fortified nature of the latest dwellings, and the protective sites chosen for them, particularly in the frontier districts of the north.[12] But eventually Chaco Canyon was abandoned; then the Mesa Verde; lastly the Kayenta plateau; and from that time on the San Juan ceased to play any significant part in Pueblo history.[13]

As to the date of the desertion of the San Juan we have no information; but from the fact that pottery of Toltecan type has been found at Pueblo Bonito, it would seem that these ruins must have been inhabited at some time between 800 and 1100 A.D.[14] Their abandonment can hardly have been much later than 1100, for, as will be shown below, a considerable length of time must have elasped between that event and the arrival of Europeans in 1540.

At the same time as the giving up of the San Juan, or shortly after, their inhabitants left the villages of the Upper Gila. At a somewhat later date the Lower Gila and Chihuahua basin settlements were abandoned. What caused this wholesale exodus of the Pueblos from their former homes we do not know. Many diverse factors

12. For example, the system of watchtowers evolved in the McElmo-Yellowjacket country (see Morley and Kidder, 1917, p. 43).

13. The occupation of the Gobernador-Largo district after the revolt of 1680 (see Kidder, 1920) and the possible use of Canyon de Chelley by the Hopi (see Fewkes, 1906) were merely temporary.

14. For a discussion of Toltecan dating, see Spinden, 1922, p. 155; the pottery mentioned above is referred to on p. 167.

doubtless operated; but from the fact that the process was merely a continuation of the concentration toward the geographical center of the Southwest which began at the close of the early Pueblo period, it seems likely that the same cause, pressure by nomads, was again responsible.[15] The result in deserted territory is obvious, but what the effect upon the actual size of Pueblo population may have been, is harder to gauge. There must have been a considerable shrinkage, but it is not likely that the entire population of the abandoned regions was riped out. Although I am disinclined to allow any great degree of historical accuracy to the Hopi and Zuñi clan migration stories, they do seem to indicate that both communities received increments of population from the north and the south. The best argument for a movement of people from the peripherae toward the center is provided by the marked increase in the number and size of pueblo ruins of relatively late date in and near that center. During the early Pueblo period and even in the Great Period that had just closed, the Rio Grande and the Little Colorado were not very densely populated. The towns of those times (i.e., the Black-on-white sites) were small when numerous, and few when they became larger; now, however, just as the northern and southern districts were being abandoned, villages became much more abundant and much greater in size. As examples of this we may name the great pueblos of the Rio Grande from Socorro to the headwaters of the Chama, and the many new towns that sprang up in the Zuñi country, along the Little Colorado, and about the Hopi mesas.

I think the connection between the two sets of phenomena, abandonment of the outlying districts and sudden increase in population in the central areas, cannot be mistaken. The puzzling thing about it is that the incoming people brought with them so little of their local cul-

15. This is also Nelson's opinion (1919, fig. 1.).

tures. No adobe "casas grandes" were built in the Little Colorado, no towns of the Mesa Verde or Chaco types were erected in the Rio Grande. The old styles of pottery became extinct, or were altered so rapidly and completely that the transitional stages have escaped identification. It would seem as if the transference of people must have been by small groups, rather than by whole communities, an infiltration rather than a migration. Each successive increment became amalgamated with the resident group that it joined, adopted the local culture, probably stimulated and strengthened it, possibly influenced it to a certain extent, but seldom, if ever, succeeded in changing it radically, or in turning its course of development sharply away from the channels in which it was already running.

As to the date of this era of redistribution we are as yet ignorant, but we must consider that it took place some centuries before 1540, because we have to allow time for the rise, development, and partial decline of the glazed pottery technique between the end of the Great Period and the coming of the Spaniards. It is reasonably certain that Glaze 1 of the Rio Grande series did not originate until after the abandonment of the Chaco ruins, for no Glaze 1 pottery, or its accompanying biscuit wares, have ever been found at a Chaco site; nor has any Chaco Black-on-white turned up in Glaze 1 Rio Grande settlements. As, however, the actual dating of many prehistoric ruins may be expected during the next few years, it is not necessary or even advisable at the present time to indulge in dating by guesswork.

When the redistribution had become well advanced, the entire Pueblo population was concentrated in the limits indicated on the map (see fig. 31). The shrinkage in territory held, and probably also to some extent in actual numerical strength, was not yet over, for many districts were abandoned between this time and the conquest. For example, a great number of large towns on the Chama and its tributaries, on the Pajarito plateau, and further south along the Rio Grande were certainly deserted before 1540. The same is true of many settlements in the Zuñi country, along the Little Colorado, and in the Hopi region. In this we seem to see merely a continuation of the pressure that had been felt ever since the early days of the true Pueblo period, rather than the working of new factors. The upshot of it was that in 1540 the entire population was gathered together in sixty or seventy towns, strung out along the Rio Grande from Socorro to Taos, and running westward in a narrow, interrupted line through Acoma and Zuñi to the Hopi villages. The still further shrinkage in the seventeenth and eighteenth centuries, the giving up of the Piro and Tano areas, and the concentration of many groups of other stocks into a smaller number of communities, are matters of documentary record. It should be noted that the extermination of the Piro was largely due to the persecution of the Apache.

To recapitulate, the Pueblo civilization owed its origin to stimuli from without, but once well on its feet it developed in its own peculiar way. It passed through an early phase of wide territorial expansion marked by great uniformity of culture. It then drew in upon itself and enjoyed a period of efflorescence characterized by strong specialization in its different branches. Finally it underwent great hardship, suffered a further diminution of territory, and in 1540 was waging a hard fight for mere existence.

Few races have gone as far toward civilization as did the Pueblos while still retaining the essential democracy of primitive life. Most other peoples, as they advanced from savagery, have first set up for themselves, and later fallen under the domination of, rulers temporal or religious; aristocracies or theocracies have sprung up, and the gap between the masses and the classes has become wider and wider. But among the Pueblos no such tendency ever made headway; there were neither very rich nor very poor, every family lived in the same sort of quarters, and ate the same sort of food, as every other family. Pre-eminence in social or religious life was to be gained solely by individual ability and was the reward of services rendered to the community.

In the sixteenth century the Pueblos had fallen upon hard times; they had been forced from many of their old ranges, were reduced in numbers, and had lost something of their former skill in material accomplishments. But their customs had not changed, and they still held out undismayed among their savage enemies. There can be little doubt that had they been allowed to work out their own salvation, they would eventually have overcome their difficulties, and might well have built up a civilization of a sort not yet attempted by any group of men. It is the tragedy of native American history that so much human effort has come to naught, and that so many hopeful experiments in life and in living were cut short by the devastating blight of the white man's arrival.

The sketch of Pueblo history which has just been presented is the merest outline. Great bodies of data have been lumped together, and no account has been taken of various complexities which are known to be present in some of the regions discussed. Many of the correlations made between one area and another are also unsatisfactorily vague, and some of them rest on the unreliable evidence of surface finds. Many corrections will have to be made, some of them, perhaps, fundamental. But whether or not our working hypothesis can stand the severe tests which we hope to apply to it in the future, it has shown how much still remains to be done. Nevertheless, we are far enough along in our studies to realize that the problems of any given district can be solved, and that accurate correlations between the different districts can eventually be made, so that in the end we shall surely be able to reconstruct with surprising fullness the history not only of the Pueblo culture in its perfected form, but also that of the early cultures from which it originated. The material is remarkably abundant, and, thanks to the dry climate of the Southwest, extraordinarily well preserved. I know of no other area in the Americas, with the possible exception of Peru, where all the steps in the development of a people from nomadic savagery to a comparatively high degree of civilization, can be traced so accurately and with such a wealth of detail.

When the long task is finished, we shall be able to tell a most interesting story, but the aim of our researchers is, or should be, a much broader one than that. We must use our results for the solution of those general problems of anthropological science without a true understanding of which we can never hope to arrive at valid conclusions as to the history of mankind as a whole.

Anthropologists, particularly those who have concerned themselves with the various manifestations of human culture, have reasoned very loosely, have been prone to draw inferences from fragmentary data, to evolve theories which fit well with preconceived ideas. In no science is the need for empirical study more keenly felt. We have had much writing upon culture growth, trait transmission, divergent and convergent evolution, the tendencies of primitive art, the influence of environment on culture, and the like. But when one examines these writings closely, one finds all too often that they are based on data insufficient in quantity or even historically incorrect.

The Southwest alone cannot, of course, give us final answers to any of these broader problems, for the Southwest was only occupied for a relatively short time by a single small branch of the human race. But as to that time, and as to that people, we can learn a great deal; and we shall have, for this area at least, full data which are also historically correct. As chronology is the basis of history, information bearing on the age of Southwestern remains is diligently to be sought for, and we must be constantly on the lookout for new methods of obtaining it.

One such new method is that of tree-ring study, devised by Professor A. E. Douglass of the University of Arizona, for determining the chronological sequence of ruins.[16] His system is based on the fact that in arid countries like the Southwest all vegetable life has a stern struggle for existence. When rainfall is adequate, growth is normal; but during the frequent dry years growth is checked in proportion to the severity of the drought. Douglass has shown that this irregularity of growth, conditioned by irregularity of rainfall, is clearly and accurately recorded in the width of the annual rings of trees. In a favorable year a broad, easily recognizable ring will be produced; in a bad year an equally characteristic narrow ring. Now let us suppose for example that six good years are followed by three rather poor ones, then by one very bad, one good, and one very good. A sequence such as this leaves a clear record in the rings added to a given tree during those years and one which is exceedingly unlikely ever to be exactly duplicated. Douglass has further proved that all, or practically all, the trees over a whole district will register in exactly the same way. He has also determined that the weather conditions which produced the observed variations in ring growth extended over very considerable areas, trees as much as two hundred miles apart often showing exactly parallel peculiarities of ring growth. To illustrate the application of this method, we will say that one examines and counts the rings in a section of a tree cut in 1922 in Flagstaff, Arizona, and finds that eighty-four rings (i.e., years) in from the bark there ended a peculiar sequence of exceptional years, producing a peculiar and easily recognizable sequence of rings. This sequence must therefore have ended in 1922 minus 84, or in other words

16. See Douglass, 1921, 1922, 1922a; Wissler, 1921.

in 1838. One now examines in section a log used, say, as a roofbeam in an old house in Santa Fe, New Mexico, and discovers that the same peculiar sequence of rings occurs twenty rings in from the bark; thus it is shown that the Santa Fe log was cut in 1838 plus 20, i.e., in 1858. Extending his investigations, Douglass has employed the same process for trees not actually datable, and has studied sections from the roof beams of prehistoric ruins. Through the cooperation of the American Museum of Natural History he was enabled to examine sections of beams from the great Aztec ruin, and recognized in each of them certain peculiar and characteristic groups of rings which allowed him to determine the relative dates of the cutting of the logs. To express these dates conveniently he assigned an arbitrary date, R.D. (Relative Date) 500 to a certain easily recognizable ring and expressed all dates with reference to that year. He found that most of the beams examined had been cut during two periods, namely, in R.D. 524–525, and in R.D. 528. The next series of beams to be examined came from Pueblo Bonito, some sixty-five miles to the south, and in these he recognized the same characteristic ring groups that he had found at Aztec. By counting from them he was able to determine that the Bonito logs had been cut between forty and fifty years earlier than those at Aztec (i.e., in about R.D. 484).

When it is remembered how much material in the way of roof beams, terracing logs, and other woodwork is still preserved in the ruins of the Southwest, it can readily be realized what vast possibilities have been opened up by Douglass's remarkable discovery; for example, we shall undoubtedly be able to make out the exact order of erection of many of the great Mesa Verde cliff houses, and even determine the relative date of building of parts of structures, such as single rooms, kivas, etc. The prospect is fairly dazzling.

In discussing the archaeological evidence, and in considering Douglass's method as well, we have confined ourselves to the relative dating of remains of man in the Southwest. It has been shown, I hope, that the outlook is bright, and that patient work will eventually enable us to arrange in approximately their proper order all the ruins that we know at the present time, or shall find in the future. We must not, however, allow ourselves to evade the issue of absolute chronology; for if we could apply dates, even if only approximate ones, to the main stages of Southwestern development, our historical perspective would not only be greatly sharpened, but we should also have acquired data of the utmost value for the solution of many of the broader problems of anthropology, such problems, for example, as those of the rate of acceleration in culture, the rapidity of the spread of culture traits, etc.

For arriving at the age of the basic stages of Southwestern culture, such as the Basket Maker, we have as yet no reliable evidence whatever. No way of applying geological methods to the problem has been discovered. Help might be derived from a correlation of the Basket Maker period with some stage in the history of Mexican culture, but the actual chronology of early Mexico is by no means clear.[17] We must for the present, therefore, be content to work back through the Pueblo and pre-Pueblo periods from our historic datum of 1540 A.D. Two lines of research seem promising: tree-ring studies, and correlation with the known chronology of the Maya area.

It has been shown above that the relative dating of prehistoric sites in the Southwest may be accomplished by Douglass's method of tree-ring study. This line of investigation has also been extended to include the great sequoias of the Pacific Coast. It has been found that in the annual rings of these exceedingly long-lived trees

17. If there is a single problem of outstanding importance for American archaeology, it is that of dating the origin of corn-growing and the rise of the Archaic culture in the highlands of Mexico.

there are preserved weather records, so to speak, reaching back for 3,000 years,[18] and it is possible that certain of the more marked peculiarities in tree-ring growth may be due to weather conditions so widespread as to have affected regions as far distant as the Southwest, and that beams used in prehistoric pueblos and cliff houses may yet be actually dated by comparing their rings with those of the sequoias.

Even should the sequoias fail us as a time index, the tree-ring method may yet, it seems to me, be used for ascertaining the actual date of many prehistoric ruins. For example, there are in the New Mexico mission churches many large beams which were cut in the early and middle parts of the seventeenth century; some of these bear carved dates, but all of them should be accurately datable by comparing their outer rings with the inner rings of the three and four hundred years old pines still growing today in the nearby mountains. We may next compare the inner rings of the mission beams with the outer rings of beams from such ruins as stratigraphic studies of the pottery show to have been inhabited during the later stages of prehistoric times. This process may be pursued indefinitely, and it is not beyond the bounds of possibility that we may eventually be able to establish reliable series of overlapping tree growths extending from the present day back to the time when the ancestors of the Pueblos first began to use large timbers in the construction of their houses.[19]

While Douglass's method gives us our best hope for absolute chronology, we must not fail to undertake a second line of investigation which, although it cannot provide us

18. Huntington, 1913.

19. There are few Southwestern ruins from which some beam material cannot be recovered by careful work. Professor Douglass informs me that he has secured useful data from badly decayed, and even from charred, logs. It is evident that no opportunity for the collection of such specimens should be overlooked.

with more than approximate dates, may still serve to throw light on the age of many Southwestern ruins, and act as a cross-check on such results as may be attained by the Douglass system. This second line of investigation must consist in an attempt to determine the time correlation between the ruins of the Southwest and those of the Maya culture of Central America. This may appear a far cry, but one bit of evidence is already at hand, and much more may confidently be expected.

The Maya people, as is well known, erected monuments bearing a wealth of contemporary dates which not only are decipherable, but have been correlated with considerable precision with the years of our own system of chronology.[20] This of course provides for students of Maya archaeology an excellent basis for working out the development of Maya pottery, lapidary work, etc. Hence it should eventually be possible to date with fair accuracy any given Maya pot, jade ornament, or other specimen. Aboriginal trade having been surprisingly active and far-reaching, it is reasonable to suppose that datable Maya objects will be found in, say, central Mexican sites. A few such finds would fix the approximate date of those sites beyond reasonable doubt. Objects characteristic of the thus datable central Mexican cultures may be expected from northern Mexico, northern Mexican specimens from southern New Mexico, and so on. Such dating naturally becomes less and less accurate as we recede from the starting point, for many as yet unassessable factors enter, such as the rate of travel for trade objects, the persistency of objects among a people as heirlooms, etc. Nevertheless much may be done, and the technological and artistic studies necessary for carrying out the attempt are in themselves well worthwhile.

As was said above, there is already one bit of evidence at hand. From Pueblo Bonito, Pepper collected sherds of

20. Spinden, 1922, p. 129.

a certain type of cloisonné pottery characteristic of one phase of the Toltec culture. Fragments of the same, or a closely allied, ware have been found at a Maya site, Chichen Itza, in Yucatan. While it cannot yet be stated just how old the Toltec ruins (which are the headquarters of this pottery) may be, there is no question but that their age will in the near future be ascertained with reasonable accuracy, and then it will be possible to give an approximate date for the occupation of Pueblo Bonito. That anything so fragile as pottery should have been carried in aboriginal trade all the way from central Mexico to northern New Mexico is very surprising. It is also encouraging, for it gives rise to the hope that many other Mexican objects less difficult of transportation will yet be found in Southwestern sites.

We have briefly summarized the data at present available for the study of Southwestern archaeology; have made an attempt to fit these data together into a historical reconstruction; and, finally, have pointed out the need for further chronological information, both relative and absolute. The place of Pecos in the general archaeological scheme is now clear, for of all the stratified sites in the Southwest, Pecos is the largest and was the longest inhabited. If a single outstanding fact has become apparent in our survey, it is the great value of stratigraphy, first for determining the sequence of local types and for solving local problems, secondly for the possibilities that it holds out for providing cross-finds of contemporaneous non-local types and so for solving the broader and more important problems of inter-area chronology. It is by work of this sort that we shall eventually be enabled to piece together the story of the Pueblos and of their ancestors, and by an extension of it shall ultimately recover the history of all the higher American civilizations.

# Bibliography


Anonymous

1918 Excavations at Hawikuh. *El Palacio,* vol. 5, no. 11, pp. 180–84. Santa Fe.

Ayer, E. A. B.

1916 The memorial of Fray Alonso de Benavides, 1630. Chicago.

Bandelier, A. F.

1881 Historical introduction to studies among the sedentary Indians of New Mexico. Report on the ruins of the pueblo of Pecos. *Papers of the Archaeological Institute of America. American Series,* no. 1. Boston.

1890 Final report of investigations among the Indians of the southwestern United States, part 1. *Papers of the Archaeological Institute of America. American Series,* no. 3. Cambridge.

1890a Contributions to the history of the southwestern portion of the United States. *Papers of the Archaeological Institute of America. American Series,* no. 5. Cambridge.

1890b The delight makers. New York.

1892 Final report of investigations among the Indians of the southwestern United States, part 2. *Papers of the Archaeological Institute of America. American Series,* no. 4. Cambridge.

1892a An outline of the documentary history of the Zuñi tribe. *Journal of American Ethnology and Archaeology,* vol. 3, pp. 1–115. Cambridge.

1910 Documentary history of the Rio Grande Pueblos of New Mexico. *Archaeological Institute of America; Papers of the School of American Archaeology,* no. 13. Santa Fe.

Bancroft, H. H.

1889 History of Arizona and New Mexico. San Francisco.

BARBER, E. A.

1876 The ancient pottery of Colorado, Utah, Arizona and New Mexico. *American Naturalist,* vol. 10, pp. 449–64. Cambridge.

1877 Stone implements and ornaments from the ruins of Colorado, Utah and Arizona. *American Naturalist,* vol. 11, pp. 264–275. Cambridge.

BARTLETT, J. R.

1854 Personal narrative of explorations and incidents in Texas, New Mexico, California, Sonora and Chihuahua. New York.

BAXTER, S.

1888 The old New World. Reprinted from *Boston Herald* of April 15, 1888. Salem.

BEAM, G. L.

1909 The prehistoric ruin of Tsankawi. *National Geographic Magazine,* vol. 20, no. 9, pp. 807–22. Washington.

BICKFORD, F. T.

1890 Prehistoric cave-dwellings. *Century Magazine,* October, 1890, pp. 896–911. New York.

BIERBOWER, S.

1905 Among the cliff and cavate dwellings of New Mexico. *Records of the Past,* vol. 4, pp. 227–33. Washington.

BIRNIE, R.

1875 Report on certain ruins visited in New Mexico. *Annual Report of the Geographical Explorations and Surveys West of the 100th Meridian,* pp. 178–80. Washington.

BLACKISTON, A. H.

1905 Cliff dwellings of northern Mexico. *Records of the Past,* vol. 4, pp. 355–61. Washington.

1906 Cliff ruins of Cave Valley, northern Mexico. *Records of the Past,* vol. 5, pp. 5–11. Washington.

1906a Casas Grandian outposts. *Records of the Past,* vol. 5, pp. 142–47. Washington.

1906b Ruins on the Cerro de Montezuma. *American Anthropologist,* n.s., vol. 8, no. 2, pp. 256–61. Lancaster.

1908 Ruins of the Tenaja and the Rio San Pedro. *Records of the Past,* vol. 7, pp. 282–90. Washington.

1909 Recently discovered cliff-dwellings of the Sierras Madres. *Records of the Past,* vol. 8, pp. 20–32. Washington.

BLAKE, W. P.

1899 Aboriginal turquoise mining in Arizona and New Mexico. *American Antiquarian,* vol. 21, no. 5, pp. 278–84. Chicago.

BLOOM, L. B.

1922 The West Jemez culture area. *El Palacio,* vol. 12, no. 2, pp. 18–25. Santa Fe.

1923 The Jemez expedition of the School. Summer of 1922. *El Palacio,* vol. 14, no. 2, pp. 13–20. Santa Fe.

BOLTON, H. E.

1916 Spanish exploration in the Southwest, 1542–1706. New York.

BRADFIELD, W.

1921 Economic resources of Chaco Canyon. *Art and Archaeology,* vol. 11, nos. 1–2, pp. 36–38. Washington.

1923 Preliminary report on excavating at Cameron Creek site. *El Palacio,* vol. 15, no. 5, pp. 67–73. Santa Fe.

BURR, R. T.

1880 Ruins in White River Cañon, Pima county, Arizona. *Annual Report of the Smithsonian Institution for 1879,* pp. 333–34. Washington.

CHAPIN, F. H.

1890 Cliff-dwellings of the Mancos cañons. *American Antiquarian,* vol. 12, no. 4, pp. 193–210. Chicago.

1892 The land of the cliff dwellers. Boston.

CHAPMAN, K. M.

1921 What the potsherds tell. *Art and Archaeology,* vol. 11, nos. 1–2, pp. 39–44. Washington.

1922 Life forms in Pueblo pottery decoration. *Art and Archaeology,* vol. 13, no. 3, pp. 120–22. Washington.

COLTON, H. S.

1920 Did the so-called cliff dwellers of central Arizona also build "hogans"? *American Anthropologist,* n.s., vol. 22, no. 3, pp. 298–301. Lancaster.

COLTON, M. R. F. and H. S.

1918 The little-known small house ruins in the Coconino forest. *Memoirs American Anthropological Association,* vol. 5, no. 4, pp. 101–26. Lancaster.

COPE, E. D.

1875 Report on the remains of population observed on and near the Eocene plateau of northwestern New Mexico *Annual Report of the Geographical Explorations and Surveys West of the 100th Meridian,* pp. 166–73. Washington.

COSGROVE, C. B.

1923 Two kivas at Treasure Hill, *El Palacio,* vol. 15, no. 2, pp. 18–21. Santa Fe.

CROTSENBURG, C. N.

1900 Cliff-dweller's ruins. *American Antiquarian,* vol. 22, no. 6, pp. 400–01. Chicago.

CUMMINGS, B.

1910 The ancient inhabitants of the San Juan Valley. *Bulletin of the University of Utah,* 2nd Archaeological number, vol. 3, no. 3, pt. 2. Salt Lake City.

1915 Kivas of the San Juan drainage. *American Anthropologist,* n.s., vol. 17, no. 2, pp. 272–82. Lancaster.

CUSHING, F. H.

1886 A study of Pueblo pottery as illustrative of Zuñi culture growth. *Fourth Report of the Bureau of Ethnology,* pp. 467–521. Washington.

1890 Preliminary notes on the origin, working hypothesis and primary researches of the Hemenway Southwestern Archaeological Expedition. *Congrès International des Américanistes, Compte-rendu de la septième session*; pp. 151–94. Berlin.

1901 Zuñi folk-tales. New York.

1920 Zuñi breadstuff. *Museum of the American Indian, Heye Foundation; Indian Notes and Monographs,* vol. 8. New York.

DONALDSON, T.

1893 Moqui Indians of Arizona and Pueblo Indians of

New Mexico. *11th Census of the United States, extra census bulletin.* Washington.

DOUGLASS, A. E.

1921 Dating our prehistoric ruins. *Natural History,* vol. 21, no. 1, pp. 27–30. New York.

1922 Some aspects of the use of the annual rings of trees in climatic study. *Scientific Monthly,* vol. 15, no. 1, pp. 5–22. Utica.

1922a Some topographic and climatic characters in the annual rings of the yellow pines and sequoias of the Southwest. *Proceedings American Philosophical Society,* vol. 61, no. 2, pp. 117–22. Philadelphia.

DUFF, U. F.

1897 The prehistoric ruins of the Rio Tularosa. *American Geographical Society Journal,* vol. 29, pp. 261–70. New York.

1902 The ruins of the Mimbres Valley. *American Antiquarian,* vol. 24, pp. 397–400. Chicago.

1904 Some exploded theories concerning southwestern archaeology. *American Anthropologist,* n.s., vol. 6, no. 2, pp. 303–06. Lancaster.

DUFFIELD, M. S.

1904 Aboriginal remains in Nevada and Utah. *American Anthropologist,* n.s., vol. 6, no. 1, pp. 148–50. Lancaster.

EMORY, W. H.

1848 Notes of a military reconnaissance from Fort Leavenworth, in Missouri, to San Diego, in California, etc., 30th Congress, 1st sess., Senate, ex. doc. no. 7. Washington.

FEWKES, J. W.

1891 Reconnaissance of ruins in or near the Zuñi reservation. *Journal of American Ethnology and Archaeology,* vol. 1, pp. 93–133. Boston.

1892 A report on the present condition of a ruin in Arizona called Casa Grande. *Journal of American Ethnology and Archaeology,* vol. 2, pp. 176–93. Cambridge.

1893 A-wa-to-bi; an archaeological verification of a Tusayan legend. *American Anthropologist,* vol. 6, no. 4, pp. 363–76. Washington.

1896 Two ruins recently discovered in the Red Rock country, Arizona. *American Anthropologist,* vol. 9, no. 8, pp. 263–83. Washington.

1896a The prehistoric culture of Tusayan. *American Anthropologist,* vol. 9, no. 5, pp. 151–73. Washington.

1896b Southern extension of prehistoric Tusayan. *American Anthropologist,* vol. 9, no. 7, p. 253. Washington.

1896c Pacific coast shells from prehistoric Tusayan pueblos. *American Anthropologist,* vol. 9, no. 11, pp. 359–67. Washington.

1896d Studies of Tusayan archaeology. *Internationales Archiv für Ethnographie,* vol. 9, pp. 204–05. Leiden.

1898 Archaeological expedition to Arizona in 1895. *Seventeenth Report of the Bureau of American Ethnology,* pt. 2, pp. 519–742. Washington.

1898a The feather symbol in ancient Hopi designs. *American Anthropologist,* vol. 11, no. 1, pp. 1–14. Washington.

1898b Preliminary account of an expedition to the pueblo ruins near Winslow, Arizona in 1896. *Annual Report of the Smithsonian Institution for 1896,* pp. 517–39. Washington.

1900 Pueblo ruins near Flagstaff, Arizona. *American Anthropologist,* n.s., vol. 2, no. 3, pp. 422–50. New York.

1904 Two summers' work in pueblo ruins. *Twenty-second Report of the Bureau of American Ethnology,* pt. 1, pp. 3–195. Washington.

1906 Hopi ceremonial frames from Cañon de Chelly, Arizona. *American Anthropologist,* n.s., vol. 8, no. 4, pp. 664–70. Lancaster.

1907 Excavations at Casa Grande, Arizona, in 1906–07. *Smithsonian Miscellaneous Collections,* vol. 50 (quarterly issue, vol. 4, pt. 3), pp. 289–329. Washington.

1908 Ventilators in ceremonial rooms of prehistoric cliff-dwellings. *American Anthropologist,* n.s., vol. 10, no. 3, pp. 387–98. Lancaster.

1909 Antiquities of the Mesa Verde National Park: Spruce-tree House. *Bulletin 41, Bureau of American Ethnology.* Washington.

1909a Prehistoric ruins of the Gila Valley. *Smithsonian Miscellaneous Collections,* vol. 52 (quarterly issue, vol. 5, pt. 4), pp. 403–36. Washington.

1909b Ancient Zuñi pottery. *Putnam Anniversary Volume,* pp. 43–82. New York.

1910 Cremation in cliff-dwellings. *Records of the Past,* vol. 9, pt. 3, pp. 154–56. Washington.

1910a Report on the excavation and repair of Cliff Palace, Mesa Verde National Park, Colorado, in 1909. *Reports of the Department of the Interior for 1909,* vol. 1, pp. 483–503. Washington.

1910b A new type of Southwestern ruin. *Records of the Past,* vol. 9, pt. 6, pp. 291–97. Washington.

1911 Preliminary report on a visit to the Navaho National Monument, Arizona. *Bulletin 50, Bureau of American Ethnology.* Washington.

1911a Antiquities of the Mesa Verde National Park; Cliff Palace. *Bulletin 51, Bureau of American Ethnology.* Washington.

1912 Casa Grande, Arizona. *Twenty-eighth Report of the Bureau of American Ethnology,* pp. 25–179. Washington.

1912a Antiquities of the Upper Verde River and Walnut Creek valleys, Arizona. *Twenty-eighth Report of the Bureau of American Ethnology,* pp. 181–220. Washington.

1914 Archaeology of the lower Mimbres Valley, New Mexico. *Smithsonian Miscellaneous Collections,* vol. 63, no. 10. Washington.

1915 Prehistoric remains in New Mexico. *Smithsonian Miscellaneous Collections,* vol. 65, no. 6, pp. 62–72. Washington.

1916 Excavation and repair of Sun Temple, Mesa Verde National Park. *Department of the Interior*. Washington.

1916a The cliff-ruins in Fewkes Cañon, Mesa Verde National Park, Colorado. *Holmes Anniversary Volume,* pp. 96–117. Washington.

1916b Prehistoric remains in Arizona, New Mexico and Colorado. *Smithsonian Miscellaneous Collections,* vol. 66, no. 3, pp. 82–98. Washington.

1916c Animal figures on prehistoric pottery from Mimbres Valley, New Mexico. *American Anthropologist,* n.s., vol. 18, no. 4, pp. 535–45. Lancaster.

1916d The relation of Sun Temple, a new type of ruin lately excavated in the Mesa Verde National Park, to prehistoric "towers." *Journal of the Washington Academy of Sciences,* vol. 6, no. 8, pp. 212–21. Washington.

1916e A Sun Temple in the Mesa Verde National Park. *Art and Archaeology,* vol. 3, no. 6, pp. 341–46. Washington.

1917 Prehistoric remains in New Mexico, Colorado and Utah. *Smithsonian Miscellaneous Collections,* vol. 66, no. 17, pp. 76–92. Washington.

1917a Archaeological investigations in New Mexico, Colorado and Utah. *Smithsonian Miscellaneous Collections,* vol. 68, no. 1. Washington.

1917b A prehistoric Mesa Verde pueblo and its people. *Annual Report of the Smithsonian Institution for 1916,* pp. 461–88. Washington.

1918 Prehistoric ruins in southwestern Colorado and southeastern Utah. *Smithsonian Miscellaneous Collections,* vol. 68, no. 12, pp. 108–33. Washington.

1919 Prehistoric villages, castles, and towers of southwestern Colorado. *Bulletin 70, Bureau of American Ethnology*. Washington.

1919a Designs on prehistoric Hopi pottery. *Thirty-third Report of the Bureau of American Ethnology,* pp. 207–84. Washington.

1920 Field-work on the Mesa Verde National Park, Colorado. *Smithsonian Miscellaneous Collections,* vol. 72, no. 1, pp. 47–64. Washington.

1921 Field-work on the Mesa Verde National Park. *Smithsonian Miscellaneous Collections,* vol. 72, no. 6, pp. 75–94. Washington.

1922 Archaeological field-work on the Mesa Verde National Park. *Smithsonian Miscellaneous Collections,* vol. 72, no. 15, pp. 64–83. Washington.

1923 Archaeological field-work on the Mesa Verde National Park, Colorado. *Smithsonian Miscellaneous Collections,* vol. 74, no. 5, pp. 89–115. Washington.

1923a Designs on prehistoric pottery from the Mimbres Valley, New Mexico. *Smithsonian Miscellaneous Collections,* vol. 74, no. 6. Washington.

1923b The Hovenweep National Monument. *American Anthropologist,* n.s., vol. 25, no. 2, pp. 145–55. Menasha, Wis.

1923c Additional designs on prehistoric Mimbres pottery. *Smithsonian Miscellaneous Collections,* vol. 76, no. 8. Washington.

Goddard, P. E.

1920 The cultural and somatic correlations of Uto-Aztecan. *American Anthropologist,* n.s., vol. 22, no. 3, pp. 244–47. Lancaster.

1921 Indians of the Southwest. *American Museum of Natural History, Handbook Series,* no. 2, 2nd ed. New York.

Gregg, J.

1845 Commerce of the prairies, 2nd ed. New York.

Gregory, H. E.

1916 The Navajo country, a geographic and hydrographic reconnaissance of parts of Arizona, New Mexico and Utah. *United States Geological Survey,* Water-supply paper 380. Washington.

Guernsey, S. J. and Kidder, A. V.

1921 Basket-Maker caves of northeastern Arizona. *Papers of the Peabody Museum of American Archaeology and Ethnology,* vol. 8, no. 2. Cambridge.

GUNCKEL, L. W.

1897 Ruins and picture writings in the cañons of the McElmo and Hovenweep. *American Antiquarian*, vol. 19, pp. 223–26. Chicago.

GUTHE, C. E.

1917 The pueblo ruin at Rowe, New Mexico. *El Palacio*, vol. 4, no. 4, pp. 33–39. Santa Fe.

"H"

1894 Recent finds in Utah. *The Archaeologist*, vol. 2, no. 5, pp. 154–55. Waterloo, Ind.

HALES, H.

1893 Prehistoric New Mexican pottery. *Annual Report of the Smithsonian Institution for 1892*, pp. 535–54. Washington.

HALL, S. M.

1895 The cliff-dwellings of the lower Verde Valley, northern Arizona. *The Archaeologist*, vol. 3, no. 5, pp. 119–22. Columbus, Ohio.

HARRINGTON, J. P.

1916 The ethnogeography of the Tewa Indians. *Twenty-ninth Report of the Bureau of American Ethnology*. Washington.

HARSHBERGER, J. W.

1893 Maize: a botanical and economic study. *Contributions from the Botanical Laboratory of the University of Pennsylvania*, vol. 1, no. 2. Philadelphia.

HEISTER, A. L.

1894 Pueblo graves. *The Archaeologist*, vol. 2, no. 5, pp. 153–54. Waterloo, Ind.

HEWETT, E. L.

1904 Studies on the extinct pueblo of Pecos. *American Anthropologist*, n.s., vol. 6, no. 4, pp. 426–39. Lancaster.

1904a Archaeology of Pajarito Park, New Mexico. *American Anthropologist*, n.s., vol. 6, no. 5, pp. 629–59. Lancaster.

1905 A general view of the archaeology of the Pueblo region. *Annual Report of the Smithsonian Institution for 1904*, pp. 583–605. Washington.

1905a Prehistoric irrigation in the Navajo desert. *Records of the Past,* vol. 4, pt. 11, pp. 322–29. Washington.

1905b Historic and prehistoric ruins of the Southwest and their preservation. *Department of the Interior.* Washington.

1906 Antiquities of the Jemez Plateau, New Mexico. *Bulletin 32, Bureau of American Ethnology.* Washington.

1908 Les communautés anciennes dans le désert américain. Geneva.

1909 The excavations at Tyuonyi, New Mexico, in 1908. *American Anthropologist,* n.s., vol. 11, no. 3, pp. 434–55. Lancaster.

1909a The excavations at El Rito de los Frijoles in 1909. *American Anthropologist,* n.s., vol. 11, no. 4, pp. 651–73. Lancaster.

1909b The Pajaritan culture. *American Journal of Archaeology,* 2nd series, vol. 13, no. 3, pp. 334–44. Norwood, Mass.

1909c Archaeology of Rio Grande Valley. *Out West,* vol. 31, no. 2, pp. 692–719. Los Angeles.

1920 The cliff maiden. *El Palacio,* vol. 8, nos. 5–6, p. 109. Santa Fe.

1921 The Chaco Canyon and its ancient monuments. *Art and Archaeology,* vol. 11, nos. 1–2, pp. 3–28. Washington.

1922 The Chaco Canyon in 1921. *Art and Archaeology,* vol. 14, no. 3, pp. 115–31. Washington.

HEWETT, E. L. HENDERSON, J., ROBBINS, W. W.

1913 The physiography of the Rio Grande Valley, New Mexico, in relation to Pueblo culture. *Bulletin 54, Bureau of American Ethnology.* Washington.

HODGE, F. W.

1893 Prehistoric irrigation in Arizona. *American Anthropologist,* vol. 6, no. 3, pp. 323–30. Washington.

1895 The first discovered city of Cibola. *American Anthropologist,* vol. 8, no. 2, pp. 142–52. Washington.

1897 The Enchanted Mesa. *National Geographic Magazine,* vol. 8, no. 10, pp. 273–84. Washington.

1897a The verification of a tradition. *American Anthropologist,* vol. 10, no. 9, pp. 299–302. Washington.

1904 Hopi pottery fired with coal. *American Anthropologist,* n.s., vol. 6, no. 4, pp. 581–82. Lancaster.

1914 Archaeological explorations in western New Mexico. *Smithsonian Miscellaneous Collections,* vol. 63, no. 8, pp. 53–58. Washington.

1918 Excavations at Hawikuh, New Mexico. *Smithsonian Miscellaneous Collections,* vol. 68, no. 12, pp. 61–72. Washington.

1920 Hawikuh bonework. *Museum of the American Indian, Heye Foundation; Indian notes and monographs,* vol. 3, no. 3. New York.

1921 Turquois work of Hawikuh, New Mexico. *Leaflets of the Museum of the American Indian, Heye Foundation,* no. 2. New York.

1922 Recent excavations at Hawikuh. *El Palacio,* vol. 12, no. 1, pp. 1–11. Santa Fe.

1923 Circular kivas near Hawikuh, New Mexico. *Contributions from the Museum of the American Indian, Heye Foundation,* vol. 7, no. 1. New York.

HOFFMAN, W. J.

1878 Report on the Chaco cranium. *Tenth Annual Report of the U. S. Geological and Geographical Survey of the Territories, 1876,* pp. 453–57. Washington.

HOLMES, W. H.

1878 Report on the ancient ruins of southwestern Colorado, examined during the summers of 1875 and 1876. *Tenth Annual Report of the U. S. Geological and Geographical Survey of the Territories, 1876,* pp. 383–408. Washington.

1886 Pottery of the ancient Pueblos. *Fourth Report of the Bureau of Ethnology,* pp. 257–360. Washington.

1905 Notes on the antiquities of Jemez Valley, New Mexico. *American Anthropologist,* n.s., vol. 7, no. 2, pp. 198–212. Lancaster.

HOUGH, W.

1902 Ancient peoples of the Petrified Forest of Arizona.

*Harper's Magazine,* vol. 105, November, 1902, pp. 897–901. New York.

1903 Archaeological field-work in northeastern Arizona, the Museum-Gates expedition of 1901. *Annual Report of the U. S. National Museum for 1901,* pp. 279–358. Washington.

1907 Antiquities of the Upper Gila and Salt River valleys in Arizona and New Mexico. *Bulletin 35, Bureau of American Ethnology.* Washington.

1914 Culture of the ancient Pueblos of the Upper Gila River region, New Mexico and Arizona. *Bulletin 87, U. S. National Museum.* Washington.

1915 The Hopi Indians. *Little Histories of North American Indians,* no. 4. Cedar Rapids.

1917 Archaeological investigations in New Mexico. *Smithsonian Miscellaneous Collections,* vol. 66, no. 17, pp. 99–103. Washington.

1918 Ancient pit dwellings in New Mexico. *Smithsonian Miscellaneous Collections,* vol. 68, no. 12, pp. 72–74. Washington.

1919 Exploration of a pit house village at Luna, New Mexico. *Proceedings U. S. National Museum,* vol. 55, pp. 409–31. Washington.

1920 Archaeological excavations in Arizona. *Smithsonian Miscellaneous Collections,* vol. 72, no. 1, pp. 64–66. Washington.

1923 Pit dwellings and square kivas of the Upper San Francisco River. *El Palacio,* vol. 15, no. 1, pp. 3–9. Santa Fe.

HULL, D.

1916 Castaño de Sosa's expedition to New Mexico in 1590. *Old Santa Fe Magazine,* vol. 3, no. 12, pp. 307–32. Santa Fe.

HUNTINGTON, E.

1912 The physical environment of the Southwest in pre-Columbian days. *Records of the Past,* vol. 11, no. 3, pp. 128–41. Washington.

1913 The secret of the big trees. *Department of the Interior.* Washington.

1914 The climatic factor as illustrated in arid America. *Publications of the Carnegie Institution of Washington,* no. 192. Washington.

JACKSON, W. H.

1876 Ancient ruins in southwestern Colorado. *Annual Report of the U. S. Geological and Geographical Survey of the Territories, 1874,* pp. 367–81. Washington.

1878 Report on the ancient ruins examined in 1875 and 1877. *Annual Report of the U. S. Geological and Geographical Survey of the Territories, 1876,* pp. 411–50. Washington.

JEANCON, J. A.

1911 Explorations in Chama basin, New Mexico. *Records of the Past,* vol. 10, pt. 2, pp. 92–108. Washington.

1912 Ruins of Pesedeuinge. *Records of the Past,* vol. 11, pt. 1, pp. 28–37. Washington.

1919 Preliminary report of the excavations at Po Shu Ouinge, near Abiquiu. *El Palacio,* vol. 7, no. 4, pp. 66–69. Santa Fe.

1921 Archaeological explorations in New Mexico. *Smithsonian Miscellaneous Collections,* vol. 72, no. 6, pp. 120–25. Washington.

1922 Archaeological research in the northeastern San Juan basin of Colorado during the summer of 1921. *State Historical and Natural History Society of Colorado and the University of Denver.* Denver.

1923 Excavations in the Chama Valley, New Mexico. *Bulletin 81, Bureau of American Ethnology.* Washington.

JUDD, N. M.

1917 Evidence of circular kivas in western Utah ruins. *American Anthropologist,* n.s., vol. 19, no. 1, pp. 34–40. Lancaster.

1917a Archaeological reconnaissance in western Utah. *Smithsonian Miscellaneous Collections,* vol. 66, no. 17, pp. 103–08. Washington.

1917b Notes on certain prehistoric habitations in western Utah. *Proceedings 19th International Congress of Americanists,* pp. 119–24. Washington.

1918 Archaeological work in Arizona and Utah. *Smithsonian Miscellaneous Collections,* vol. 68, no. 12, pp. 74–83. Washington.

1919 Archaeological investigations at Paragonah, Utah. *Smithsonian Miscellaneous Collections,* vol. 70, no. 3. Washington.

1920 Archaeological investigations in Utah and Arizona. *Smithsonian Miscellaneous Collections,* vol. 72, no. 1, pp. 66–69. Washington.

1922 The Pueblo Bonito expedition of the National Geographic Society. *National Geographic Magazine,* vol. 41, no. 3, pp. 322–31. Washington.

1922a Archaeological investigations at Pueblo Bonito, New Mexico. *Smithsonian Miscellaneous Collections,* vol. 72, no. 15, pp. 106–17. Washington.

1923 Archaeological investigations at Pueblo Bonito, New Mexico. *Smithsonian Miscellaneous Collections,* vol. 74, no. 5, pp. 134–43. Washington.

KENDALL, G. W.

1844 Narrative of the Texan Santa Fe expedition. New York.

KIDDER, A. V.

1910 Explorations in southeastern Utah in 1908. *American Journal of Archaeology,* 2nd ser., vol. 14, pp. 337–59. Norwood, Mass.

1915 Pottery of the Pajarito plateau and of some adjacent regions in New Mexico. *Memoirs American Anthropological Association,* vol. 2, pt. 6, pp. 407–62. Lancaster.

1916 The pottery of the Casas Grandes district, Chihuahua. *Holmes Anniversary Volume,* pp. 253–68. Washington.

1916a Archaeological explorations at Pecos, New Mexico. *Proceedings of the National Academy of Sciences,* vol. 2, pp. 119–23. Baltimore.

1916b The pueblo of Pecos. *Archaeological Institute of America; Papers of the School of American Archaeology,* no. 33. Santa Fe.

1917 Prehistoric cultures of the San Juan drainage. *Pro-*

*ceedings 19th International Congress of Americanists,* pp. 108–13. Washington.

1917a The old north pueblo of Pecos. *Archaeological Institute of America; Papers of the School of American Archaeology,* no. 38. Santa Fe.

1917b A design-sequence from New Mexico. *Proceedings of the National Academy of Sciences,* vol. 3, pp. 369–70. Baltimore.

1919 Review of Spier, "An outline for a chronology of Zuñi ruins." *American Anthropologist,* n.s., vol. 21, no. 3, pp. 296–301. Lancaster.

1920 Ruins of the historic period in the upper San Juan Valley, New Mexico. *American Anthropologist,* n.s., vol. 22, no. 4, pp. 322–29. Lancaster.

KIDDER, M. A. AND A. V.

1917 Notes on the pottery of Pecos. *American Anthropologist,* n.s., vol. 19, no. 3, pp. 325–60. Lancaster.

KIDDER, A. V. AND GUERNSEY, S. J.

1919 Archaeological explorations in northeastern Arizona. *Bulletin 65, Bureau of American Ethnology.* Washington.

1920 Review of Morris, "Preliminary account of the antiquities of the region between the Mancos and La Plata rivers in southwestern Colorado." *American Anthropologist,* n.s., vol. 22, no. 3, pp. 285–88. Lancaster.

1921 Peabody Museum Arizona exploration, 1920. *Proceedings of the National Academy of Sciences,* vol. 7, pp. 69–71. Easton, Pa.

KROEBER, A. L.

1916 Zuñi culture sequences. *Proceedings of the National Academy of Sciences,* vol. 2, pp. 42–45. Baltimore.

1916a Zuñi potsherds. *Anthropological Papers of the American Museum of Natural History,* vol. 18, pt. 1. New York.

1917 Zuñi kin and clan. *Anthropological Papers of the American Museum of Natural History,* vol. 18, pt. 2. New York.

LOEW, O.

1875 Report on the ruins of New Mexico. *Annual Report of the Geographical Explorations and Surveys West of the 100th Meridian,* pp. 174–78. Washington.

LUMHOLTZ, C.

1891 Report of explorations in northern Mexico. *Bulletin of the American Geographical Society,* no. 3, pp. 386–402. New York.

1891a Explorations in the Sierra Madre. *Scribner's Monthly Magazine,* November, 1891, pp. 532–48. New York.

1902 Unknown Mexico. New York.

LUMMIS, C. F.

1889 Mysterious ruins, a visit to the Pueblo Alto. *San Francisco Sunday Chronicle,* January 27.

1906 The land of *poco tiempo.* New York.

1910 Pueblo Indian folk-stories. New York.

LYON, M. W.

1906 Mammal remains from two prehistoric village sites in New Mexico and Arizona. *Proceedings U. S. National Museum,* vol. 31, pp. 647–49. Washington.

MARTIN, H. T.

1909 Further notes on the pueblo ruins of Scott County. *Kansas University Science Bulletin,* vol. 5, no. 2, pp. 11–22. Lawrence.

MATTHEWS, W.

1894 Explorations in the Salado Valley. *The Archaeologist,* vol. 2, no. 12, pp. 351–66. Waterloo, Ind.

MEARNS, E. A.

1890 Ancient dwellings of the Rio Verde Valley. *Popular Science Monthly,* October, 1890, pp. 745–63. New York.

MINDELEFF, C.

1895 Cliff ruins of Canyon de Chelly, Arizona. *American Anthropologist,* vol. 8, no. 2, pp. 153–74. Washington.

1896 Aboriginal remains in Verde Valley, Arizona. *Thirteenth Report of the Bureau of Ethnology,* pp. 179–261. Washington.

1896a Casa Grande ruin. *Thirteenth Report of the Bureau of Ethnology*, pp. 289–319. Washington.

1897 The cliff ruins of Cañon de Chelly, Arizona. *Sixteenth Report of the Bureau of American Ethnology*, pp. 73–198. Washington.

1898 Origin of the cliff dwellings. *Bulletin of the American Geographical Society*, vol. 30, no. 2, pp. 111–123. New York.

MINDELEFF, V.

1891 A study of Pueblo architecture: Tusayan and Cibola. *Eighth Report of the Bureau of Ethnology*, pp. 3–228. Washington.

MONTGOMERY, H.

1894 Prehistoric man in Utah. *The Archaeologist*, vol. 2, nos. 8, 10, 11, pp. 225–34, 298–306, 335–42. Waterloo, Ind.

MOONEY, J.

1893 Recent archaeologic find in Arizona. *American Anthropologist*, vol. 6, no. 3, pp. 283–84. Washington.

MOOREHEAD, W. K.

1898 Some objects from the Salado Valley, Arizona. *American Archaeologist*, vol. 2, no. 8, pp. 207–210. Columbus, Ohio.

1902 The field diary of an archaeological collector. Andover.

1906 A narrative of explorations in New Mexico, Arizona, Indiana, etc. *Bulletin of Phillips Academy, Dept. of Archaeology*, no. 3. Andover.

1908 Ruins at Aztec and on the Rio La Plata, New Mexico. *American Anthropologist*, n.s., vol. 10, no. 2, pp. 255–63. Lancaster.

MOOREHEAD, W. K. AND GUNCKEL, L. W.

1892 In search of a lost race. *Illustrated American*, vol. 10, no. 116; vol. 11, nos. 119, 121, 122, 124–30. New York.

MORGAN, L. H.

1880 On the ruins of a stone pueblo on the Animas River in New Mexico. *Reports of the Peabody Museum*, vol. 2, pp. 536–56. Cambridge.

1881 Houses and house life of the American aborigines. *Contributions to North American Ethnology,* vol. 4. Washington.

MORLEY, S. G.

1908 The excavation of Cannonball ruins in southwestern Colorado. *American Anthropologist,* n.s., vol. 10, no. 4, pp. 596–610. Lancaster.

1910 The South House, Puyé. *Southwest Society, 6th Bulletin.* Los Angeles.

MORLEY, S. G. AND KIDDER, A. V.

1917 The archaeology of McElmo Canyon, Colorado. *El Palacio,* vol. 4, no. 4, pp. 41–70. Santa Fe.

MORRIS, E. H.

1915 The excavation of a ruin near Aztec, San Juan county, New Mexico. *American Anthropologist,* n.s., vol. 17, no. 4, pp. 666–84. Lancaster.

1917 The place of coiled ware in Southwestern pottery. *American Anthropologist,* n.s., vol. 19, no. 1, pp. 24–29. Lancaster.

1917a Discoveries at the Aztec ruin. *American Museum Journal,* vol. 17, no. 3, pp. 169–79. New York.

1917b Explorations in New Mexico. *American Museum Journal,* vol. 17, no. 7, pp. 461–71. New York.

1918 Further discoveries at the Aztec ruin. *American Museum Journal,* vol. 18, no. 7, pp. 603–10. New York.

1919 Preliminary account of the antiquities of the region between the Mancos and La Plata rivers in southwestern Colorado. *Thirty-third Report of the Bureau of American Ethnology,* pp. 155–206. Washington.

1919a The Aztec ruin. *Anthropological Papers of the American Museum of Natural History,* vol. 26, pt. 1. New York.

1921 Chronology of the San Juan area. *Proceedings of the National Academy of Sciences,* vol. 7, pp. 18–22. Easton, Pa.

1921a The house of the great kiva at the Aztec ruin. *Anthropological Papers of the American Museum of Natural History,* vol. 26, pt. 2. New York.

NELSON, E. W.

1884 Explorations in southern Arizona. *Annual Report of the Smithsonian Institution for 1884*, pp. 20–24. Washington.

NELSON, N. C.

1913 Ruins of prehistoric New Mexico. *American Museum Journal*, vol. 13, no. 2, pp. 63–81. New York.

1914 Pueblo ruins of the Galisteo basin, New Mexico. *Anthropological Papers of the American Museum of Natural History*, vol. 15, pt. 1. New York.

1916 Chronology of the Tano ruins, New Mexico. *American Anthropologist*, n.s., vol. 18, no. 2, pp. 159–80. Lancaster.

1917 Archaeology of the Tano district, New Mexico. *Proceedings 19th International Congress of Americanists*, pp. 114–18. Washington.

1917a Excavation of the Aztec ruin. *American Museum Journal*, vol. 17, no. 2, pp. 85–99. New York.

1919 The archaeology of the southwest: a preliminary report. *Proceedings of the National Academy of Sciences*, vol. 5, pp. 114–20. Baltimore.

1919a The Southwest problem, *El Palacio*, vol. 6, no. 9, pp. 132–35. Santa Fe.

NEWBERRY, J. S.

1876 Report of the exploring expedition from Santa Fe, New Mexico, to the junction of the Grand and Green rivers of the Great Colorado of the West, in 1859. *U. S. Engineering Dept.* Washington.

NORDENSKIOLD, G.

1893 The cliff-dwellers of the Mesa Verde. Translated by D. Lloyd Morgan. Stockholm.

NUSSBAUM, J. L.

1922 A Basket-Maker cave in Kane County, Utah; with notes on the artifacts by A. V. Kidder and S. J. Guernsey. *Museum of the American Indian, Heye Foundation; Indian Notes and Monographs* (no. 29). New York.

PALMER, E.

1876 Exploration of a mound in Utah. *American Naturalist*, vol. 10, pp. 410–14. Cambridge.

1880 Cave dwellings in Utah. *Reports of the Peabody Museum,* vol. 2, pp. 269–72. Cambridge.

PALMER, F. M.

1905 A land of mystery. *Out West,* vol. 23, no. 6, pp. 525–38. Los Angeles.

PATRICK, H. R.

1903 The ancient canal systems and pueblos of the Salt River Valley, Arizona. *Phoenix Free Museum Bulletin,* no. 1. Phoenix.

PEPPER, G. H.

1899 Ceremonial deposits found in an ancient Pueblo estufa in northern New Mexico. *Monumental Records,* vol. 1, no. 1, pp. 1–6. New York.

1902 The ancient Basket Makers of southeastern Utah. *American Museum Journal,* vol. 2, no. 4, suppl. New York.

1905 Ceremonial objects and ornaments from Pueblo Bonito, New Mexico. *American Anthropologist,* n.s., vol. 7, no. 2, pp. 183–97. Lancaster.

1905a The throwing-stick of a prehistoric people of the Southwest. *International Congress of Americanists, 13th Session, New York, 1902,* pp. 107–30. Easton, Pa.

1906 Human effigy vases from Chaco Canyon, New Mexico. *Boas Anniversary Volume,* pp. 320–34. New York.

1909 The exploration of a burial room in Pueblo Bonito, New Mexico. *Putnam Anniversary Volume,* pp. 196–252. New York.

1920 Pueblo Bonito. *Anthropological Papers of the American Museum of Natural History,* vol. 27. New York.

PRUDDEN, T. M.

1897 An elder brother to the cliff-dweller. *Harper's Monthly Magazine,* vol. 95, June, 1897, pp. 56–63. New York.

1903 The prehistoric ruins of the San Juan watershed in Utah, Arizona, Colorado and New Mexico. *American Anthropologist,* n.s., vol. 5, no. 2, pp. 224–88. Lancaster.

1914 The circular kivas of small ruins in the San Juan watershed. *American Anthropologist*, n.s., vol. 16, no. 1, pp. 33–58. Lancaster.

1918 A further study of prehistoric small house ruins in the San Juan watershed. *Memoirs American Anthropological Association*, vol. 5, no. 1, pp. 3–50. Lancaster.

PUTNAM, F. W. AND OTHERS.

1879 Reports upon archaeological and ethnological collections from the vicinity of Santa Barbara, Cal., and from ruined pueblos in Arizona and New Mexico, and certain interior tribes. *Report of the U. S. Geographical Surveys West of 100th Meridian*, vol. 7, Archaeology. Washington.

REAGAN, A. B.

1917 The story of Jemez and Zia. *El Palacio*, vol. 4, no. 2, pp. 24–72. Santa Fe.

1919 The ancient ruins in Lower and Middle Pine River Valley, Colorado. *El Palacio*, vol. 7, nos. 9–12, pp. 170–76. Santa Fe.

1922 Additional notes on the Jemez-Zia region. *El Palacio*, vol. 12, no. 9, pp. 120–21. Santa Fe.

ROBERTS, F. J. J. JR.

1922 Report on the work of the 1922 season in the Piedra Parada archaeological field. *University of Denver Bulletin*, vol. 23, no. 9. Denver.

SAPIR, E.

1916 Time perspective in aboriginal American culture; a study in method. *Geological Survey of Canada, Anthropological Series*, no. 13. Ottawa.

SAUNDERS, C. F.

1912 The Indians of the terraced houses. New York.

SAVILLE, M. H.

1894 The plumed serpent in northern Mexico. *The Archaeologist*, vol. 2, no. 10, pp. 291–93. Waterloo, Ind.

SIMPSON, J. H.

1850 Journal of a military reconnaissance from Santa Fe, New Mexico, to the Navajo country. Reports of the

Secretary of War, 31st Congress, 1st sess., Senate, ex. doc. 64, pp. 56–139. Washington.

Spier, L.

1917 An outline for a chronology of Zuñi ruins. *Anthropological Papers of the American Museum of Natural History*, vol. 18, pt. 3. New York.

1918 Notes on some Little Colorado ruins. *Anthropological Papers of the American Museum of Natural History*, vol. 18, pt. 4. New York.

1919 Ruins in the White Mountains, Arizona. *Anthropological Papers of the American Museum of Natural History*, vol. 18, pt. 5. New York.

Spinden, H. J.

1922 Ancient civilizations of Mexico and Central America. *American Museum of Natural History, Handbook Series*, no. 3, 2nd ed. New York.

Starr, F.

1900 Shrines near Cochiti, New Mexico. *American Antiquarian*, vol. 22, no. 4, pp. 219–23. Chicago.

Stevenson, J.

1883 Illustrated catalogue of the collections obtained from the Indians of New Mexico and Arizona in 1879. *Second Report of the Bureau of Ethnology*, pp. 307–422. Washington.

1883a Illustrated catalogue of the collections obtained from the Indians of New Mexico in 1880. *Second Report of the Bureau of Ethnology*, pp. 423–65. Washington.

1884 Illustrated catalogue of the collections obtained from the pueblos of Zuñi, New Mexico, and Wolpi, Arizona, in 1881. *Third Report of the Bureau of Ethnology*, pp. 511–94. Washington.

1886 Ancient habitations of the Southwest. *Bulletin American Geographical Society*, no. 4, pp. 329–42. New York.

Taylor, W.

1898 The pueblos and ancient mines near Allison, New Mexico. *American Antiquarian*, vol. 22, no. 5, pp. 258–61. Chicago.

TWITCHELL, R. E.

1911 The leading facts of New Mexican history. Cedar Rapids, Iowa.

1914 The Spanish archives of New Mexico. Cedar Rapids, Iowa.

WALTER, P. A. F.

1916 The cities that died of fear. *El Palacio*, vol. 3, no. 4, pp. 12–73. Santa Fe.

WEBSTER, C. L.

1912 Some burial customs practiced by the ancient people of the Southwest. *Archaeological Bulletin*, vol. 3, no. 3, pp. 69–78. Madison, Ind.

1912a Archaeological and ethnological researches in southwestern New Mexico. *Archaeological Bulletin*, vol. 3, no. 4; vol. 4, nos. 1, 2; vol. 5, nos. 2, 3. Madison, Ind., and Ottawa, Kansas, 1912, 1913, 1914.

WETHERILL, L. W. AND CUMMINGS, B.

1922 A Navaho folk tale of Pueblo Bonito. *Art and Archaeology*, vol. 14, no. 3, pp. 132–36. Washington.

WETHERILL, R.

1894 Snider's well. *The Archaeologist*, vol. 2, no. 9, pp. 288–89. Waterloo, Ind.

WILLISTON, S. W.

1899 Some prehistoric ruins in Scott County, Kansas. *Kansas University Quarterly*, vol. 7, no. 4, pp. 109–14. Lawrence.

WILSON, L. L. W.

1916 Excavations at Otowi. *El Palacio*, vol. 3, no. 2, pp. 28–36. Santa Fe.

1916a A prehistoric anthropomorphic figure from the Rio Grande basin. *American Anthropologist*, n.s., vol. 18, no. 4, pp. 548–51. Lancaster.

1918 Hand sign or avanyu, a note on a Pajaritan biscuit-ware motif. *American Anthropologist*, n.s., vol. 20, no. 3, pp. 310–17. Lancaster.

WINSHIP, G. P.

1896 The Coronado expedition, 1540–1542. *Fourteenth Report of the Bureau of Ethnology*, pt. 1, pp. 329–613. Washington.

WISSLER, C.

1919 The Archer M. Huntington survey of the Southwest. Zuñi district. General Introduction. *Anthropological Papers of the American Museum of Natural History,* vol. 18, pp. i-ix. New York.

1921 Dating our prehistoric ruins. *Natural History,* vol. 21, no. 1, pp. 13–26. New York.

1922 Pueblo Bonito as made known by the Hyde expedition. *Natural History,* vol. 22, no. 4, pp. 343–54. New York.

# Schwartz References


Abbott, David R.

1994. Hohokam social structure and irrigation management: The ceramic evidence from the Central Phoenix Basin. Ph.D. diss., Arizona State University. Ann Arbor, Mich.: University Microfilms.

Adams, E. Charles.

1991. *The origin and development of the Pueblo Katsina cult.* Tucson: University of Arizona Press.

———.

1994. The Katsina cult: A western pueblo perspective. In Schaafsma, Polly, ed. 1994.

Adler, Michael A.

1989. Ritual facilities and social integration in non-ranked societies. In *The Architecture of Social Integration in Prehistoric Pueblos,* ed. W. D. Lipe and M. Hegmon. Occasional Paper No. 1 of the Crow Canyon Archaeological Center, Cortez, Colorado.

Aldana, Barbara Kidder.

1983. The Kidder Pecos expedition, 1924–1929: A personal memoir. *The Kiva* 48 (4):243–50.

Bandelier, Adolph F.

1881a. *Report on the ruins of the Pueblo of Pecos.* Boston: A. Williams.

———.

1881b. *A visit to the aboriginal ruins in the Valley of the Rio Pecos.* Papers of the Archaeological Institute of America, American Series 1. Boston.

———.

1883. Report by A. F. Bandelier on his investigations in New Mexico in the spring and summer of 1882. *Bulletin of the Archaeological Institute of America* 1:13–33.

———.

1884. Reports by A. F. Bandelier on his investigations in New Mexico during the years 1883–1884. In *Fifth Annual Report of the Executive Committee, Archaeological Institute of America.* Cambridge.

———.

1890a. *Contributions to the history of the southwestern portion of the United States.* Papers of the Archaeological Institute of America, American Series 5. Cambridge: John Wilson and Son.

———.

1890b. *Final report of investigations among the Indians of the southwestern United States, carried on mainly in the years from 1880–1885.* Part 1. Papers of the Archaeological Institute of America, American Series 3.

———.

1892. *Final report of investigations among the Indians of the southwestern United States, carried on mainly in the years from 1880–1885.* Part 2. Papers of the Archaeological Institute of America, American Series 4.

Beals, Ralph L., George W. Brainerd, and Watson Smith.

1945. *Archaeological studies in northeast Arizona.* University of California Publications in American Archaeology and Ethnology, vol. 44, no. 1. Berkeley and Los Angeles: University of California Press.

Bishop, Ronald L., and Frederick W. Lange, eds.

1991. *The ceramic legacy of Anna O. Shepard.* Niwot: University Press of Colorado.

Breternitz, David.

1983. *Mesa Verde National Park: A history of its archaeology.* Essays and Monographs in Colorado History, no. 2. Denver: Colorado Historical Society.

Brew, John Otis.

1946. *The archaeology of Alkali Ridge, Southeastern Utah.* Papers of the Peabody Museum of American Archaeology and Ethnology, no. 21. Cambridge: Harvard University.

Bunzel, R.

1932. Introduction to Zuni ceremonialism. In *47th Annual report of the Bureau of American Ethnology.* Washington, D.C.: Government Printing Office.

Chapman, Kenneth M., F. W. Hodge, Jesse L. Nusbaum, and Ina Sizer Cassidy.

1955. *Reminiscences of four oldtimers.* Conversations recorded September 9, 1955. Santa Fe: Laboratory of Anthropology.

Cordell, Linda S.

1996. Big sites, big questions: Pueblos in transition. In *The prehistoric Pueblo world, A.D. 1150–1350,* ed. M. A. Adler. Tucson: University of Arizona Press.

———.

1997. *Archaeology of the Southwest.* 2d ed. San Diego: Academic Press.

Cordell, Linda S., David E. Doyel, and Keith W. Kintigh.

1994. Processes of aggregation in the prehistoric Southwest. In *Themes in Southwest prehistory,* ed. G. J. Gumerman. Santa Fe: School of American Research Press.

Cordell, Linda S., and George J. Gumerman, eds.

1989. *Dynamics of Southwest prehistory.* Washington, D.C.: Smithsonian Institution Press.

Creamer, Winifred.

1993. *The architecture of Arroyo Hondo Pueblo, New Mexico.* Santa Fe: School of American Research Press.

Crown, Patricia L.

1991. The Hohokam: Current views of prehistory and the regional system. In *Chaco and Hohokam,* ed. P. L. Crown and W. J. Judge. Santa Fe: School of American Research Press.

———.

1994. *Ceramics and ideology: Salado polychrome pottery.* Albuquerque: University of New Mexico Press.

Daifuku, Hiroshi.
1952. A new conceptual scheme for prehistoric cultures in the southwestern United States. *American Anthropologist* 54 (2):191–200.

Dean, Jeffrey S.
1970. Aspects of Tsegi phase social organization: A trial reconstruction. In *Reconstructing Prehistoric Pueblo Societies,* ed. W. A. Longacre. Albuquerque: University of New Mexico Press.

———.
1996. Kayenta Anasazi settlement transformations in northeastern Arizona, A.D. 1150–1350. In *The prehistoric Pueblo world, A.D. 1150–1350,* ed. M. A. Adler. Tucson: University of Arizona Press.

DiPeso, Charles C.
1974. *Casas Grandes: A fallen trading center of the Gran Chichimeca.* Vols. 1–3. Ed. Gloria J. Fenner. Dragoon: The Amerind Foundation.

DiPeso, Charles C., John B. Rinaldo, and Gloria J. Fenner.
1974. *Casas Grandes: A fallen trading center of the Gran Chichimeca.* Vols. 4–8. Dragoon: The Amerind Foundation; Flagstaff: Northland Press.

Dozier, Edward P.
1970. *The Pueblo Indians of North America.* New York: Holt, Rinehart and Winston.

Eggan, Fred.
1950. *Social organization of the western Pueblos.* Chicago: University of Chicago Press.

Elliott, Melinda.
1995. *Great Excavations.* Santa Fe: School of American Research Press.

Ellis, F. H.
1951. Patterns of aggression and war cult in southwestern pueblos. *Southwestern Journal of Anthropology* 7:177–201.

Fewkes, Jesse Walter.
1900. Tusayan migration traditions. In *19th Annual Report of the Bureau of American Ethnology,* ed. J. W. Powell. Washington, D.C.: Government Printing Office.

———.
1912. Casa Grande, Arizona. In *28th Annual Report of the Bureau of American Ethnology.* Washington, D.C.: Government Printing Office.

Gilman, Patricia A.
1987. Architecture as artifact: Pit structures and Pueblos in the American Southwest. *American Antiquity* 52:538–64.

Givens, Douglas.
1992. *Alfred Vincent Kidder and the development of Americanist archaeology.* Albuquerque: University of New Mexico Press.

Gladwin, Harold Sterling.
1947. *Men out of Asia.* New York: McGraw-Hill.

Guernsey, Samuel J., and Alfred V. Kidder.
1921. *Basket-maker caves of northeastern Arizona.* Papers of the Peabody Museum of American Archaeology and Ethnology, vol. 12, no. 1. Cambridge: Harvard University.

Gumerman, George. J., ed.

1988. *The Anasazi in a changing environment.* School of American Research Advanced Seminar Series. Cambridge: Cambridge University Press.

———.

1994. *Themes in Southwest prehistory.* Santa Fe: School of American Research Press.

Guthe, Carl E.

1959. Review of *Pecos, New Mexico: Archaeological notes,* by A. V. Kidder. *El Palacio* 66 (1):33–36.

Hammond, George Peter, and Agapito Rey.

1940. *Narratives of the Coronado expedition, 1540–1542.* Albuquerque: University of New Mexico Press.

Haury, Emil W

1950. *The stratigraphy and archaeology of Ventana Cave.* Tucson: University of Arizona Press.

———.

1958. Evidence at Point of Pines for a prehistoric migration from northern Arizona. In *Migrations in new world culture history,* ed. R. H. Thompson. Tucson: University of Arizona Press.

———.

1976. *The Hohokam, desert farmers and craftsmen: Excavations at Snaketown, 1964–1965.* Tucson: University of Arizona Press.

———.

1985. Reflections: Fifty years of Southwestern archaeology. *American Antiquity* 50 (2):383–94.

Hewett, Edgar Lee.

1902. Archaeology [of New Mexico]. In *Report of the Governor of New Mexico to the Secretary of the Interior, 1902.* Washington, D.C.: Government Printing Office.

———.

1903. Archaeology [of New Mexico]. In *Report of the Governor of New Mexico to the Secretary of the Interior, 1903.* Washington, D.C.: Government Printing Office.

———.

1904a. *Circular relating to historic and prehistoric ruins of the southwest and their preservation.* Issued by the Department of the Interior, General Land Office. Washington, D.C.: Government Printing Office.

———.

1904b. Studies on the extinct Pueblo of Pecos. *American Anthropologist* 6 (4):425–39.

———.

1904c. The archaeology of Pajarito Park, New Mexico. *American Anthropologist* 6 (5):629–59.

———.

1905. A general view of the archaeology of the Pueblo region. *Annual report of the Smithsonian Institution for 1904,* 583–605. Washington, D.C.: Government Printing Office.

———.

1906. Antiquities of the Jemez Plateau, New Mexico. *Bureau of American Ethnology Bulletin* 32. Washington, D.C.: Government Printing Office.

———.

1908a. Archaeology of Rio Grande Valley. *Out West* 28:1–29.

———.

1908b. Les Communautés Anciennes dans le Désert Américain. Recherches Archaéologiques sur le distribution et l'organisation Sociale des Anciennes Populations au Sudoest des Etats-Unis au Nord du Mexique. Geneva: Librarie Kundig. (Dissertation presented for degree of Doctor of Social Sciences, University of Geneva, Switzerland.)

———.

1909a. *Ancient ruins of the Southwest.* Issued by the Passenger Department, Denver and Rio Grande Railroad. Denver: Carson-Harper.

———.

1909b. The excavations at El Rito de los Frijoles. *Papers of the School of American Archaeology,* no. 10:651–73.

———.

1909c. *The Pajaritan culture.* Papers of the School of American Archaeology, no. 3.

———. 1930. *Ancient life in the American Southwest.* Indianapolis: Bobbs-Merrill Co.

Hooton, Earnest Albert.

1930. *The Indians of Pecos Pueblo: A study of their skeletal remains.* Papers of the Southwestern Expedition, no. 4. New Haven: Yale University Press for the Department of Archaeology, Phillips Academy, Andover, Mass.

Jennings, Jesse D., and Erik K. Reed.

1956. The American Southwest: A problem in cultural isolation. In *Seminars in archaeology: 1955.* Memoirs of the Society for American Archaeology, no. 11. Salt Lake City: Society for American Archaeology.

Judd, Neil M.

1954. Byron Cummings, 1860–1954. *American Anthropologist* 56 (5):871–72.

———.

1964. *The architecture of Pueblo Bonito.* Smithsonian Miscellaneous Collections, vol. 147, no. 1. Washington, D.C.: Smithsonian Institution Press.

Kessell, John.

1979. *Kiva, cross, and crown: The Pecos Indians and New Mexico, 1540–1840.* Washington, D.C.: National Park Service.

Kidder, Alfred Vincent.

1914. Southwestern ceramics: Their value in reconstructing the history of the ancient Cliff Dwelling and Pueblo Tribes: An exposition from the point of view of type distinctions. Ph.D. diss., Harvard University.

———.

1916. *The Pueblo of Pecos.* Papers of the School of American Archaeology, no. 33.

———.

1925a. Introduction to *Pueblo pottery making: A study at the village of San Ildefonso,* by C. E. Guthe. New Haven: Yale University Press for the Department of Archaeology, Phillips Academy, Andover, Mass.

———.

1925b. *Pecos explorations in 1924*. Papers of the School of American Research, no. 11. [Santa Fe]: El Palacio Press.

———.

1927. Southwestern Archaeological Conference. *El Palacio* 23 (22):554–61. Also published in *Science* 66:489–91.

———.

1931. The dull-paint wares, with a section on the black-on-white wares by C. A. Amsden. Vol. 1 of *The pottery of Pecos*. Papers of the Southwestern Expedition, no. 5. New Haven: Yale University Press for the Department of Archaeology, Phillips Academy, Andover, Mass.

———.

1932. *The Artifacts of Pecos*. Papers of the Southwestern Expedition, no. 6. New Haven: Yale University Press for the Department of Archaeology, Phillips Academy, Andover, Mass.

———.

1936a. The glaze-paint, culinary, and other wares. Part 1 of *The pottery of Pecos,* vol. 2., by Kidder and Anna O. Shepard. Papers of the Southwest Expedition, no. 7. New Haven: Yale University Press for Phillips Academy, Andover, Mass.

———.

1936b. Discussion. Part 3 of *The pottery of Pecos,* vol. 2, by Kidder and Anna O. Shepard. Papers of the Southwest Expedition, no. 7. New Haven: Yale University Press for Phillips Academy, Andover, Mass.

———.

1951. Pecos Pueblo. *El Palacio* 58 (3):82–89.

———.

1957. Interview by Gordon R. Willey. Transcript, parts 1 and 2. Pecos, New Mexico: National Park Service files, Pecos National Historical Park.

———.

1958. *Pecos, New Mexico: Archaeological notes*. Papers of the Robert S. Peabody Foundation for Archaeology, no. 5. Andover, Mass.: Phillips Academy.

———.

1960. Reminiscences in Southwest Archaeology: I. *The Kiva* 25 (4):1–32.

———.

1962. *An introduction to the study of Southwestern archaeology, with a preliminary account of the excavations at Pecos*. 1924. Rev. ed., with a Summary of Southwestern archaeology today, by Irving Rouse. New Haven: Yale University Press.

Kidder, Alfred Vincent, and Samuel J. Guernsey.

1919. *Archaeological explorations in northeastern Arizona*. Bulletin of the Bureau of American Ethnology, no. 65. Washington, D. C.: Government Printing Office.

Kidder, Alfred Vincent, and M. A. Kidder.

1917. Notes on the pottery of Pecos. *American Anthropologist* 19:325–60.

Kroeber, A. L.

1916. *Zuni potsherds*. Anthropological Papers of the American Museum of Natural History, vol. 18, pt. 1. New York: American Museum of Natural History.

Lange, Charles H., and Carroll L. Riley, eds.

1966. *The Southwestern journals of Adolph F. Bandelier, 1880–1882*. Albuquerque: University of New Mexico Press.

Lekson, Stephen H., Thomas C. Windes, John R. Stein, and W. James Judge.

1988. The Chaco Canyon community. *Scientific American* 259 (1):100–09.

Lipe, W. D.

1995. The depopulation of the northern San Juan: conditions in the turbulent 1200s. *Journal of Anthropological Archaeology* 14:143–69.

Lister, Florence C., and Robert H. Lister.

1968. *Earl Morris and Southwestern archaeology*. Albuquerque: University of New Mexico Press.

Longacre, William A., ed.

1970. *Reconstructing prehistoric Pueblo societies*. Albuquerque: University of New Mexico Press.

Martin, Paul S., and John B. Rinaldo.

1951. The Southwestern co-tradition. *Southwestern Journal of Anthropology* 7:215–29.

McNitt, Frank.

1966. *Richard Wetherill: Anasazi*. Rev. ed. Albuquerque: University of New Mexico Press.

Mera, H. P.

1935. *Ceramic clues to the prehistory of north central New Mexico*. Laboratory of Anthropology Survey of Archaeology, Technical Series Bulletin, no. 8. Ann Arbor, Mich.: Edwards Brothers.

Mindeleff, Victor.

1891. A study of Pueblo architecture in Tusayan and Cibola. In *Eighth Annual Report of the Bureau of Ethnology, 1886–87*, 12–228. Washington, D.C: Government Printing Office.

Minnis, Paul E.

1989. The Casas Grandes polity in the International Four Corners. In *The Sociopolitical Structure of Prehistoric Southwestern Societies*, ed. Steadman Upham, Kent G. Lightfoot, and Roberta A. Jewett. Boulder: Westview Press.

Nelson, Nels C.

1914. *Pueblo Ruins of the Galisteo Basin, New Mexico*. Anthropological Papers of the American Museum of Natural History, vol. 15, no. 1. New York: American Museum of Natural History.

———.

1916. Chronology of the Tano Ruins, New Mexico. *American Anthropologist* 18:159–80.

Noble, David Grant.

1981. Pecos Pueblo, December 31, 1590. Excerpted from the journals of Castaño de Sosa. *Exploration, Annual Bulletin of the School of American Research*.

Nordby, Larry.

1981. The prehistory of the Pecos Indians. *Exploration, Annual Bulletin of the School of American Research,* 5–11.

Ortiz, Alfonso.

1969. *The Tewa world.* Chicago: University of Chicago Press.

———, ed. 1979. *Southwest.* Vol. 9 of *Handbook of North American Indians,* ed. William C. Sturtevant. Washington, D.C.: Smithsonian Institution.

Palkovich, Ann M.

1980. *The Arroyo Hondo skeletal and mortuary remains.* Santa Fe: School of American Research Press.

Parsons, Elsie Worthington Clews.

1939. *Pueblo Indian religion,* 2 vols. Chicago: University of Chicago Press.

Reed, E.

1956. Types of village-plan layouts in the Southwest. In *Prehistoric settlement patterns in the New World,* ed. G. R. Willey. Viking Fund Publications in Anthropology, no. 23. Westport, Conn.: Greenwood Press.

Reff, Daniel T.

1991. *Disease, depopulation, and culture change in northwestern New Spain, 1518–1764.* Salt Lake City: University of Utah Press.

Roberts, Frank H., Jr.

1935. A survey of Southwestern archaeology. *American Anthropologist* 37:1–33.

Rouse, Irving.

1962. Southwestern archaeology today. In *An introduction to the study of Southwestern archaeology,* by A. V. Kidder, 1–55. Rev. ed. New Haven: Yale University Press.

Schaafsma, Polly.

1979a. *Indian rock art of the southwest.* Santa Fe: School of American Research Press; Albuquerque: University of New Mexico Press.

———.

1979b. Prehistory: Hayataya. In *Southwest,* ed. Alfonso Ortiz. Vol. 9 of *Handbook of North American Indians,* ed. William C. Sturtevant. Washington, D.C.: Smithsonian Institution.

———, ed.

1994. *Kachinas in the Pueblo world.* Albuquerque: University of New Mexico Press.

Schroeder, Albert H.

1979. Prehistory: Hakataya. In *Southwest,* ed. Alfonso Ortiz. Vol. 9 of *Handbook of North American Indians,* ed. William C. Sturtevant. Washington, D.C.: Smithsonian Institution.

Schwartz, Douglas.

1963. The Southwest. In *Early Indian farmers and village communities,* 174. National Park Service.

———.

1968. *Conceptions of Kentucky prehistory, 1661–1657: A case study in the history of archaeology.* Studies in Anthropology, no. 6. Lexington: University of Kentucky Press.

———.

1979. A Conceptual Framework for the Sociology of Archaeology. In *Archaeological Essays in Honor of Irving B. Rouse,* ed. Robert C. Dunnell and Edward S. Hall. The Hague: Mouton.

———.

1983. Havasupai. In *Southwest.* Vol. 10 of *Handbook of North American Indians,* ed. William C. Sturtevant. Washington, D.C.: Smithsonian Institution Press.

———.

1989. *On the edge of splendor: Exploring Grand Canyon's human past.* Santa Fe: School of American Research Press.

———.

1993. Foreword to *The pottery from Arroyo Hondo Pueblo, New Mexico: Tribalization and trade in the northern Rio Grande,* by Judith A. Habicht-Mauche. Arroyo Hondo Archaeological Series, vol. 8. Santa Fe: School of American Research Press.

Schwartz, Douglas W., Michael P. Marshall, and Jane Kepp.

1979. *Archaeology of the Grand Canyon: The Bright Angel site.* Grand Canyon Archaeological Series, vol. 1. Santa Fe: School of American Research Press.

Schwartz, Douglas W., Richard C. Chapman, Jane Kepp.

1980. *Archaeology of the Grand Canyon: Unkar Delta.* Grand Canyon Archaeological Series, vol. 2. Santa Fe: School of American Research Press.

———.

1981. *Archaeology of the Grand Canyon: The Walhalla Plateau.* Grand Canyon Archaeological Series, vol. 3. Santa Fe: School of American Research Press.

Simmons, Marc.

1981. Pecos Pueblo on the Santa Fe trail. *Exploration, Annual Bulletin of the School of American Research,* 2–4.

Spier, Leslie.

1917. *An outline for a chronology of Zuni ruins.* Anthropological Papers of the American Museum of Natural History, vol. 28, pt. 3. New York: American Museum of Natural History.

Taylor, Walter W.

1948. A Study of Archeology. *American Anthropologist* 50 (3, pt. 2), American Anthropological Association Memoir 69.

Thomas, David Hurst.

1994. *Exploring ancient Native America: An archaeological guide.* New York: Macmillan.

Trimble, Stephen.

1993. *The people: Indians of the American Southwest.* Santa Fe: School of American Research Press.

Vivian, R. Gwinn.

1990. *The Chacoan prehistory of the San Juan Basin.* San Diego: Academic Press.

Wauchope, Robert.

1965. Alfred Vincent Kidder, 1885–1963. With a bibliography compiled by M. A. L. Harrison. *American Antiquity* 31 (2):149–71.

Wendorf, Fred.

1953. *Salvage archaeology in the Chama Valley, New Mexico.* School of American

Research Monographs, no. 17. Santa Fe: School of American Research Press.

White, Leslie A., ed.

1940. *Pioneers in American anthropology: The Bandelier-Morgan letters, 1873–1883*. 2 vols. Albuquerque: University of New Mexico Press.

Wilcox, David R.

1991a. Changing contexts of Pueblo Adaptations. In *Farmers, hunters, and colonists: Interaction between the Southwest and the Southern plains,* ed. Katherine A. Spielmann. Tucson: University of Arizona Press.

———.

1991b. The Mesoamerican ballgame in the American Southwest. In *The Mesoamerican Ballgame,* ed. Vernon. L. Scarborough and Wilcox. Tucson: University of Arizona Press.

Willey, Gordon R.

1967. Alfred Vincent Kidder, October 29, 1885–June 11, 1963. In *National Academy of Sciences Biographical Memoirs,* vol. 39, 292–322. New York: Columbia University Press.

Willey, Gordon R., and Jeremy Sabloff.

1974. *A history of American archaeology*. San Francisco: W. H. Freeman.

———.

1980. *A history of American archaeology*. 2d ed. San Francisco: W. H. Freeman.

Williams, Stephen.

1998. A critical review of some of the history of American archaeology. Paper presented to the 2d Willey HOAC Symposium. Seattle: SAA Meetings.

Wissler, Clark.

1917. The new archaeology. *American Museum Journal* 17 (2):100–01.

Woodbury, Richard B.

1960a. Nels C. Nelson and chronological archaeology. *American Antiquity* 25 (3):400–01.

———.

1960b. Nelson's stratigraphy. *American Antiquity* 26 (1):98–99.

———.

1973. *Alfred V. Kidder*. New York: Columbia University Press.

———.

1979. Prehistory: Introduction. In *Southwest,* ed. Alfonso Ortiz. Vol. 9 of *Handbook of North American Indians,* ed. William C. Sturtevant. Washington, D.C.: Smithsonian Institution.

———.

1981. From chaos to order: A. V. Kidder at Pecos. *Exploration, Annual Bulletin of the School of American Research,* 17–25.

———.

1993. *Sixty years of Southwestern archaeology: A history of the Pecos Conference*. Albuquerque: University of New Mexico Press.